Adolescent Personality and Behavior

MMPI PATTERNS OF NORMAL, DELINQUENT, DROPOUT, AND OTHER OUTCOMES

by STARKE R. HATHAWAY
and ELIO D. MONACHESI

THE UNIVERSITY OF MINNESOTA PRESS, MINNEAPOLIS

ACKNOWLEDGMENTS

THE research on which the data presented in this volume are based has had two main sources of support. We have received liberal grants from graduate school research funds of the University of Minnesota, and even larger grants from the National Institute of Mental Health. For this support we express our appreciation.

It is obvious that we cannot properly accept full credit for the great amount of work in the completion of so extensive a project as this. Our first measure of thanks is to the school personnel, police officials, judges, ministers, and others who have so believed in the significance of our work that they have given freely of facilities, time, and confidential information. It is our greatest wish that the findings we make available to aid in understanding the problems related to delinquency and mental health that confront these contributors may meet their expectations.

We also owe a debt to the ninth-grade students who were the original subjects and who continue to provide data on their lives toward a mutually desired better, more healthy society. We recognize with gratitude the freedom we have had to administer a personality test that touches upon matters private to students and their families. We have soberly accepted the responsibility this entails, and we believe that the data provided will adequately repay our subjects for their trust in us through the broadening of understanding of the psychological and social events that affect many families and individuals.

We continue to be aware of our dependence upon the field workers who have collected and organized the data, and to be deeply grateful to them. Alta Nupson, now long with us, has again contributed in inimitable fashion, both in keeping track of subjects in her part of the state and in providing us with field bulletins.

The handling of data in the central office and the general coordination of work have, by now, involved a host of persons individually remembered and valued but too numerous to name here.

This manuscript comes particularly from the collaboration of Phyllis Reynolds and the, by now, indispensable special editorial skills of Jeanne Sinnen.

STARKE R. HATHAWAY and ELIO D. MONACHESI

Minneapolis, September 1963

TABLE OF CONTENTS

List of Tables

Adolescent Personality and Behavior

INTRODUCTION

THIS report, covering a period of nearly fifteen years, provides a great deal of information about the behavior in late adolescence of thousands of boys and girls. Much of the behavior is shown here in relation to personality test data obtained from these young people when they were in the ninth grade, which was the point of our first contact with them.

The ninth-grade test data are hundreds of responses that the boys and girls made about themselves to items concerning daily interests, attitudes toward home and society, physical ills, and sex. The facts about behavior that are brought into relation with these personal evaluations are contrastingly public and mostly come from reports by teachers, police, ministers, and others of the society around the adolescents.

These overt views of the young people in our studies are our primary interest. We wished to portray these boys and girls as they were seen by themselves and by the society about them. We are aware of the common belief that there are true personality constructs that exist independently of the reports of self or of others. To put it in other terms: A person may believe that he has a real headache and most of us believe in the existence of such real headaches. Nevertheless we may say of someone who complains of a headache that he does not have a *real* headache. We imply that a headache can have a reality independent of the personal report. By the same token it is frequently asserted or implied that what a person says he is, likes, or feels can be contrasted to what he really is, likes, or feels, and that the "real" person has to be found out through projective tests or clinical inferences rather than self-report personality tests since false assertions or misleading statements are possible in response to the latter.

There is an interesting epistemological issue involved here. But given the purpose of our study and the limitations of our resources, we chose to base our research upon the overt world, without attempting to define "real" personalities — if such there are. We depended upon what our adolescent subjects said about themselves and what others said about them. In so doing we must admit that we will not satisfy many psychologists, psychiatrists, and sociologists who look askance at the collection of personality data without the application of modern clinical skills and theory. We wanted, however, to collect replicable and practically available data. We have used simple two-dimensional analyses, comparing no more than two variables at one time. Ours was a purposeful attempt to establish the limits of such data and analyses. To the degree that we show certain useful relationships, we also point to a way of meeting, in part, the increasing shortage of professional mental health personnel through the use of survey tests and other data-collecting devices to guide effectively teachers and others who are concerned with the mental health of their charges but who do not have specialized clinical training.

Our chief hope for the report lies in any evidence that bears upon the predictive and analytic value of survey data at the ninth-grade level as measured against later careers. If routine surveys can provide premonitory signs of later good adjustment in certain children, it would seem possible to concentrate educational effort more unequivocally toward preparing them for adult living in the community. Conversely, if signs can be discovered as early as the ninth grade that are premonitory of later personal or social trouble, particular attention could be devoted to the boys and girls thus marked, in the hopes of preventing trouble or ameliorating the cost of it to the individual and to society.

Possibly the clearest data emerging from our complex of tables are evidences predicting normal adjustment. This study, unlike most of those that have been reported, follows all the boys and girls with similar effort. We gathered the laconic and rather colorless comments about the normal majority of adolescents, illustrated by remarks like "Nice boy," or "She'll be just a regular housewife and mother," with as much care as we gathered the lurid news accounts of rare exploits of others. The average lives turn out to be more solidly predictable than are deviant lives. There was some evidence that this is true whatever the direction of the deviancy — toward outstanding and useful achievement or toward unacceptable behavior.

Personality, home conditions, intelligence, place of residence, and other variables proved in our study to relate to school dropout, delinquency, and other outcomes. And these variables also interact with each other. Bright boys are more likely than average or dull ones to stay in school, but if the personality test of a particular boy shows him to be masculine and energetic, he may well quit school in spite of high intelligence. However, if he lives in a suburban area, he is more likely than not to finish high school in spite of being restless and uninterested in schoolwork. In many ways it is a good thing for a child to come from an upper socioeconomic level home, but boys from middle-level homes made up a much larger proportion of all our delinquents than did those from homes at the day-laborer level.

The intricacies of interaction among the variables we report in our tables defy our ability to report. If we had collected less information, we probably could have given a better synthesized and more theoretically coherent report. Our efforts at synthesis have been unrewarding. Nearly every relationship seems complex. We found, for example, that boys or girls of broken homes who lived with the mother were more likely to be delinquent than those who lived with the father or another person. One could assume from this datum that mothers are bad for children. If, however, this is an unpalatable idea, it is not difficult to think of an alternative explanation. For example, when a family breaks up, it may be that disturbed children are selectively much more likely to be placed with the mother and normal children with the father.

The data, despite the large number of cases, are often not statistically reliable. We are only moderately apologetic on this point. A review of the literature on delinquency and other social behavior reveals such a wealth of elaboration from such small samples that our feeling of statistical virtue because of our large number of cases is an antidote to our unhappiness with the limitations of our data. An example of these limitations which may point to both the strengths and the weaknesses of this work is to be found in Chapter 5, pages 50 and 52. We discuss there tables which show that schizophrenic symptoms (as defined, at least, by the personality test used) are closely related to poor school grades and school dropout. In other tables these latter outcomes are also related to low test scores in school ability and English usage. Still another table shows that the social class of the parents is not as closely related to high schizophrenia scores as are low grades. There would seem to be an early defect in amount of schooling and achievement during schooling which contributes to a regression of these children, to their ending up in the lower classes; as adults they become more uniformly lower class than their parents were. This interesting line of interpretation may, however, be erroneous because of deficiencies in our sampling or classifications. We cannot more than state the data and their hypothetical expansion. With another ten years of follow-up we would be more positive.

Definitive statements in social science, we have come to feel, are less readily made as the data behind them are better and more complete. Faced with a welter of interrelated evidence, we have provided a report with little by way of summary or other broad, conclusive statements. We surely recognize the present crisis in juvenile delinquency and the magnitude of other social problems. It is tempting to select out special findings and, without tracing through all the related data, tell what should be done by parents, schools, and others to prevent undesirable outcomes in the transition to adult life. But we feel obliged to stress that our work has led us to believe that the problems of delinquency and other maladjustment are complicated results of multiple personal and social variables. We think that the extensive data in this report lead more clearly to this conclusion than to any other. This idea is not new, but the consequences of it are frequently overlooked. If we develop this idea, for example, it becomes apparent that no one community or special interest program will sharply affect the rate of juvenile delinquency. Clear out all slum areas, keep all families intact — our data show that there would still be a substantial rate of delinquency. It appears that some unfortunate outcomes are related to nearly every variable that we investigated, and we certainly did not look at every possible aspect.

The significant findings of research are dependent upon the methods and rules of observation adopted. We are properly accustomed to be critical of biased or inaccurate data and of faulty processes for deriving conclusions no matter how accurate the raw data may be. All this is most pertinent to research in the social sciences. Since the material presented in this report suggests many important relationships, we are particularly constrained to provide critical readers with the routine and often boring details of our procedure. Reading of these details is not essential unless positive or negative evidences in the tables or the discussion seem to need evaluation against the details of experimental design.

The report is organized in the general sequence of the development of the research itself. We tell why we used the design, give details of the design itself, pointing out some strengths and weaknesses, describe the variables collected, and finally get to the findings.

Unfortunately, it has not seemed to us possible or fair to the strength of our data to avoid certain professional jargon in the presentation of the results. For example, the personality test used, the Minnesota Multiphasic Personality Inventory (MMPI), provides profiles that are cumbersome to present in tables or description, and we have been forced to translate the test results into "codes." The coding system, which may seem complex at first glance, is not difficult and can be adequately mastered with brief study. Again, our data had to be evaluated statistically if they were to be useful for other researchers; and the most efficient way to order the details of the data was to put them in tabular form. Yet many persons deeply concerned with juvenile delinquency and active in the field have had little formal training in the use of statistical terms and devices. We have deliberately avoided elaborate statistical analysis and we have tried to avoid a highly technical language that would unnecessarily hamper easy reading. But we found it unwise to adopt a popular writing style — what would have been gained in interest and in number of readers would have been adversely balanced by the improper generalizations and part-truths necessary for such simplification. We expect that we shall later be able, in shorter publications, to develop some of the more useful findings for a wider audience.

We anticipate that many persons will reject our findings, and their reaction is understandable. Evidence that children differ in personality so that some are handicapped by being less attractive or more prone to hostility and delinquency tends to meet with resistance. Environmental explanations of deviant behavior are often more acceptable, possibly because there is in them less imputation of personal weakness or fundamental defect. The statement that children from broken homes are handicapped finds ready concurrence, but if a personality test suggests that certain boys and girls are warped or weak in some way, this implication is likely to be unpopular. It is the teacher, the psychiatrist, the psychologist, the counselor, the social worker, the minister, and all others whose work brings them into contact with the individual child who will recognize most clearly the implications of our findings and how the data may be applied when working with a particular child. We shall return to this issue of personal versus environmental approach in Chapter 1.

New and more critical evaluations of the present programs of prevention and treatment of adjustment disorders should guide us in the use of our limited resources even if it becomes apparent that certain favorite programs are not worth support. We hope that our findings will give impetus to the reappraisal of the effectiveness of much that is now being done. We do not want to appear merely destructive; we hope that the practical effects of this research will be to encourage the development of both more efficient and more effective methods for dealing with the problems of adolescents.

In addition to providing data for the analysis and prediction of adjustment, our findings also make available useful norms. Most of the children who were part of the original sample are represented here; as pointed out earlier, no appreciable neglect of the normal or of the exceptional child in the school-attending population occurred. Further, data on outcomes are not much dependent upon changing emphases in, say, police work. We rated delinquency by our own standard and tended to eliminate the variability that often affects published delinquency rates. We were also able to avoid the difficulty encountered when rate calculation must depend upon an estimate of the population from public records — for example, our population data are unusually accurate because our sample sizes are known and our rates are the actually observed values in the samples. The combined sample is a reasonably good cross section of adolescents. The rates of delinquency, of nervous disorders, of family and school difficulty are therefore based upon a relatively defined and representative population, and this normative aspect of our findings alone may justify the work.

❶

PRELIMINARY CONSIDERATIONS

ALTHOUGH it is evident that most boys and girls live through their teens with only minor difficulties, one has only to look at newspapers, magazines, and social science and medical journals to realize the extent and severity of adolescent maladjustment. The consequences of technological developments and of a rapidly expanding population, such as the increased number of binding rules and laws established to safeguard complicated property and personal rights, place a heavy burden on boys and girls as they become more and more a part of the outside world in their teens. Moreover, these years are the period of the most rapid and radical physiological change for the individual.

Sharply aware as we all are of the troubles many adolescents have, we unfortunately know little about how, in any adequate way, to predict or prevent their difficulties. The problem is a complex one, and it may be its very complexity that leads to the numerous and often contrasting theories of cause and treatment. These theories underlie many of the community, agency, and individual youth programs of the past and present that are emotionally defended despite their lack of demonstrated effectiveness.

The persistent reluctance of those persons and groups who work with young people to come to grips with the fact that there is no convincing evidence for or against the value of their preventive efforts on problems such as juvenile delinquency (failure to find such evidence is reported in reference 26) may stem partly from the fact that with few exceptions these persons are in close touch with only a select number of boys and girls — the probation officer sees his assigned cases (see reference 2), the church worker sees those who participate in his program, and a psychologist sees those referred to him. Their opinions are understandably guided by their experiences with their own case data, data that unfortunately are seldom analyzed to see if, for example, "successful prevention" is perhaps no more than an outcome of natural maturation or a unique occurrence, not replicable because of features peculiar to either the worker or the sample, or a combination of both. Our own data show that the trend is strong for those who have been delinquent to stay out of trouble as they get older. In fact, as better controlled data, such as the Cambridge-Somerville Youth Study (26), are made available, it becomes increasingly clear that a treatment or prevention program applied to delinquents or even to those teen-agers assumed to be predelinquent must be very powerful in order really to improve upon the outcomes following from mere passage of time. Kvaraceus (20) states the problem well: "Even today much of the writing on this topic barely comes in the classification of scientific research. A majority of the journal articles still fall in the category of descriptive reporting of personal experience, with heavy dependence on subjective evaluation. Many articles and books on the 'causes and cures' of juvenile delinquency put forth assertions, opinions, claims, and hypotheses that cannot be supported by the data presented (or available) on the point at issue."

Attempts to develop tests or other devices predictive of personal and social adjustment have in almost all instances contrasted a group already identified as maladjusted with a control or normal sample (for example, those reported in 9, 10, 11, and 28). Differentiating items of information about the remote or recent past in the lives of these subjects are sought under the assumption that such items would also have separated the groups before they were identified as maladjusted and control — and that, therefore, these items could be used to predict the behavior of other youths. This type of study is the source of the data usually available to social workers, probation officers, and others working with deviant children and adults. Such studies provide us with useful classificatory information, but they are an unreliable source of predictive items, since the personalities of the subjects before they were placed in the normal or maladjusted sample are only indirectly studied.

The present fact of a person's being abnormal or normal inevitably confuses description of the past environment and behavior; knowing that someone has had trouble encourages him and those about him to errors of memory and emphasis. Both the observer and the subject are modified by the implications of the undesirable behavior. Prison inmates, for example, understandably are likely not to be accurate in reporting earlier autobiographical dispositions or events. Nor can interviewers correct for the defect; the interviewer usually knows the fact of the prisoner's offenses and will unconsciously modify and selectively record items. When such sources of error are not recognized or controlled, the evidence can appear to provide simple explanations of delinquency and crime: for ministers these outcomes might seem to be due to defective early religious training; for sociologists, to defective family or social structure; for psychiatrists, to faulty expressions of love of parents for their children.

It is infrequent that a person or agency possesses information on a truly representative cross section of adolescents, for they lack the opportunity to collect adequate data on those who are most elusive of all — the boys and girls who make unobtrusive and good adjustment. Even when well-adjusted children are in a position to be more conspicuous, like the well-behaved siblings in a notoriously bad family, their case histories are often neglected in assessment of the causative background of those who are delinquent. Furthermore, it seems that having normal children of one's own or observing normal adolescents in the everyday world does not provide a properly balanced control group against which to formulate hypotheses about the causes of delinquency. What is needed, then, to avoid the pitfalls of faulty logic in our thinking about the causes and prevention of maladjustment is the opportunity to evaluate all adolescents in a large sample of the general population where equal attention can be given to those who are well adjusted and those who do not do so well. One of the major advantages of the present study is a research design that allows an almost equal look at every child in a large random sample of adolescents.

Design of Research on Psychological Maladjustment

The predictive statements we might make about a particular child can take three different forms. Assuming that the environment is constant and that we have data about him, we could say: "This is what he is now and he will continue to be this way," "This is what he is now and he will be something specifically different in the future," or, finally, "This is what he is now but all we can predict is that he will become different." Only by tracing the lives of children over a fairly long period can the valid statement be identified. And if one of the first two statements can be made, only longitudinal data will indicate the degree of its validity.

Longitudinal research is relatively easy to design; it is, however, difficult and costly to execute because of the large numbers of cases and the sustained effort that are necessary to carry the research over months or years. Such research when designed to study delinquency or mental illness involves the collection of a mass of what it is hoped will be pertinent information on a very large number of subjects. Large numbers are needed because so many members of the group will never show some of the critical symptoms, and because there is an inevitable attrition in sample size. This kind of research becomes impractical if the base rate of incidence of the critical event is very low. The more advanced stages of a longitudinal research design are exemplified by the programs for prevention of poliomyelitis. Whole communities were used as sources of experimental and control groups in order to get reliable data about morbidity rates for this disease of low incidence. Fortunately, some of the difficulties posed by work with a disease of low incidence rate such as poliomyelitis may be avoided through preliminary experiments on animals. However, many psychological problems can be studied only in humans. Delinquency, as an example, is not a physiological disease. Rats, even monkeys, if they become delinquent at all, do so in rat or monkey — not human — ways.

There is another important aspect of designing research on psychological maladjustment, the source of the data. The sources may be divided into two major categories. On the one hand, information for classifications can be derived from data emphasizing environment. For example, groups might be made up of children from slum neighborhoods or from broken homes. Contrastingly, classifying information can be derived from introspective personal data that tell of the individual's interests, attitudes, or aptitudes. Most studies of behavioral outcomes have depended upon classificatory information about the environment — neighborhood, home, or school conditions.

Few would deny that some of the most important differences among children are those that are indicated by the value-freighted words describing elements that constitute the personality. But many would emphasize the critical importance of environment as an influence on personality and hence the value of approaching personality problems through environmental forces. Much recent psychological and psychiatric theory depends heavily on the concept that environment is the chief molder of individual personality. Major attention has been given to the mother and her formative role in the development of the personality of a child. Fathers and teachers also are seen as determining influences. But there are two ways in which we may still consider personality to have intrinsic aspects that should be recognized. First, even if the mother and other significant persons about a child are chiefly responsible for the later disposition that characterizes him, nearly everyone recognizes that the personality that emerges can in turn be a significant determinant of environmental situations. To some degree a boy or girl can set up opportunities to get into trouble. The child influences the formative treatment he receives. Secondly, it may be that the trend to place the origins of personality on the behavior of parents has gone much too far. Perhaps babies from birth have reaction systems that, if not yet acceptable under the term *personality*, are still differentiated in ways that make it possible to say that mothers, for example, are "formed" by their babies. Such a view would certainly make it easier to explain the fact that a mother of several children seems much more constant in personality than are the personalities of her children.

In any case, while we did not neglect environmental data in our study, we chose to come at the problem of research into psychological maladjustment through personal data, which allows us always to keep the individual in view. A society, if it is to be strong, and families, if they are to be devoted to the welfare of their children, must be concerned about the *individual* needs and attitudes of each child — his personality — as he matures. When we ignore what each child thinks about or feels, we are likely to apply invariant rules, punishing and rewarding children without discrimination. Such an approach also encourages attempts to give general rules about how parents should behave toward their children — toward *any* child. Many parents and others appear to equate all children; what they believe to be good or bad in training or treatment is universally good or bad, for one and all. But children cannot all be treated alike and still become as adults the self-reliant individuals who are the basis of our social structure. Of course, we cannot treat children differentially, helping one with praise, another with disapproval, and another with teaching in a certain way or with a certain content according to needs, if we do not know the children as individuals — their reactions about, for, and against the world they must live in. We may also find it useful to know, more or less objectively, what that world, their environment, has been and is, but in this study we are primarily looking at our fifteen-year-olds as persons having individualities that are significant enough to justify an individualization of our efforts to influence them, rather than as members of a group defined by a certain kind of environment who are assumed to respond similarly to a similar outside influence and whose responses hence can be modified merely by manipulation of that influence.

There is a simple way to highlight the difference between the personal and the environmental approach to the prediction and understanding of behavior. With the environmental approach one does not need to examine or question the individual child to get the pertinent information. If a group of one hundred boys from broken homes is found to include eighty delinquents, any boy from a similarly selected and treated sample can be assigned an 80 per cent chance of becoming delinquent. In contrast, with the personal approach one must question the individual child about his interests, attitudes, or aptitudes to get the needed information. Should eighty out of one hundred boys (whether or not they come from broken homes) who say they like to race autos have a later history of delinquency, then any boys from a similarly selected sample (those boys who say they like to race autos) could be assigned an 80 per cent chance of becoming delinquent. Admittedly, these two approaches to prediction — environmental and personal — are ultimately similar in principle. They do, however, employ significantly different operations in deriving the data for study.

The Problem of Behavior Prediction

It is interesting that one seldom encounters any doubt that delinquency and many other maladjustment patterns are predictable. One constantly hears it said that broken homes and other background stresses permit a prediction about the individual children exposed to the specific condition. Also one hears often that personal problems can be prevented "if we get them in time," a phrase implying that one should be able to recognize early symptoms.

On the other hand, it has not been disproved that mental breakdown, delinquency, and other behavior deviations appear in a current situation with no premonitory signs. Many of our actions do seem to come about in this way. We say that we had no idea we were going to act as we did; we did it on impulse. It is true, by definition, that we cannot do things we have no potential for doing, but it seems that a sudden, unforeseeable opportunity or inducement can, at times, greatly change our activities.

To reject the hypothesis that most maladjustment originates from current conditions rather than from a long development in the person, it would be necessary to find that we can accurately make individual predictions from a time well before the trouble develops. However, because of the complexity of the contributing factors behind such problems as delinquency, we may find ourselves confronted with the situation of being unable either to accept or to reject the hypothesis of predictable outcomes. A particular boy's delinquency may be due to so large a number of factors of varying weights that his behavior is unpredictable by any practical analysis, although it is determined and predictable in an ultimate sense.

Even if it is possible to accept the hypothesis of predictable outcomes in some instances, we would still be faced with the problem of knowing the time range over which the predictions could come true. Could an individual's later delinquency be predicted with any confidence from data gathered at the time he is in kindergarten? Is it even conceivable that a usefully accurate predictive statement of delinquent acts to occur by age twenty-one could be made from study of a newborn child? Affirmative responses to these questions certainly suggest an acceptance of continuity of a trend during many years of life. Considering how little we know, it would appear that the most efficient experiments should explore short-time predictions first. If the short-time evidence supports the hypothesis of predictability, then one could search at earlier ages.

There is another problem that can be foreseen in longitudinal studies started at earlier ages. If the interval between prediction and outcome included an active program of psychotherapy or of school or community efforts toward the prevention of delinquency and if these intervening activities were effective, then the predictive accuracy would be lowered because there would be less delinquency. In the degree, therefore, that children are influenced after the age at which predictions are made, one expects less accuracy of the predictions.

We know little about the psychological forces that mold individual behavior or about the relative effect of heredity and experience. It is naive to assert that thieves are born, but it may be reasonable to assume that some persons are more prone to thievery and require more training or more restraint than do others if they are to resist becoming thieves. If heredity or early conditioning established a proneness to thievery, then the discovery of signs or symptoms of the proneness in children should permit the identification of those most affected.

In contrast, if heredity or early conditioning does not establish a proneness, the development of a thief would only be detectable after onset of the immediate influences that operate to generate the behavior. In this instance a personality study should not be expected to reveal individual dispositions or resistance before the experiences in the individual's life that lead him into wrongdoing. Finally, it would be expected that all children would be potential misbehavers or relatively equal to one another in potential for good and happy adjustment.

We have, then, two related goals in our study of prediction using personality data: to develop evidence for or against the hypothesis that some children are more prone than others to become maladjusted; and if such premonitory signs or symptoms are found, to isolate these to produce reasonable accuracy in prediction.

Preventive Programs from Use of Personal Data

If we find that personality traits suggest proneness to develop psychological maladjustment, individually prescribed preventive work seems likely to be the preferential method of procedure. The diversity of personality among children becomes a center of emphasis. The emphasis upon personality does not ignore the environmental sources of maladjustment, but this kind of thinking does suggest why various environmentally centered programs for the prevention of delinquency can seem to work for some children and be ineffectual for others.

From the personal approach it is apparent that putting a certain boy into a Boy Scout troop or a good foster home could actually increase the probability that the boy will get into trouble. To illustrate further the difference in the application of personal and environmental data in preventive programs, we might make contrasting statements. We might say, first, "Boys who belong to this gang are under bad influences. It has been found that such boys are likely to be delinquent and it is therefore necessary to destroy the gang." This would imply that the gang environment affected all boys adversely, leaving out of consideration the possibility that various boys react quite differently to the same influence. Conversely, a statement that says "This boy in the gang has personality characteristics which have been found to be predictive of good behavior; he will probably not yield to the bad influences of the gang, but he may gain needed self-confidence" is based on the recognition that boys are susceptible in different degrees to what are bad influences. To destroy the gang in this case would conceivably do harm rather than good for some boys.

The Present Study

In the present longitudinal studies of school children, reporting the relationships between personality and other data collected in the ninth grade and emotional and behavioral events that occurred up to four years later, the modal age of the subjects changed from fifteen to nineteen years. Among the problems that developed for our subjects during the period, no single one was as prominent as delinquency. Other difficulties were also encountered. Sometimes severe or dramatic, they involved school, social, or personal emotional adjustment. All these problems were usually interrelated in varying degrees.

Although some of our data show the well-known relationships between undesirable social behavior and such environmental variables as low socioeconomic status and unstable homes, we are concerned chiefly with the boy or girl as an individual person who more or less successfully withstands such environmental influences. For the specific problem of juvenile delinquency, the work of Wirt and Briggs (34) is very important. Their data suggest that the most powerful approach to understanding delinquency comes from combining knowledge about the personality traits of the individual with facts concerning his environmental situation.

Ball (1) has published a compilation of studies that provides a basic source for method and findings parallel to the work we are presenting. Although he was handicapped by the small numbers available to him, comparisons with our report will show many instances where he deserves precedence for pointing out trends.

Implicit in our report is the assumption that there are large differences from child to child in the degree of their personality change during the late adolescent period. Some at middle age have much the same personality characteristics they had at age fifteen, but others become very different persons at age eighteen from what they were at age fifteen.

Our sample of children was homogeneous to the extent that it was composed of ninth-graders who, except for a small number, attended public schools. We collected environmental data on each child: status of the family economically and socially, facts about the family structure, and the population density of the place of residence. We also had teachers indicate who were problem children, and we recorded grades and other school facts. All this information was about the child as a passive subject.

The MMPI was used to collect the personality data from the child. Each boy and girl responded "True" or "False" to statements about himself and his environment. The children were told that they could leave items unanswered if they wished. These statements ranged in subject matter from interests in things such as flowers or mechanics to reports on physical pains or sensations, to liking policemen, and to feelings about sex. It is our intention in this study to focus attention upon the personality types that the test identifies rather than on study or demonstration of the test itself. We have used the test as an established tool. When a child has answered the 566 test items, he has become an individual, and no one is likely to be identical with him. Yet some of the children are similar enough in personality type as identified by the test so that they may be classified together and group data can be used. In the present context, when we write of the child's personality, we define it by the items and scales of the MMPI, but these data will only be used in relation to his later adjustment as seen by those about him.

THE SAMPLES AND THE VARIABLES

THE subjects for our studies were ninth-grade pupils in Minnesota public schools (plus a small group of Roman Catholic parochial students). The MMPI is, it has been shown, easily enough read by boys and girls at this level, and the ninth-grader is already aware of most of the adult problems referred to in the MMPI either through his own experience or vicariously from parents and others.

We began our studies in 1947. It was assumed that the delinquency rate began its steep rise at about the time youngsters reached the ninth grade and achieved its maximum level a year or two later. We hoped to get our data early enough so that most of the delinquent behavior we expected to study would occur after the time of the testing. Since the initiation of the study, the peak of the incidence rate for delinquency has slipped toward lower ages, at least in urban areas. There has been a similar shift toward earlier marriage. These changes illustrate one kind of cultural variation that will probably affect the meaning of some of our data.

Minnesota has certain advantages as a source for population samples. Its people are predominantly native born and at least second generation. There are no important minority problems in the state. Negroes and American Indians appear among our subjects but not in such important numbers as to force us to control for possible race-linked differences. The economic position of the state in comparison to other states is neither extremely high nor low. Farming slightly outweighs manufacturing as the dominant economic activity.

The original adult normative data for the MMPI were also based upon samples of the population of Minnesota. In many of the subsequent studies with this test, the Minnesota norms were compared with those for samples from other states, and it has seemed that the Minnesota population is fairly average in the variables represented.

A crucial aspect of the study to be reported here was the search for early symptoms of a variety of subsequent psychological adjustment problems. Since some of these difficulties are infrequent in occurrence, and since a sample inevitably becomes smaller with the passage of time, the initial sample from which the original data were to be drawn had to be large, heterogeneous, and broadly representative of the population — the general requirement of longitudinal research mentioned in Chapter 1.

Our combined sample of more than 15,000 subjects is large and diverse. However, even with this number, subsamples become distressingly small. Of course, a first division into boys and girls was necessary for nearly all analyses. The backgrounds of the subjects were highly variable. Schools, communities, homes all differed in ways that suggested subgroup analysis. Several different psychometric instruments had been used in the schools to measure intelligence, interests, and aptitude. With so many variables, it has rarely been possible for us to use large groups of subjects for an analysis. We now realize that although our sample seemed large in the planning stages, the study should be repeated on a tenfold larger scale.

The Samples

The Minneapolis Sample. The first ninth-grade MMPI testing program was initiated in the Minneapolis public school system during the 1947–48 school year. At the beginning of the school year there were 4572 ninth-graders registered in the sixteen Minneapolis public high schools. The MMPI was administered to 3971, or 87 per cent, of this group. Most of the testing was done during March, April, and May of 1948. Considerable effort was made to test every student in the schools. At each school the entire ninth-grade population was scheduled for testing, and return trips were made to reach students missed during the original session. Still, as must be expected, some students because of absence, dropout, or transfer during the school year were not tested and could not be included in the samples. At the time of the MMPI testing we collected other data by microfilming each student's school record.

These 3971 cases from the Minneapolis public schools will hereafter be referred to as the Minneapolis sample. They represent the most urban of the groups. For sundry reasons the total sample numbers used in the tables in this book vary. When the variations are small, we give no explanation since their effects are of little consequence.

In 1950 and again in 1952, two and four years after testing, the files of the Hennepin County Probation Office and the Juvenile Division of the Minneapolis Police Department were examined for the names of the Minneapolis boys and girls who were tested as ninth-graders.

The Statewide Sample. Preliminary work with the data from the Minneapolis sample quickly showed how inadequate the sample was in size. For example, classification into approximately one hundred categories based on MMPI results produced few groups containing as many as ten pupils. It was apparent that a much larger sample was needed, and it seemed desirable to obtain data on rural ninth-graders as well as on urban children.

During the spring of 1954, 11,329 additional ninth-graders were tested. The testing was done in 92 schools situated in 86 communities, in 47 of Minnesota's 87 counties. Sampling was actually broader than is suggested by these figures, for Minnesota school district boundaries do not always coincide with political and other subdivisions. Many schools serve several communities, and not infrequently a school draws pupils from two or more counties. Schools were selected to represent so far as possible Minnesota's diverse economic and geographic areas. The sample actually includes 28 per cent of the entire ninth-grade public school population of Minnesota in 1954, 36 per cent of all ninth-graders outside the Minneapolis and St. Paul public school systems. In addition there are 101 boys and girls from two Roman Catholic parochial schools in the sample.

This larger sample, derived with procedures similar to those used for the Minneapolis sample, will hereafter be referred to as the statewide sample. Unfortunately, a number of factors, among which is the six-year time difference, make parallel analyses for every variable on the Minneapolis and statewide samples impossible.

At the time of statewide MMPI testing we collected other data from several sources. Microfilms were made of the school records; the students filled out a Personal Data Sheet (see Appendix B); and their teachers filled out a report form on which they were asked to predict which students were likely to have legal or emotional difficulties (see Appendix C).

Three years after the testing of the statewide sample, in 1956–57, a student-by-student follow-up survey was made in each community from which subjects had been drawn, and police and court files were searched for names and records. These data were used in making a "delinquency rating." Ratings of school conduct and adjustment were based on teacher reports, also obtained at this time.

At this time too an intensive follow-up was done in twelve schools representative of the statewide sample. The students, now by normal school progress in the twelfth grade, were again tested with the MMPI, and further personal data were collected on each. In order to secure a sufficient number of retests, an additional 2000 twelfth-grade students from the original ninth-grade sample were also tested again with the MMPI.

Characteristics of the Samples (Tables 1–15)

Chronological Age. Table 1 shows the distribution of ages among the ninth-graders. (The tables are gathered together at the end of this volume.) For the Minneapolis group, the figures are derived from random samples of two hundred cases to represent each sex, and the age at the subject's nearest birthday is used. The ages of the statewide ninth-graders in Table 1 are those given by the pupils. The true chronological mean age would be approximated by adding one-half year to the values shown, since the children reported their age as it was at their last birthday. More than 90 per cent of these subjects were age fourteen or fifteen at the time of testing. The ages are so homogeneous that we have made no analyses on this variable. The mean ages for the statewide sample were nearly identical with those of the Minneapolis sample of six years earlier.

Size of Community. The community of residence for subjects in the statewide sample was determined from the Personal Data Sheet and verified by the microfilmed school record. Community size was taken from the 1950 official census.

The number of ninth-graders placed in each category of community size is shown in Table 2. With the exception of the farm category, the classifications actually refer to the community in which the school was situated. All youngsters living on farms, regardless of the location of the school, were put in the farm category. The class called suburb was used exclusively for suburban schools located within the greater Twin Cities (Minneapolis and St. Paul) metropolitan area. It should be noted here that this category does not necessarily represent typical middle-class suburbia since it includes some rooming house and manufacturing areas. If the two cities (Minneapolis and Duluth) and the suburban communities are considered as urban and the towns and farms as rural, the total sample is approximately equally divided. For analysis, we have usually combined all towns to provide three classes of population density: city, town, farm.

Socioeconomic Status. A rough estimate of the socioeconomic status for the families of subjects in the Minneapolis sample was made on the basis of the rent level for the area of residence. Immediately after the ninth-grade testing the address of each student was located on a map procured from the 1940 Housing Supplement of the Bureau of the Census which gave rent levels by city blocks. Four arbitrary categories of rent level — high to low — were set up, with a separate category for students living outside the city limits.

Table 3 shows the distribution of the sample from highest to lowest rent level. These data are given to provide the reader with a normative view of the sample. The levels themselves were used in our analysis only as one of a group of variables since any differences associated with them are attenuated by the fact that average rent levels do not represent the individual family economic status and, further, by the fact that the data on average rent levels were out of date.

To consider socioeconomic differences in the Minneapolis sample in another way, we divided the schools into three groups on the basis of combined data on families in each school district: rent level, the proportion of welfare contacts, the income level, and an estimation of social welfare services needed. Two schools became the "high group," i.e., highest income and rent levels and smallest proportion of welfare contacts and potential social need, and three schools became the "low group." Analyses on these groups were done only for boys since we were primarily interested in the incidence of delinquency. The high group numbered 331 boys and the low group 321 boys. Possibly differences between these groups would better be termed neighborhood rather than socioeconomic differences.

The microfilmed school records for the statewide sample gave us the father's occupation, which we used to determine socioeconomic status for these subjects (see Table 4). The classification was made in accordance with the Minnesota Scale for Parental Occupations (24) and was usually based on the true father's occupation, even when he was deceased or otherwise out of the home. In case there was no information on the true father's occupation, either the stepfather's or the mother's occupation was substituted. If the father had two jobs, his primary occupation was chosen. When the information was indefinite, all available data, in particular the educational level of the father, were utilized in making a decision. For example, if the father had a college education, he was arbitrarily rated in Class II, as is shown in the list below, which illustrates in more detail how the socioeconomic level was linked to educational level.

I = Professional (B.A. or B.S. degree and advanced graduate or professional school training)

II = Semiprofessional (college graduate)

III = Clerical, skilled, and retail business (high school graduate and special training)

IV = Farmer (A: large commercial farm, e.g., dairy, truck, with above average income; uses progressive farming methods;

well managed and maintained; etc. B: average, substantial farm. C: unusually small farm; low income, marginal or submarginal income; substandard farming procedures; management and maintenance below standard.)

V = Semiskilled, clerks, and minor business positions (grade school and some high school)

VI = Slightly skilled (grade school)

VII = Day laborer (grade school)

For many of the later analyses, it was necessary to form larger classes from the data on socioeconomic status. As indicated in Table 4, we combined professional and semiprofessional, the three farmer groups, and skilled and slightly skilled. The clerical and day-laborer categories were not combined with others.

Family Status. The family status of subjects in the Minneapolis sample was determined from the microfilmed school records. Nine categories were then formed: (1) normal, (2) divorced parents, (3) separated parents, (4) father deceased, (5) mother deceased, (6) both parents deceased, (7) stepparent, (8) foster parents, (9) one parent unknown. The frequencies in each of these categories are given in Table 5.

Family status for subjects in the statewide sample was determined from the Personal Data Sheet. From responses to the question "With whom do you live?" each student was placed in one of five categories: (1) both parents, (2) mother, (3) father, (4) neither parent, (5) stepparent. Additional responses from this sheet indicated whether the father and mother were living or not living and the parents' marital status (separated or divorced; not separated or divorced). Tables 6 and 7 show the distribution of the sample on these variables. About two and one-half times as many children of this age have fathers not living as have mothers not living.

Finally, the Personal Data Sheet asked for the number of brothers and number of sisters. No determination of the subject's birth order was made at this time. Table 8 shows the distribution of number of siblings.

Intelligence Ratings. Intelligence ratings for the Minneapolis sample were obtained from the microfilms of school record cards. The majority of scores were Otis IQ's because this test had been recently administered. Stanford-Binet scores from earlier grades were used where the Otis score was not available. The scores were classified into three groups: (1) high, 111 and above, (2) medium, 90 to 110, (3) low, 89 and below. Table 9 shows the number and percentage of ninth-grade boys and girls in the various categories.

Scores on the American Council on Education Psychological Examination (ACE), 1952 College Edition, were obtained for the statewide sample when the subjects were in the eleventh grade. If this score was not available, the ninth-grade ACE, 1947 High School Edition, was used. When neither score was available, we substituted an IQ score from the time nearest to the ninth-grade testing. This score was obtained from our microfilmed school record and was prorated to a roughly equivalent ACE percentile score. Table 10 shows the distribution of the sample according to arbitrarily grouped percentiles.

Cooperative English Test, Form Z. Cooperative English Test scores (eleventh grade) were also collected for the statewide sample. If this score was not available, the ninth-grade English test score was used. Arbitrary percentile categories were selected and Table 11 shows the frequency and percentage of students in each category.

High School Rank. Table 12 gives the distribution of the statewide sample according to the high school percentile rank of each subject. The eleventh-grade rank was used for almost all the students. When the percentile rank was not available from eleventh-grade data, a twelfth-grade rank was used. All analyses using these data will, of course, omit students who dropped out of school before they had gone far enough to provide data for ranking.

School Status at Follow-Up. During the 1956–57 follow-up, interviewers established the school status of each student of the statewide sample from school personnel records. Each student was placed in one of six classifications: (1) ninth-grade dropout, (2) tenth-grade dropout, (3) eleventh-grade dropout, (4) twelfth-grade dropout, (5) transfer and status unknown, (6) attending the twelfth grade (which included the following cases: expelled and back in school again, held back a grade because of illness, etc., transferred during the intervening period and returned to the same school to graduate with the class, transferred to another school and known to be attending or to have graduated from the twelfth grade, still in the twelfth grade in the second part of the senior year but may not have graduated — this last does not apply to the twelve schools in the intensive follow-up where we ascertained the graduation status). Placement in a classification indicated that the student had completed the preceding year in school. Table 13 gives the normative results.

When a student of the statewide sample was found to have left school, he was placed in one of nine categories according to the reason for his dropping out. The reason assigned was decided upon by the interviewers, usually on the basis of information from a teacher. Table 14 gives the numbers and percentages in each dropout category for those who left school.

Teacher Predictions. At the time of the ninth-grade testing for the statewide sample, the teachers in the school who were familiar with the students were asked to list five students they thought most likely to get into serious difficulty with the school authorities or the law within the next four years and to list five students most likely to show evidence of emotional maladjustment within the next four years. The names from the one or more teachers of each school were then combined in final lists in the two prediction categories. Some names appeared on both lists. In a given school the percentage of all students so named might be large, as was likely in a small school, or small, as was more likely in a large school. Teachers were asked to give five names for each list merely to assure that they would make some predictions. No real effort was made to get exactly ten or to restrict the number named. As a result the teachers usually listed the names of all the pupils that seemed to them likely to have trouble. Table 15 shows the number and percentage of boys and girls who were named by teachers in each category and of those who were named in both categories.

The Follow-Up Data (Tables 16–20)

Conduct and Adjustment Ratings. After the general 1956–57 statewide follow-up the interviewers gave each student ratings on school conduct and school adjustment based chiefly on information collected from school personnel. In order to keep the amount of variation on these ratings at a minimum, the interviewers were given a detailed explanation of what to look for in determining the ratings.

The school conduct rating range was from 0 to 4; a separate rating, 5, was used exclusively for girls with a history of illegitimate pregnancy or forced marriage. A rating of 0 meant good school conduct with no difficulties. A rating of 4 was assigned when it had been necessary to go outside of the school for help in dealing with the student's problem. A rating of 2 or 3 depended primarily on the extent or degree that a student's conduct interfered with his over-all efficiency and effectiveness.

The school adjustment rating range was also from 0 to 4. Students showing maladjustive behavior that, although significant in the view of the raters, could not be appropriately included in the category of school conduct were given an adjustment rating. Obviously the difference lay in an emphasis upon emotional problems rather than upon troublesome behavior. For example, students rated in this group included those judged to be excessively irritable, petulant, anxious, fearful, shy, unhappy, moody, or lacking in self-confidence. A rating of 4 was used exclusively to designate those students who received psychological treatment outside of the normal school setting. Again, a rating of 0 meant good school adjustment with no difficulties and ratings of 2 and 3 depended primarily on the extent or degree that a student's maladjustment interfered with his over-all efficiency and effectiveness. Tables 16 and 17 give the numbers and percentages of students rated in each of the categories.

Delinquency Ratings. For all the follow-up surveys the files of the probation office, juvenile police, and juvenile courts in each community where ninth-grade testing was done were examined. Each student received a severity of delinquency rating based on the records or on any other pertinent information. A rating indicating some degree of delinquency could be given for subjects who had no official record, but this was rarely done.

The delinquency levels ranged from 0 to 4, with 0 signifying no evidence of delinquent acts and 4 signifying a clear pattern of delinquency.* The system guiding this classification is outlined below:

0 = No delinquency.

1 = Names of subjects placed in this classification were found in police records for at least one minor difficulty such as a traffic violation like overtime parking or being picked up by the police. In the latter case, involvement was either poorly established or the individual contributed to whatever disturbance occurred in such a minor way that classification into level 2, 3, or 4 was not justified.

2 = The youngsters placed in this class had committed minor offenses such as destruction of property (especially when this was connected with play activities), drinking, one or more traffic offenses (escapades involving speeding, driving without a license, and/or going at high speed through a stop light or sign), curfew violation, and immoral conduct of a severity or frequency that did not require a rating of 3 or 4. The misbehavior was

---

*In the report of Minneapolis 1950 follow-up data in *Analyzing and Predicting Juvenile Delinquency with the MMPI* (15), levels 2, 3, and 4 appear as levels III, II, and I respectively.

relatively nondelinquent in comparison to that of the other two categories. Nevertheless, these boys and girls as a group had all behaved in clearly undesirable ways.

3 = This level of misconduct involves the commission of one serious offense such as auto theft, grand larceny, or gross immorality, or more than one less serious offense such as petty larceny, immoral conduct, assault, disorderly conduct, malicious destruction of property, shoplifting, flagrant curfew violations, truancy, and incorrigibility. The youngsters placed in this class were therefore not established as severely delinquent, but, nevertheless, their offenses were worse or more numerous than those of subjects classified in level 2.

4 = This classification is used to denote those who committed repeated offenses such as auto theft, burglary, grand larceny, holdup with a gun, gross immoral conduct (girls), accompanied by less serious offenses. In this category were placed all youngsters who were considered to have demonstrated a well-established delinquent pattern.

The Delinquency Rates. Table 18 shows the percentage of subjects who were delinquent (at level 2, 3, or 4) at the indicated ages. Because of the timing of the follow-ups, the two samples can be combined to show the rates at ages fifteen, seventeen, eighteen, and nineteen. Of course, the samples are of very different composition. In the statewide sample, which included about as many rural cases as it did urban, the rural children had a large influence on the rates. In the chapter on delinquency below, we will show that the rural rates are very low, especially for the earlier age levels. In Table 18 it can be seen that the rates of the two samples appear to be about equal by age nineteen if one extrapolates the statewide sample by one year.

The accumulated percentage for delinquency by age nineteen was 28.4 among the boys and 9.0 among the girls. These rates, as is true of all published rates, depend upon the definition of the delinquency levels. There is one point of special significance which was mentioned earlier but should be stressed here. Unlike the usually given rates, these are based upon a known total sample that includes the nondelinquent. Most published rates use a questionable estimate for determining the population size.

Table 19 shows a breakdown of the rates over the four delinquency levels. Since the statewide sample data are more stable because of larger numbers, they are the basis for the table. The rates of delinquency for the boys are from three to four times those of the girls except at level 1. Nearly one among every four boys and one among every sixteen girls were reported to have been clearly in trouble — rated at level 2 or higher. By this early age, twenty-four among every thousand boys and seven among every thousand girls are guilty at our most severe level of offense.

Table 20 provides some interesting data on the time of delinquency. We have tabulated the delinquency rates (combined levels 2, 3, and 4) for the Minneapolis boys as observed within each of three periods. The first rate, 3.2, is that for boys who committed delinquent acts before the time of testing, in the two years following, and also in the next two years. The third line shows that 161, or 29.0 per cent, of the delinquent boys had already been delinquent at the time of testing but did not continue so. These 161 boys were 8.2 per cent of the total sample of boys; such figures serve to emphasize the obvious fact that delinquent youngsters do not all continue to get in trouble. As a further illustration, it may be pointed out that those who commit offenses serious enough to be rated as delinquent before the twelfth grade but who do not do so thereafter constitute about 58 per cent of the whole sample of delinquent boys.

❸

THE MMPI

THE measurement of personality in a large number of subjects presents some practical problems. The size of the sample in itself calls for an easily administered test in order to produce the data sought with a minimum investment of time by professional workers. In our study we assumed that it was impractical to assess hundreds of boys and girls through individual interviews by trained investigators such as psychologists, psychiatrists, or social workers. We also assumed that it was impractical to use tests that required much professional time for administration. The primary virtue of an objective test lies in the fact that the subjects themselves directly provide the information. The test responses produce data free from the biases of interviewer or test interpreter.

The MMPI, chosen as our basic instrument for collecting personality test data, is an objective personality inventory and the prototype for a number of similar inventories. Many research reports have demonstrated that MMPI scales are useful in assessing psychological adjustment in certain personal and social areas. The following is a brief description of it.*

Of the 550 items in the inventory (566 in the booklet form — 16 items are repeated to facilitate machine scoring), only about two-thirds contribute to the basic set of three validity and ten clinical scales that are used in the usual profile derived from the test. More than two hundred other scales have been developed from the items, and new scales are constantly being reported. Our analyses of MMPI data for each of the variables will generally be done in one or more of three ways: by scale averages, by code patterns, which are symbolic of profiles, and by test items. Both theoretically and practically we have found that average profiles made up from the averages on separate scales are not very effective in developing such research data as we have. Averaged data lose the information contained in the relative scale values of the individual profiles used in the calculations. Codes retain some of the profile shape information and we will mainly use these in our analyses.

Test Validity and the Validity Scales

A student who is a poor reader might be unable to understand some crucial words in the MMPI items and would mistake the meaning. Also, if a subject

---

*A more complete analysis can be found in *Basic Readings on the MMPI in Psychology and Medicine* (33), *An MMPI Handbook* (6), and other sources.

loses his place and puts answers in the wrong places, his test is not valid. Similarly, a boy or girl who deliberately modifies responses in a highly individual way will probably produce an invalid test. One boy ostentatiously tossed a coin to determine his answers; a few boys boasted that they had treated the statements as jokes and responded with what they considered humorous answers. Any teacher experienced with teen-agers can suggest additional ways in which responses to the test items may be improperly made.

As used here, the term *invalidity* refers to conditions such as those mentioned above, when the test is not responded to in a standard manner. Where a test is invalid any interpretation of the scores must be done with caution. But even invalid tests tell some things about the person. If a boy can read well enough, does not lose his place in answering, yet responds to items in a pattern that suggests invalidity of his test, one can at least say that, unlike most boys in the test group, he is uncooperative or individual in some way.

The scales symbolized by L, F, and K (see the summary of scale characteristics on page 28) are called validity scales. These three scales aid in the formation of assumptions about the validity or truthfulness of the profile pattern produced by the ten clinical scales. These validity scales are complex and need to be separately described.

The L Score. High L scores signify an assumption of ostentatious virtue in the person's responses. In effect, he says that he does not share common human faults. Persons of this type respond "True" to items like "I am always sharp and alert" and "I never say a gossipy thing." Most people can claim a few virtues, but an L score higher than 9 from among the scale's 15 items is arbitrary evidence that some of the items that make up the clinical scales were probably responded to in what the person would consider to be the socially desirable direction. Profiles with L scores greater than 9 are called high L. Such profiles have to be interpreted with extra caution.

The F Score. The F score is made up of 64 items such as "I have convulsions," "I don't think people are basically good." These items are rarely marked "True." To answer many F items in the affirmative suggests overemphasis upon faults and complaints. A person might do this as a prank or as an appeal for help through claiming to be in great trouble. A high F score can also be the result of poor reading ability and poor comprehension of items. This should have been rare among the ninth-grade samples we used because the reading comprehension needed for the MMPI is well below that necessary for schoolwork at this level; however, some high F scores must have come from poor reading. High F scores can also occur as a symptom of severe mental disturbance, shown in part by a distortion and miscomprehension of the items. Finally, carelessness or uncooperative behavior, such as marking answers in the wrong place and answering items with deliberate disregard of instructions, will also produce high F scores. The boy who tossed a coin to determine his answers would have a profile invalid with high F and probably a high L as well.

Whatever the reasons for a high F score, such a profile is of doubtful validity. We have arbitrarily called invalid all profiles with F greater than a raw score of 15 items. A further subdivision separates these into "high F" and "ultra high F" (UHF). The high F profiles have scores from 16 to 21, inclusive. Although we have analyzed them separately, the scales of many high F profiles would probably be acceptable for inclusion in the data. UHF profiles with raw F scores of 22 or greater are not acceptable and are not analyzed. There is little doubt that many of those students who got a high F were uncooperative.

The K Score. The scale called K is composed of thirty items that were derived by elaborate study to sharpen the discriminatory power of some of the clinical scales (23, 33).

Edwards (8) has extensively explored a test factor that he has called Social Desirability (SD). This factor correlates highly with K. High K scores, therefore, are best described as indicating a response set favoring choice of the socially desirable response. It is allied to the L scale, but the measure is more subtle.

Low scores on K suggest more than average candor and tend to have a meaning similar to that of high F.

K is combined with clinical scales 1, 4, 7, 8, and 9 to improve their validity. Selection of K items depended upon analysis of MMPI profiles obtained from persons judges felt should have a high score on an MMPI scale but who did not, and of profiles from persons who were judged to be more normal but, paradoxically, obtained high scores. These items helped to push low scores higher for persons judged to be disturbed and to lower the scores of persons judged to be better adjusted. All this means that the K score is directed toward better differentiation of borderline mental adjustment. The borderline used in derivation was a T score of 70, so that the application of K is most justified in scores around 70.

The Clinical Scales

On page 28 are listed the ten clinical scales that are basic for the use of the MMPI. Although interpretation of these scales is based partly on knowledge of the mental disorders that the scales represent, as is illustrated in the following paragraph describing how scale 3 was constructed, it is not adequate or always meaningful to depend heavily upon clinical knowledge derived from mentally ill people. We have tried in our study to minimize the narrow diagnostic clinical approach. Although some meaning of what each scale measures is given by the diagnostic type of its derivation, many persons with high scale scores are not mentally ill. The scales also suggest components of personality that, although related to mental illness, are more typically expressed in patterns of normal behavior. The descriptions in the list suggest some of the common adjectives associated with high scores for each scale and with low scores for several scales. (See *An Atlas of Juvenile MMPI Profiles* (17), Tables 7 and 8, for added information.)

Scale 3 can be used to illustrate the origins of all the scales. The items of this scale were selected from response frequencies differentiating a group of patients whose mental illness included classical symptoms of conversion hysteria. These patients seem to attempt solution of their psychological problems or frustrations by developing such symptoms as pain, paralysis, or sensory defect. It has been said of them that the psychological symptom is converted into a physical one. When the frequency of the "True" response to an item by hysteria patients was clearly different from the frequency observed among normal persons, the item was considered to be one symptom of similarity among hysteria patients

THE THREE VALIDITY SCALES AND THE TEN CLINICAL SCALES OF THE MMPI

Scale Number	Scale Name	Clinical Expression	Normal Expression
	L	Unlikely degree of virtue	Score <10
	F	Many unusual symptoms	Score <16
	K	None	Circumspect; social desirability set; or, with low score, candid; low self-esteem
1	Hs	Hypochondriasis	Tired; inactive; lethargic; feels physically ill
2	D	Depression	Serious; low in morale; unhappy; self-dissatisfied
3	Hy	Hysteria	Idealistic; naive; articulate; ill under stress; social
4	Pd	Psychopathic deviation	Rebellious; cynical; disregards rules; socially aggressive; selfish
5	Mf	Interest pattern of the opposite sex	High score: sensitive. Low score: exaggerated own sex interest pattern. High score in males: gentlemanly; scholarly; feminine. High score in females: rough; ambitious
6	Pa	Paranoia	Perfectionistic; stubborn; hard to know; or, with moderate scores, socially acceptable
7	Pt	Psychasthenia	Dependent; desires to please; feelings of inferiority; indecisive; anxious
8	Sc	Schizophrenia	Negative; difficult; odd; apathetic; lacks social grace
9	Ma	Hypomania	Expansive; optimistic; decisive; not bound by custom
0	Si	Social introversion	Unassertive; self-conscious; shy; or, with low score, socially active

and, if it met a number of other requirements, it was assigned to scale 3. With experience it was soon observed that the scale measured aspects of personality only loosely correlated with the obvious clinical symptoms of hysteria. The words *idealistic, naive, articulate*, in addition to *ill under stress*, as found in the list, give a more meaningful characterization of a person with a moderately high 3 score than the clinical term. This does not deny the possibility that high-scoring people are prone to develop the symptomatic syndrome of hysteria if they must face psychological stress. Familiarity with the published research and accumulated clinical knowledge on scale 3 establishes a much richer meaning for the scale than can be conveyed here.

Every one of the nine other clinical scales was similarly derived; scale 0, however, used another test rather than a clinical diagnosis as the criterion. The list suggests the meanings well enough to give the reader some comprehension, but other source books should be used to learn extended scale meanings.

The Profile and Code

Among our thousands of collected MMPI profiles very few are alike. Despite this variety, profiles are probably not as variable as are the personalities of the children that they describe in a simplified manner.

For the analysis and description of MMPI experimental data it is necessary to simplify the profiles so that groups with a definite similarity among the members can be formed, and these groups must have enough members to permit statistical generalizations. One simplification is produced by coding, which is an arbitrary method of selecting and emphasizing part of the information in a profile in order to decrease the variability of profile types. Coding disregards some information in favor of simplification of the process of profile analysis. It is assumed that important information in the profiles is carried by the few scales on which the subject is most different from the average. Coding focuses on high and low scales of the profile and underemphasizes scores near the average. The near average scores are part of the information that is sacrificed; but coding emphasis upon deviant scores does not completely ignore average scores. If one scale among the ten MMPI profile scores is most extreme, it is obvious that other scores are not so much so and that they are nearer to the mean value. A profile with a certain scale named as most deviant is immediately known to be more clearly average on every one of the remaining nine scales. In coding, scales are exclusively referred to by the ten digits associated with the scales as shown in the list above.

The reader should become familiar with the numbers and names for the scales and with the coding process. The following brief account is intended to be only a general review of coding. More information can be found in *An MMPI Handbook* (6).

A code representing the clinical scales of an MMPI profile having one or more T scores at values greater than 54 always starts with the number of the scale on which the person has obtained his highest score. This number thus denotes the highest peak of the profile. Following this number, in order of height, are the numbers of all (if any) other scales for which the profile shows a score greater than 54. If T scores on any successive two or more of these ordered scales are equal or within one point of one another, these digit symbols of the code are underscored to show that they are interchangeable in position. When the profile has a score or scores that exceed 70, the digit symbols for these scales are separated from the rest of the code by a prime. (We use a double prime to separate a T score of 80, a triple prime at 90, etc.) The completed series of scale digit symbols and underscoring and primes, representing in descending order the scores that exceed 54, is called the high-point code.

A high-point code might be written, for example, 9′4–. This means that for this profile two clinical scales had a larger T value than 54; one of them, the score for scale 9, was 70 or greater. The score for scale 4 fell between 55 and 69, inclusive. The dash indicates the end of the high-point code.

As another example, the code ′413– would indicate that on this profile three scores were greater than 54, but none was as large as 70. Scale 4 was the highest, with scales 1 and 3 somewhat lower and equal in value or within one point of each other. (This high-point code can be read equally correctly as ′431–.) The dash again indicates that the high-point code has ended. This therefore means that scores on all scales not in the high-point code had T values of 54 or less. If no scale score exceeds the T value of 54, then the profile is referred to as a "no-high-point" profile (NHP).

Complete coding includes the writing of a low-point code if there is one. To write the low-point code, one begins with the lowest point of the profile. The digit symbols of scales are written following the dash of the high-point code in order as determined now by ascending values. This process, beginning with the lowest point, is continued upward to include a T score of 45. When the ordered digits that represent all scales with scores below 46 have been written, the low-point code is complete. Underscoring is used as in the high-point code to indicate scores that are equal or within one point of one another. A prime is used to separate scales of T score below 40.

A low-point code, for example, might read –2′90. The dash indicates the beginning of the low-point code and the 2 means that scale 2 was the lowest point of the profile. (The prime in this case shows that the scale 2 score was less than 40.) Scales 9 and 0 were at higher values but were still less than a T of 46. In the complete coding of a profile, scales having T scores of the values 46 to 54, inclusive, are not indicated in the code. These scores, lying near the average (a T of 50), are presumably less definitive than are the deviant scores that appear in the high-point and low-point codes. When there are no coded low points (below a T score of 46) the profile is referred to as a "no-low-point" profile (NLP).

A completely coded profile with both high- and low-point codes might read 6′84–′259. This would indicate that scale 6 was 70 or above in the profile; scales 8 and 4 were in the range 55–69, inclusive; scales 2, 5, and 9 were below 46 with scale 2 lower than 5 and 9, which were equal or within one point of each other. Finally, the remaining four scales (1, 3, 7, and 0) had values in the range 46–54, inclusive, since they do not appear among the digits.

Only the ten clinical scales are included in the high-point and low-point codes. Since, however, the validity scales are very important in the interpretation of a profile, the raw scores for these are listed following the codes. A fourth validity score, called Cannot Say, which gives the number of unanswered items, is usually omitted under the assumption that it is satisfactory (fewer than 40 unanswered items). No profiles with high Cannot Say scores are ever included in our research data, and hence these scores are not provided in the code data. On the other hand, L, F, and K values are always given. Thus, if the code above were followed by the numbers 4:2:18, it would mean that 4 was the raw score for L, 2 the raw score for F, and 18 the raw score for K. T scores for the raw scores can be obtained by looking in the tables of the MMPI *Manual*.

Application of Codes

Most of the personality test data of this report were analyzed to show how single-point codes (that is, codes showing only the highest or lowest scale) or selected code combinations are associated with the criterion, or behavioral, items. For example, the high 49 . . . profile type will be associated with delinquency. Simplified code analysis leaves some statistical problems. Even the two-digit codes (those showing the two highest scales on the profile) in combinations and permutations over the ten scales provide about one hundred discrete classes of profile and at least ten cases need to be in each class so that an observed relationship between the group in the class and some item of behavior will be reliable. If boys and girls are separated, as is usually necessary, then a hundred code types would require at least 1000 cases of each sex to provide ten cases for every code type. But the case profiles cluster; a relatively few code types are very frequent and many types are uncommon. Unfortunately, counselors and clinicians are usually more interested in deviant and rarer types than in the common ones, which are more often characteristic of well-adjusted, normal subjects. Another even more difficult problem arises when boys or girls are to be contrasted among themselves on another variable. For example, starting with the group in a certain code class and breaking them into several levels of socioeconomic status and again dividing these several socioeconomic subgroupings to show the rates of delinquency requires a large initial number of cases with the code type. The only solutions to the statistical study of relationships between code classes and criterion behavior lie either in reducing the number of code types to make larger groups or in having a very large population to study.

In our work, despite the fact that we started with a fairly large sample, we have often been forced to use very simple profile classes defined merely by the single highest or lowest score of the profiles. This grouping provides ten scale classes (plus the class for the no-high-point or no-low-point profiles) which are often too heterogeneous to allow many significant relationships to show in the analysis. In effect, this procedure amounts to saying that the whole MMPI permits the recognition of only eleven personality types. When the MMPI identifies one hundred personality types (by codes showing the first two high points), many of the code classes contain populations that are too small for study.

One of the best methods by which one can develop an appreciation of the behavior associated with code types is to use the MMPI atlases (14, 17). The principle of an atlas is simple. A large number of coded profiles are placed in numerical order so that any given code pattern can be easily found. With each profile is included a short descriptive history of the person who obtained it. There are about a thousand persons in each atlas. Since the histories were written independently of the codes, reading of these histories both permits some generalizations about code type and ensures some control of any tendency that the reader may have to over-interpret the MMPI profile.

Why the MMPI?

Our choice of the MMPI as the primary instrument for gathering data may strike the reader as unwarranted parochialism. The choice, however, was based on very practical considerations. At the time that our study was planned, late in 1945, there did exist other procedures and techniques that could have been used in addition to the MMPI to collect data. Studies by Burgess (3), the Gluecks (9, 10), Laune (22), Vold (31), Monachesi (25), Sanders (27), Weeks (32), and others had demonstrated by various procedures the probable existence of personality traits associated with delinquent and criminal behavior. When we considered the evidence, however, the data on the validity of the available devices were not very convincing and did not promise sharper discrimination than did the MMPI as reported by Capwell (4). Also, several of the tests required special administration or special decisions about each case and could not have been used in a routine manner except with considerably more expense than was practicable. As indicated above, we were interested in the limits of usefulness of testing that could be regularly done by schools in survey programs.

Our intention also was to explore maturational outcomes much more broadly than just in the field of delinquency. This report discusses other problems and we hope that reports will follow this one emphasizing mental illness and other problems of later life. The MMPI was the only test available that had some demonstrated validity across several of the numerous variables that may provide useful information. Even if the existing scales of the MMPI should be of little value for a given problem, the large and varied pool of items would permit exploration of new patterns.

By the time our study was extended to the statewide group in 1953–54, more devices for the prediction of deviant behavior had come into existence which might have been incorporated in our project. The Gluecks' 1950 experience tables had been published (11), the Gough delinquency proneness and social responsibility scales were known (13), and a revised edition of Kvaraceus' *K D Proneness Scale and Check List* had appeared in 1953 (19). But even if we had been interested in comparing the validities of prediction among these devices, we could not have engaged more time from school routines. We found that our testing program required two class periods. To ask for any more time would have led to appreciably more resistance to participation with us. We have meant only to survey the field; future work can be more definitive.

We hope that our data will provide tentative steppingstones to more definitive work. The significant questions we ask are not merely centered upon whether the available MMPI scales are related to later behavior but more broadly upon whether later behavior is foreshadowed by verbal statements like those elicited in the MMPI. Our data should either indicate the existence of positive relationships and encourage more intensive study of mental hygiene programs using objective tests or show that at least one objective test method is not sufficiently useful to warrant further experimentation.

The scales of the MMPI, derived from major syndromes of adult maladjustment, have some correlation with the degree of psychological maladjustment in mental disturbance areas broadly characterized by three terms — *neurotic, psychotic,* and *character disorder.* The use of the MMPI to estimate the relative strengths of these syndromes in the personality patterns of adolescent youngsters represents a compromise; we know of no other practical way to do this.

The establishment of correlation or other interaction between MMPI profiles and delinquency or another of our follow-up behavioral criteria in the material that follows does not permit elaborate interpretation. Statements about causal relationships are avoided, since we consider that at this point in the analysis such statements would be premature. For example, there is repeated evidence that scale 4 of the MMPI is correlated with the appearance of delinquent behavior. This relationship suggests, but does not prove, the existence of some overlapping of delinquency and the known clinical correlates of scale 4 among adult sociopathic disorders. That is, our data do not prove that scale 4 identifies sociopathic cases among the juveniles; the data agree with but do not closely support a hypothesis that there is a similarity of personality between some misbehaving juveniles and adults with syndromes of sociopathy. In summary, it seems that asocial sociopathy, the syndrome recognized in adult clinical work and partly identified with scale 4, contributes to the occurrence of juvenile delinquency. But even if the correlations between juvenile behavior and scale 4 were regarded as an expression of the syndrome of sociopathy, juvenile delinquency and adult diagnostic patterns may simply share two symptomatic expressions of some more general class or classes of disorder such as imperfect nervous system development or latent schizophrenia.

Where crucial issues like delinquency are involved, we have done item studies in order to determine which of the 550 items discriminate. This adjunct to the scale and code analyses best illustrates our real interest in laying a foundation for other work investigating objective tests. We could not explore the utility of all the more than 200 published scales of the MMPI, although there are many of these less known scales that seem to be promising. We have assumed that if items do not differentiate a group — for instance, delinquents — with much better than chance expectancy, then it is unlikely that any of the published scales would do so since item studies can be thought of as being the "atomic" level of differentiation.

To the degree to which we believe at all in the hypothesis of predictable outcomes, we have more faith in the discovery of some really new psychometric method than in further refinement of the general methods exemplified by the MMPI. Although the foregoing discussion is intended to show that we are not satisfied with the data we have, we do feel that our findings have practical applications and constitute promising bases for future work.

The MMPI Testing Procedure

The setting and attitude of the subject are of paramount importance for administration of a personality test. Also, where young people are the subjects, school authorities and parents must be in sympathy with the purposes of the testing so that they will be cooperative and understanding. Many personality testing programs have run into difficulty because those in charge neglected to inform all persons involved about purposes and procedures. The MMPI contains items that can be offensive unless the test is presented properly and assurance is given that the data will be used legitimately. The acceptable approach emphasizes the professional integrity of the investigators and respect for the persons providing the data.

We have never treated our testing program lightly. Trained field workers went to the schools. They first established contact with the superintendent, principal, and teachers. Superintendents or principals had previously received a letter explaining the general plan. When they came to a school, the project workers answered questions straightforwardly and honestly, and they tried to explain any technical issues that came up. School personnel who helped in the program were instructed how to answer questions from students during testing or later from parents. Every effort was made to develop really cooperative interest and participation.

Apparently this preparation for the testing was successful, since almost no difficulty developed. Despite the fact that many communities were known to be especially alert to protect their children from potential dangers in the measurement of personality and in exposure to the subject matter suggested by a few MMPI items, only one telephone call and two letters from parents reached the central office. The parents' letters stated that their child had told them of a "test" that was given at school and respectfully requested a copy of the test. These letters were carefully and honestly answered, but the test copy was refused on the grounds of confidentiality. It was explained that most children were normal but that data gathered on normal children were of great importance in the recognition of variations from normal. In other words, this test was justified on the same grounds that we justify inspection of teeth, chest X-rays, or any other examination made in the best interest of the pupil, without implication that he is abnormal.

It may be of some general interest that we clearly found this generation of children not as concerned about responding to personal items relating to sex or health as was expected by many adults with whom we worked. Adult concern over certain items seemed to indicate a contrast between the two generations. Sex items, for instance, rarely produced evident reaction among the younger generation. What did appear to trouble the boys and girls were affectional items and items concerning security. Their questions and doubts centered about self-confidence and interpersonal issues that related to social standing.

The testing was carefully planned to ensure a quiet and orderly setting. The examiner's procedural guide is given in Appendix A. Often the whole ninth-grade class was assembled in one room, but sometimes the class was large enough to require sectioning. Teachers helped in these arrangements. Not only were they instructed before the testing period on how to answer questions from the pupils, but they were cautioned not to stand so that any pupil would feel that his answers could be seen. If the teacher appeared to be especially nervous or doubtful, a careful effort was made to clarify the procedure. Most of the pupils' questions concerned word definitions. Some asked for help in making decisions. All were clearly told that they could leave blank any item that they felt they could not or should not answer. Teachers made every attempt to say no more than "Answer just as you feel" or "Leave it blank if you wish, but try to decide on an answer even if you are not sure it really describes you." As a result, few pupils left many items unanswered. Incomplete tests were usually from slow readers or pupils who for some other reason worked slowly. Teachers were also cautioned not to emphasize discipline. The professional bearing and ease of the project representatives was designed to contribute dignity and significance to the work.

Most important of all, the pupils themselves were fully instructed in the task required of them. The instructions to them took the following lines:

"This is a test to study personality. The study is being made by people at the university and your records will be kept by them. No one will look at your answers to individual questions because the grades depend on counting up the marks only. The test has a great many statements about people, what they like, and what they think. It is used to aid in advising men and women about jobs and other problems. We want to see if it will be a help when taken by persons who are younger. So we are asking you to do it. You may find that some of the statements don't fit you at all, or they won't fit you until you are older. If you find any of these, answer them the best you can or leave them blank, but try to answer every statement. Work quickly but don't be careless. Some of the statements will be in the past tense; for example: 'My father was a good man.' Answer as though in the present if your father is living and you are with him."

These instructions were given informally. Some time was allowed for students to ask questions in order to ensure understanding, but the test was started with little delay and individuals were permitted more questions after the group had settled down to work.

Any contributions to knowledge from our project should be considered as a tribute to the interested cooperation of school people, of parents, and of other responsible people in the community. Our task is to justify this cooperation. We again emphasize our conviction that unless research projects using personality tests are carefully designed and executed, the data will be less valid and social complications may result from actions of well-meaning but uninformed people.

THE NORMATIVE MMPI DATA

IT IS important that the subjects responding in MMPI testing have a standard attitude and expectation about the statements or questions so that they make their answers seriously and properly. This standard relationship, often called "response set," requires most obviously that the test situation be perceived similarly by the original subjects and those tested for routine clinical application of the test. We have described in Chapter 3 how we tested. The conditions of testing largely determine the response set that must be reproduced to assure standard responses.

Most MMPI statements are in the form "I liked school." The expected response is "True" or "False." Research data of this report do not depend entirely upon the subject's response being absolute or true. It may be merely a sign of qualified decision and still be valid for the test situation. A subject might answer "True" meaning "sometimes" or he might answer "True" because he considered that answer to be politic. Data such as we are presenting show relationships between follow-up behavior and the item responses given by the subject; it is not necessary that the individual item responses be assumed to be clear or true, only that they cross-validate. For example, one cannot say that the boys who respond "True" to the item stating that they liked school will show by other evidence that they really did like school. To establish their true attitude is a different problem. What is proper to say — and this is what is reported in our data — is merely that the item response "True" predicts or correlates with other behavior.

Validity Frequencies (Table 21)

In general the boys had more invalid profiles, with slightly more than one in every ten. The frequency of invalidity among the girls was approximately 50 per cent of that among boys. If the high F profiles are accepted as valid, the rate for invalid profiles of boys drops to 5.4 per cent; for girls the rate is 2.9.

No direct data are available to explain the higher incidence of invalid profiles among boys. In nearly every behavior area we studied, the boys were less cooperative and obedient — in school, home, and society. As already noted, a high F score on the MMPI is often due to failure to answer cooperatively and probably the frequency of high F profiles among boys represents one more example of general male perversity. It is consistent that high F boys have one of the highest rates of delinquency.

The rates for invalid profiles vary considerably with place of residence of the respondents (see Table 21). Rural residence tends to be the most productive of invalid profiles. When the rates for invalid profiles are grouped on the basis of chronological age, there is a consistent increase for every form of invalidity with increasing age among both the boys and the girls. For example, the rate of high F profiles was more than doubled among the sixteen-year-olds in comparison to those who were thirteen or fourteen years old. High L invalidity rates for age sixteen were higher in a comparable degree. These data are probably related to the special circumstances that contribute to older boys and girls being in the ninth grade.

It has been suggested that profession of unusual social conformity in responses to personality inventory items has a relationship to neurosis. The MMPI scales considered to be indicative of neuroticism do tend to be higher for persons with high L profiles. In contrast, the profiles of the high F cases were high on scales suggestive of schizophrenia or, more generally, of psychosis. The rates for both high L and high F invalidity are inversely correlated with intelligence and with scores on the Cooperative English Test. For example, the relative frequency of high F profiles for those with ACE scores below the fifteenth percentile is three or four times that among those with scores above the eightieth percentile. The corresponding relative rate for high L is similar to that of high F but even greater in magnitude.

Normative Data on Scales (Table 22)

The scale norm values for the Minneapolis and statewide valid profiles are listed in Table 22. For L, F, and K, the raw scores are given, while the statistics on the other scales are in T-score form. Statistical reliabilities of differences from adult norms (mean T score 50, standard deviation 10) are not shown because the large numbers in the sample assure the reliability of even the smaller differences which do not have much meaning.

The Intercorrelations of Scales (Table 23)

Table 23 presents intercorrelation matrices on MMPI scales for samples of the Minneapolis ninth-graders. The correlation between scales 7 and 8 and between scales 1 and 3 is high. A number of other high correlations may be observed, most of which are consistent with routine interpretation of the variables correlated. As should be expected, F and K are negatively correlated as are scales 0 and K. Most of the correlations obtained between a given pair of variables for boys were similar in value to the corresponding pair for girls. Although some of the sex differences approach statistical significance, we do not feel justified at this point in attempting interpretations of their possible meaning.

Code Frequencies (Tables 24 and 25)

Code frequencies provide the best expression of the MMPI data on personality. Table 24 gives the frequency rates (per thousand) of the combinations and permutations of the two-high-point codes.

This two-point code table clearly demonstrates the problems in research that arise with multiple classification. Most users of the MMPI who have had practical experience with two-point code classification of cases feel that it permits identification of very useful differences among the subjects. As an example, code 46 ... shows a rate of 19 boys per thousand. In our sample this means a total of 93 actually observed boys. Of these boys, 51 per cent were delinquent and 20 per cent dropped out of school (see Table 116). By contrast, code 50 ... occurred at a rate of only 5 per thousand, 23 boys in our sample. Of these boys, only 9 per cent were delinquent and only 9 per cent dropped out of school.

On the face of it, this seems to be a striking difference between groups — and it is one that most persons familiar with MMPI research data would have expected, that 50 ... boys would show lower rates of delinquency and dropout than 46 ... boys. But the number of 50 ... boys actually observed is too small for us to rely on the percentages, however rational and potentially useful they seem. And, of course, if these two-point code groups are further subdivided by any other variable, such as socioeconomic status or intelligence, then the numbers become impossibly small.

The difficulties stem from the fine classification that is provided by two-point codes. Even if subjects were to divide evenly among the 100 classes of Table 24, it would require 2000 in the sample to assure 20 in each class. In our study it is an advantage that some classes get many more than this, but the division still leaves the maximum number of boys at 311, which occurs for code 98 ...; even this number is too small for reliable analysis after the subjects are distributed on other variables. For the less common two-point codes, like 50 ..., any analysis must be done with great caution.

In summary, the two-point code tables — those giving the general frequencies and those giving frequencies for delinquency and dropout — contain much information which we have hesitated to develop although readers will find it profitable to look at the data against their own experience and make interpretations at their own risk.

For this report we have chiefly used the ten one-point code classes and the no-high-point (NHP) class, plus a no-low-point (NLP) class for the low-point tables, to develop our findings. At the cost of neglecting the finer two-point code information, our samples are thus much enlarged (see Table 25). It is these groups that provide the data for most of our tables relating the MMPI to other variables. We regret the loss of information that results from this grouping into one-point code types, but total samples would have had to be twice as large, at least, to permit use of the finer divisions. Drake (7) has used another method of analysis that is a compromise. We did not have this method available at first and later could not readily change.

Item Frequencies (Table 26)

The standard frequencies for the response of "True" to each item of the MMPI are given in Table 26. These figures were derived from a stratified sample of 100 boys and 100 girls with valid profiles taken from the statewide group. No information is provided on the frequency with which items were left unanswered since the selection of records for the analysis excluded those with many unanswered items. A comparison of these data with other item counts indicates that the values presented are representative and fairly stable.

Adult-Juvenile Differences (Tables 27–29)

We do not advocate the use of special juvenile norms with the MMPI, since to do so would arbitrarily erase much of the contrast between adolescents and adults. Persons concerned with children should be constantly aware of the degree to which special cultural conditions determine and modify evaluation of juvenile behavior. When test results are under study, use of adult norms keeps the amount and nature of the contrast always in view. We do provide normative data giving means in Table 22 and code frequencies in Table 24. A good practice for those working with juvenile cases is to overprint the regular MMPI profile charts with dotted lines showing the juvenile means and the juvenile means with 2 S.D.s added. For example, on scale 4 the mean would show a T score 59 and the corresponding 2 S.D. T score, comparable to the adult norm of 70, would be at 59 plus 21, which is T score 80.

Adolescents are not easy to absorb into our culture. A large number of them get test profiles suggesting that they are resisting their environmental restraints, and many other test profiles give the impression that these youngsters are suffering from some mental disturbance. If a profile drawn from the means shown in Table 22, several of which are well above the adult normal T score of 50, is interpreted as valid, there are clear similarities to the averaged data from adult patients who have been classed as having a schizophrenic or a sociopathic disorder. The average values of scales 8 and 4 are well above the normal value of 50.

Coded profiles provide more meaningful comparisons of adolescents and adults. Unfortunately, because of later modifications in the item structure of the MMPI, the records of the adult normative samples cannot be scored for scales 5 and 0. Our code comparisons are therefore based upon the remaining 8 scales. Table 27 lists the major contrasts.

The comparative data show that adults, especially women, get many more codes that suggest neurosis, scales 1, 2, and 3. Where other differences occur, most of them indicate that teen-agers more often have sociopathic or psychotic types of profile patterns than do adults, scales 4, 8, and 9.

One of the clearest differences in code frequency between juvenile and adult norms is found in the no-high-point profiles. By definition, these profiles have no T score on a scale higher than 54. To the degree that such profiles are indicative of normal personality, then normal personality is much more frequent among adults than among adolescents. To have a no-high-point profile the subject must not express enough complaints in any area encompassed by one or another of the MMPI scales to place him much above the adult normative average. The observation that so many young people show similarity to psychotic patients in their response patterns is interesting when contrasted to the data on the neurotic scales indicating that symptoms of depression, physical complaint, and psychasthenia are less common in the adolescent. Maturation appears to lead the average adolescent from a pattern of sociopathy or psychosis toward neurosis as an adult.

We are self-consciously lenient with children and unwilling to criticize or judge them by adult standards, but we often ambivalently treat even the ninth-grader as an adult. A fifteen-year-old who kills someone or who burns down a school or who is guilty of indecent sexual assault is subject to punitive or at least vigorous suppressive action. This must be so, and it takes a pathologically sympathetic adult to permit children, simply because they are children, freely to exhibit extremes of unrestraint or antisocial behavior. Society can afford only limited freedom to the adolescent; yet while complete freedom is never granted him, complete compliance with adult norms is rarely required of him either. Between these extremes there exists a great variety of limiting and governing, with the extent and rigidity of the rules differing from culture to culture.

Another view of the difference between adults and adolescents is provided by looking at the contrasting responses to individual items of the MMPI. Tables 28 and 29 list the items on which the largest differences in frequency of the response "True" occurred. (See also item differences between ninth- and twelfth-graders, Tables 79 and 80, and the discussion in Chapter 7.) These very interesting differences are in part merely what one would expect. Worry over money and business seems more appropriate to adults, but hunting lions in Africa is a juvenile wish. One highly differentiating element stands out for both sexes. Liking for poetry and history comes with maturity.

The boys, in contrast to male adults, appear to want adventure, but they feel themselves to be under family rule. They have fewer general worries; they do worry about their looks, yet they do not want expensive clothes. Love stories or serious subjects are relatively unpopular with them.

The items point to a greater variety of differences between girls and female adults than between boys and men. Although they do not choose to engage in adventuresome activity, girls do read adventure stories and newspaper articles about crime more than adult women. Like boys, they react against family and societal controls more than do adults, even to the point of hatred for such controls. Like the boys, they are freer from fears and worries than are adults, but they too worry about their looks. They blush more frequently than either boys or adult women. They try more openly to avoid boredom. More overtly religious than adults, they are also more tolerant. They endorse feminine vocational items and they like to flirt to a greater extent than women. Over half the adolescent girls would prefer working with women, but only 6 per cent of the adult women express this preference.

Sex Differences (Tables 30 and 31)

The normative tables show many sex differences. The adult norms that are used for T scores were adjusted to eliminate sex differences but small differences appear in the average norms for the adolescents (see Table 22).

Many of the high-point code frequencies in Table 24 show sex differences, some of the largest of which are pointed up in Table 30. We have published similar data on the Minneapolis sample (15). In both studies the girls display more feeling of social inferiority (scale 0). Although scale 2 (depression) is not a frequent high score among teen-agers of either sex, more boys than girls react with depression (see also Tables 77 and 78). Boys in the middle teens are often aggressively masculine (low scale 5). Girls exhibit a masculine role pattern (high scale 5) more often than boys exhibit femininity of interests (high scale 5). Girls frequently wish they were boys (70 per cent) and want the independence that society accords to the boys. When these girls become a little older, their average scores on scale 5 change to more feminine levels. Evidence on this point is also given in Chapter 6 where the stability of the personality pattern over the period from the ninth to the twelfth grade is discussed.

Profiles of boys are more likely than those of girls to have scale 8 coded high. This code trend occurs consistently in our data, and it is difficult to interpret. Perhaps it is not too wrong to say that at this point in their lives boys in contrast to girls have a greater need to establish their individuality, to be different, to be independent of the controls of their society.

Among the girls, feelings of social inferiority and reaction against their own sex along with being sensitive, easily hurt, and a little resentful (codes 0 and 5 with codes 64 and 67) combine to make a rather coherent middle teen-age pattern.

The sex differences in item response frequency shown in Table 31 specify the trends revealed by the scale and code differences. The separate items provide illustrations of the contrasts in sex role. Each reader may state his own generalizations from these item lists. The items are not isolated bits of behavior; each item suggests an area of sex difference that could be developed by additional items. Thus it is not very helpful to say simply that boys more often than girls like to read mechanics magazines or to repair a door latch. Boys like many other such activities. Similarly, to characterize girls as being afraid of mice or storms is too limited a description. It is more informative to employ generalizing adjectives like *sensitive* or *fearful* or *candid*. Such adjectives organize the pattern of correlated items expressing the feminine role, whereas *inquisitive* or *desirous of active outdoor activities* or *aggressive* might better characterize the male role.

The Omitted Items (Table 32)

As indicated earlier, when the MMPI testing was done, all the subjects were permitted to omit answers to items. Table 32 lists some of the most frequently unanswered items. These items are also interesting because they show sex differences in omission. Religion and sex appear to be the areas which produced the frequent omissions for both boys and girls. Sex items are more often left unanswered by the girls, possibly because girls have less information or experience in this area.

THE VARIABLES RELATED TO PERSONALITY

IN THIS chapter we shall show the MMPI personality characteristics of groups selected on the basis of other data and in the following chapter we shall start from MMPI classes and show how the other variables relate to personality. The first approach will be most useful to those seeking to identify personality patterns associated with various common categories of adolescents, such as those from broken families or from farms. The second approach will be most valuable for counselors and others who need to understand or predict the weak and strong aspects of an individual boy or girl classified by the MMPI.

As stated above, the ten types of single-high-point profiles plus those profiles with no high points provide the main MMPI categories (see Table 25). The profiles have also been classified on the basis of the lowest code point, with those profiles that have no coded low point in a separate category. Even with this extreme restriction on the fineness of division into MMPI types, the sample size is often too small; and when no relationship is reported, the reader should remember that the reason may be that there were not enough cases for a reliable statement. We are using very simple statistical methods for this profile analysis, since our purpose is to employ a level of complexity which is easily followed by readers without special statistical skills, and the system is probably not maximally discriminatory.

Explanation of the Tables

The main tables provide chi-square information. Each table cell shows three values: the observed population of the cell; the expected population hypothesized from the marginal total; and finally, the cell chi-square (χ^2) contribution to the total for the table, column, or row. Also indicated are the reliabilities of the differences from marginal expectations for the rows and columns. The individual cells are marked by daggers where the observed number of cases differs considerably from the expected values.

The chi-square analysis is so important in the results reported here that the reader not familiar with the technique should follow a detailed example. Table 34 provides illustrative figures, and a portion of that table is reproduced here to help the reader follow the explanation in the text.

High Scale	Duluth and Suburbs		Towns		Farm		Total N	χ^{2a}
	o	e	o	e	o	e		
4	297	243	344	335	147	210	788	
	12.15†		.25		19.10†			31.50***
Total N	1226		1693		1061		3980	
χ^{2a}	26.36**		6.78		51.40***			84.54***

$$^{a}\chi^{2} = \Sigma \ \frac{(o - e)^{2}}{e} = 12.15 + .25 + 19.10 = 31.50.$$

In the Total N column, one finds the total number of boys distributed in this row, which is 788. This means that among the 3980 boys in the sample with valid profiles, 788 had profiles with scale 4 highest among the ten scales. This total high 4 number is about 20 per cent of the 3980 boys. The second item from the bottom of Table 34 in the column labeled Duluth and Suburbs shows that 1226 boys lived in those urban regions. Now, if 20 per cent of all boys were high 4, under the hypothesis that place of residence has no selective effect, the expectation is that 20 per cent of the Duluth and suburbs boys would score highest on scale 4; this would amount to 243 boys, which is the figure appearing in the High 4–Duluth and Suburbs cell under the subheading e. The number 243 is the *expected* number of boys from urban areas who would get a high 4. In the left side of this cell under the column symbol o appears the number 297. This is our *observed* number of urban boys who actually had high 4 profiles. There were, then, 54 more boys actually observed than the 243 that were to be expected if place of residence had had no selective effect. It appears that some influence led more urban boys to get high 4 than could have been predicted by applying the total row-derived value of 20 per cent. The χ^{2} is starred, which means it is probably a statistically true (not due to chance) finding that urban boys more often have the personality suggested by high 4. Finally, since the cell High 4–Duluth and Suburbs contributes 12.15 to the χ^{2}, which is a large value adding into the column and row χ^{2} values, we have placed a dagger by that value. The criterion determining whether a dagger is assigned is the value of χ^{2} that would suggest a significance level of .05 with one degree of freedom. This procedure is an arbitrary one but serves to highlight the cells with larger differences. We also arbitrarily chose not to use this cell-marking system unless, first, the whole table and, next, either the column or row developed a χ^{2} that suggested significant variation with a probability of .05.

Searching the tables for reasonably established trends in the data, one can look at columns and rows where there is one asterisk or more and, within the column or row, the cell or cells marked with a dagger, for the main evidence. The asterisks by the numbers 31.50 and 26.36 in the column and row signify that the High 4 row and the Duluth and Suburbs column both show a high probability that they are distributed significantly differently from the distributions that would be expected from the margin totals. One can say that both the way the high 4 boys fall into the three population density categories and the way the urban boys fall into the eleven personality categories are unlikely to be a result of random variation from the over-all distribution.

The chi-square values are measures of the amount of observed variation from the expected values. In reading the tables, one should attend to these values. When they are large, one may expect to find a selective factor operating; when there is little variation, one assumes there is no strong selective factor. Both the large and small values can therefore be interpreted. In the same table, for example, the χ^2 values of 6.78 for the Towns column is not starred and is not significantly large. One concludes that the personality types of boys living in towns are distributed in a way not appreciably different from the general expectation. The data in the Farm and the Duluth and Suburbs columns suggest that the forces operating to cause variation in the urban sample and in the farm sample balance out so that towns fall between, as they actually do in density of population.

Finally, although we have used the distributions of the totals as hypotheses, one could imagine other hypotheses. We give the observed values so that readers may judge for themselves. Cells that do not appear significant at the e values we use could be very significant against some other hypothesis. This is an important consideration in the data. Suppose, for example, that one were to assume that the personality factor represented by high 4 boys is almost exclusively a result of urban living. This hypothesis would place possibly 90 per cent of the high 4 boys in the Duluth and Suburbs cell. The e value would then be 90 per cent of 788 which would be 709 instead of 243 as we have it. Obviously the observed value 297, although it is convincingly larger than 243, is not nearly so large as the 90 per cent hypothesis would require. One ends by concluding that, although there are more high 4 boys in the cities than one expects on the basis of the general population, there are not enough more to support the hypothesis that most all high 4 boys will be found in cities.

Interpretation of Results (Table 33)

The suggested meanings of the MMPI code classes are derived both from the criterion group data on which the scales were based and from published material suggesting correlates of the codes and scales. Clinical experience with the MMPI as reported in the atlases (14, 17) and in other sources can provide the reader with richer evidence about what the profiles mean (see Chapter 3).

We do not know how much information about personality is contained in the statement that a profile belongs to a certain code class. From the rules for coding, a profile coded high 0, for example, has scale 0 as the highest point among the ten coded MMPI scales and the T value of scale 0 is at least 55. But if scale 0 is the highest scale point on the profile, this tells us that the other nine scales have T-score values less than that of scale 0. How much more this additional fact tells us about the personality is dependent on a complex of the validities and covariances among the other scales. We are confident, however, that the use of codes provides at least some access to the combined information in the profiles contrasted to the information carried by each scale score considered separately. We are confident that saying a profile is of the high 0 type is more meaningful as a personality classification than is the usual approach which depends upon classes determined from each scale separately. We have come to consider the separate scale method to be so weak that we have relied on it very little. Our use of codes means that our findings cannot be replicated unless similar code type or other configural classes are used.

Each profile has only one code and there is an advantage in this. If one must describe a given person from his separate scores on several scales, then the interpretation is made complex by the fact that he can be classed differently by each scale; he does not belong to a single class. Replication of personality descriptions from the separate multiple viewpoints of several scales with different meanings is not easy — the integration of the several scale meanings and their observed values for an individual comes from arbitrary judgments by the one offering the description. By contrast, the use of a single code class for each profile makes an objective classification for most individuals, and descriptions of personality characteristics for each class can be accumulated to apply to all those who fall into it because one has a meaningful group for generating the descriptive statements.

Table 33 summarizes some of the most significant information from the series of chi-square tables that follow. The rows show the main categories of each of the variables and the column headings consist of descriptive terms that can be associated with the code high or low points. The numbers in parentheses identify the scales referred to. To illustrate the way the table may be read, consider the first row. Urban homes differ from rural homes in that, in urban families, daughters (F) are more enthusiastic or optimistic, more socially extroverted, but also more rebellious and selfish. Comparatively more boys from urban homes than from rural are also socially extroverted and rebellious, but the overactive component is not so common as for the girls. For another illustration consider the second column from the right. Masculine interests as suggested by this MMPI scale, often described as roughness or aggressiveness, are more commonly observed among rural girls and among girls with poor English test scores than among girls in other categories. For the boys, the MMPI masculine traits are more frequent among those with low ability, low English scores, and poor grades, those who drop out of school, those for whom delinquency is predicted, and those who become delinquent.

Place of Residence and Personality (Tables 34–37)

The size of the community resided in is associated with some large average variations in frequency of personality type, communities being arbitrarily grouped, by population density, into three classes: Duluth and the Twin Cities suburbs, towns, and farm.

Among the larger observed deviations to be noted in the tables are those related to scale 4. City and farm boys and girls are strongly differentiated on this indicator of psychopathic personality traits. Scale 4 is frequently interpreted as an indicator of revolt and resistance toward home and community controls. These traits are often considered to emerge in response to a complex system of social expectations coupled with too little real place for youth in the affairs of community and family. The data clearly agree with the formulation that this is so, since urban living is characterized far more than farm living by numerous social rules and regulations.

Table 37 shows an interesting trend for farm girls. There are more low 4 profiles than would be predicted. The low scale 4, especially for girls, is often associated with behavior that is passively responsible almost to a fault. Such girls may give up school and marriage in order to care for their parents or to take on some other family or religious duty. This dutiful role is perhaps a little too old-fashioned to show up with prominence among city girls.

Urban and rural youngsters also show differences in the degree of their social response. The scale 0 data in all four tables indicate that the trend is toward social ease and participation as a characteristic of those living in the city contrasted with feelings of social inferiority among those in rural areas. The tables suggest that both boys and girls in rural areas are likely to suffer appreciably more often socially than their urban counterparts, the girls showing the clearer trend.

The more isolated life in rural areas has been thought to engender schizoid personality traits. To the degree that scale 8 is an indicator, Table 34 supports this hypothesis, for rural boys more frequently than urban have high scale 8. The trend is not very strong, however. Contrasting to schizophrenia, affective disorders, particularly manic-depressive states, have been shown to be more frequent in urban and suburban localities. This trend appears among the girls in the sample. Those in urban areas more often get high 9 profiles than those in rural communities. Also, low scale 9 profiles are more common for girls living on farms (see Table 37). The combination of low scale 9 with low scale 4 noted above implies that girls in rural areas have a more passive personality makeup than city girls.

It is probably not surprising that farm girls get more high masculine scores, high scale 5 (see Table 35). Rural living often encourages girls to assume masculine roles. There is no contrast, however, among farm and city boys on this measure of masculine or feminine interests.

Socioeconomic Status and Personality (Tables 38–42)

As noted earlier, for the Minneapolis sample we used the rent level of blocks of residence as a rough measure of socioeconomic status and selected two Minneapolis school districts with high average socioeconomic status for contrast with three school districts with low average socioeconomic status. The selection of these schools is described more completely in Chapter 2. It is well to remember that socioeconomic status may not be the proper name for the differences between the families of these contrasted school areas. The contrast is between neighborhoods. These "high" neighborhoods contrast with the "low" in the usual way that a suburban middle- and upper-class area would differ from an area of rooming houses, apartments, and generally low income. A relatively large number of Negro families live in the "low" area.

Table 38 shows the personality contrast for the boys of the two neighborhoods. So far as can be seen from the data here, there is little evidence to support the idea that these contrasting neighborhoods generate or encourage sharply different personality trends — this despite the evidence that will be detailed in Chapter 8 that there is a fairly marked difference in delinquency rate. Although the most significant point of the table lies in the absence of indicated personality differences, the boys in the poor neighborhoods do show up as likely to be depressed. Possibly these boys react to the economic and social limitations of their surroundings.

The five socioeconomic classes of the statewide sample show some interesting and strong differences in the frequency of personality patterns. To a considerable extent these findings are in accord with various sources that have reported association of social class with mental illness.

There is some overlapping of the findings in these tables on the statewide sample with those concerning place of residence as developed in the previous section. For instance, to have a farmer for a father suggests living on a farm, and the data on the farmer socioeconomic status are, of course, generally consistent with those on farm as place of residence. There is some variation, however. Farmers sometimes live in town or in suburban areas; and, conversely, although some of the subjects lived on farms, their fathers had other occupations than farming.

The sons and daughters of farmers show a distinctly lower rate of the high scale 4 psychopathy than is true for any other group. With the concentration of observed difference showing mainly in the farmer columns, there is more reason to think that children of farmers are better adjusted in respect to whatever this scale measures than to think that any other group is worse adjusted. The data in tables to follow show that delinquency rates fall into this same pattern: the children of farmers are definitely less likely to be delinquent. The low delinquency rate is even more marked for the children of farmers than it is for boys and girls who live on farms but whose fathers are not farmers. But see the data on ninth- and twelfth-grade tests as presented in Chapter 7. It may be that both high scale 4 and delinquency rates are delayed a year or two and then rise to levels similar to those for other groups. Note also Table 18 where the delinquency rates for nineteen-year-olds seem to be identical for the Minneapolis and statewide samples.

The tables also show a tendency for the boys and girls from semiskilled families to get more high 4 profiles than do the other urban groups. The difference reaches probable significance for the girls. If such evidence is accepted, a reasonable hypothesis would be that the scale 4 expression of socioeconomic stress is most sharply demonstrated in the middle socioeconomic ranges rather than at the day-laborer level. From the semiskilled level the reactive stress decreases through the clerical down through the professional and farmer levels.

Data in Chapter 8 show that delinquency rates, usually correlated with rates of high scale 4, are higher among the day-laborer families. Again, if the data are accepted, one may assume that delinquency is a compound of low socioeconomic class status and the personality reaction of high 4. Both lower socioeconomic levels have higher rates of scale 4 and delinquency than the professional level, but the expression of the scale 4 through delinquency is more characteristic in the day-laborer families.

As was found in the preceding tables, high scale 0 is frequently characteristic of children of farmers. This is clearer for the girls. It is interesting that from among the other classes, the girls with clerical-level fathers are least likely to feel socially inferior (see Table 40).

If one considers a low scale 0 to be indicative of social extroversion, then the most dramatic finding is the rate of this characteristic among professional and semiprofessional families (see Tables 41 and 42). This extroversion rate gains interest when one considers the increasing emphasis upon the development of socialization in modern life. At the other end of the socioeconomic groupings, children of day laborers do not appear to be often handicapped by feelings of social inferiority, nor for that matter are they contrastingly characterized by social extroversion.

The femininity of interest patterns suggested by high scale 5 is clearly more marked for the boys from professional and semiprofessional homes than for others (see Table 39). For the girls whose fathers are farmers a masculine interest pattern is common (Table 40), although the trend is not so strong as was characteristic of the girls classified by farm residence (Table 35). The fact that the day-laborer and semiskilled fathers do not have more than the predicted number of sons who are highly masculine may be contrary to general expectation. The Minneapolis data for boys demonstrate only a weak tendency for feminine boys to be found in schools of high socioeconomic status (see Table 38). This variable seems more strongly related to verbal abilities and good grades (see Tables 51 and 55).

Scale 3, besides being connected with the neurotic trait of hysteria, is often interpreted as indicating a domination of middle-class cultural values. In part it is a measure of conformity. It might be expected that there would be relatively more high scale 3 children from professional homes, which does appear to be true for the boys, although the numbers are small. This trend is opposite that among boys from the day-laborer homes who very rarely have high 3 (see Table 39). A clearer finding that fits in is that low scale 3, a personality pattern not readily interpreted except as a lack of highly assimilated middle-class socialization standards, occurs definitely less frequently among the upper-class girls and definitely more frequently among the girls whose fathers are day laborers (see Table 42). The Minneapolis sample data are consistent. High 3 is a little more frequent among boys in the higher socioeconomic neighborhoods than among the other groups, but the general frequency rate is low (see Table 38). In summary, these data show that, although the pattern of social conformity and of physical illness as a solution to psychological stress is not a dominant feature in children of upper-class families, it ranks definitely higher among them than among the lower-class families.

One item that we found surprising was the failure of high scale 8 to be closely related to socioeconomic status. Neither the statewide nor the Minneapolis data show more than a weak correlation. High scale 8 codes suggest symptomatic similarity to schizophrenia, and this disorder has repeatedly been considered to be the modal psychiatric illness among adults of low socioeconomic status. High scale 8 does relate closely to low high school rank (Tables 59 and 60), low intelligence (Tables 51 and 52), and school dropout (Tables 130 and 131). All these factors would tend to affect the socioeconomic status of the high 8 children as they become adults — their lack of competitive assets would lead to a progressively lower socioeconomic standing. The reported low socioeconomic levels of origin for adult patients called schizophrenic appear to result in part, at least, from a downward socioeconomic mobility of the affected persons as they grow older. We consider these suggestions to be consistent with reports of Lane and Albee (21) who show by comparing childhood intelligence test performance to intelligence tests taken during psychosis that no significant deficit was found as a consequence of schizophrenia. The deficit predated the illness by many years.

A final point of interest is suggested in Tables 38 and 39 when we attend to scale 2, depression. The Minneapolis boys from "low" neighborhoods tend to show a little more than the expected amount of depression. This trend is not shown in Table 39, the table for the statewide boys. In the Minneapolis study, the "low"-status boys, by definition, come from urban areas of poor environment; for the statewide sample, classification in the low socioeconomic group was dependent upon income, not neighborhood lived in. There may well be a psychically depressing effect on boys peculiar to life in a bad neighborhood.

Marital Status of Parents and Personality (Tables 43–46)

The tables showing the relation of the parents' marital status to personality are dominated by the normative preponderance of intact families. At the time of the test, assuming that the children's reports were reasonably accurate, there were more than sixteen ninth-grade children from an intact family to every one from a broken family. Differences can be described with either reference, but we chose the usual emphasis and consider the tables to express the personality trends in the broken family against the intact family as a norm.

The data on scales 4 and 0 in Tables 43 and 44 show a sharply increased rate of psychopathic personality and a relative infrequency of feelings of social inferiority among both boys and girls from broken families. It is a little surprising that social inferiority is less observed than would be expected. Since Tables 45 and 46 do not have an excess of scale 0 low points, neither social extroversion nor introversion appears as a marked outcome of a broken family.

In contrast to the boys, the girls with separated or divorced parents get profiles that show a high 8, or schizoid, trend (see Table 44). For most comparisons this profile is typical of boys in contrast to girls, but here the pattern is reversed and the girls seem to be the ones adversely affected on this measure. The magnitude of the effect on the girls suggests a sharp sex difference that should influence our evaluation of the meaning of a broken home to the children in it. It would seem, for example, that the daughters in these homes deserve special attention in the hope of preventing at least the symptoms of scale 8 and possibly the later development of mental illness.

The mere fact that a family is broken does not appear to operate nearly so powerfully as do some other factors in producing children with personality deviations. This becomes apparent if one looks among the various tables to compare its effects with those of other variables.

Effect of Absence of Family Member(s) on Personality (Tables 47–50)

When the children from broken families are divided on the basis of the person with whom they live, it is interesting that no significant deviations among the groups can be observed in terms of the personality traits. Apparently the effects on personality of living with neither parent, with a stepparent, or with the mother or father alone as compared to living with both parents are not dramatic. But most of the cells of the tables have very small expected numbers, and it is therefore not possible to draw firm conclusions.

Later data will indicate that living with the mother alone is related to an increased delinquency rate (see Tables 92 and 93). Throughout Tables 47–50 there is a slight consistent trend, though unreliable, for boys who live with only their mother to show a greater amount of psychopathy than expected. Another unreliable trend shows that girls who live with neither parent have more of the schizoid personality than other girls. This finding may be related to the corresponding data on Table 44 that show the effect of broken families.

Intelligence and Personality (Tables 51–54)

Intelligence test scores, for the most part from the ACE, were available for a large number of the subjects. For purposes of analysis, the raw scores were first converted to percentiles and then grouped into three samples roughly equal in number.

A finding of interest appears for scale 5 where, among boys, intelligence is closely related to femininity of interests. Tables 51 and 53 both show this among the boys. Masculine boys are more common at the lower ability levels and boys with feminine interests are more common at the higher ability level. In our culture, recognized male scholars tend to be interested in art, literature, education, and cultural stability. These areas of interest describe main areas of sex differences on tests such as the MMPI. Among the girls, the effect of intelligence is most noticeable in Table 54, where many girls in the high-ability group have 5 as their lowest profile point, low 5 signifying femininity and the areas of interest described above in girls as does high 5 in boys. Girls in the low intelligence group do not show masculinity by high 5 in Table 52. However, low Cooperative English scores do seem to relate to high scale 5 among the girls (see Table 56).

The behavior of scale 8 among the tables on intelligence and related variables (Tables 51, 52, 56, 57, and 58) shows a very significant concentration of high scale 8 in relation to low intelligence, poor verbal ability, and low high school grades. In Tables 130 and 131, school dropouts also have a much higher frequency of high 8 profiles than those who do not drop out of school. The reader is referred to page 48 where the relation of socioeconomic status and schizophrenia is discussed.

It may be maintained that the common element between scale 8 and the ability measures is chiefly reading ability. Poor ability to read, it might be assumed, makes for a high scale 8 score and is the meaningful factor in the related measures. No direct refutation of this is available. The cases for the tables all had valid F scores on the MMPI (see Chapter 3). Since the F score had to be low, it is hard to believe that high scale 8 scores could come from poor reading ability. With the evidence available, we believe that the better choice is to consider that the symptomatic syndrome of schizophrenia (not the psychotic illness) is the meaningful variable in the intellectual deficiencies.

That frequencies of most forms of maladjustment are inversely related to ability comes out in the comparative rates of no-high-point and no-low-point profile types, especially in the data of Tables 53 and 54. Another significant item is the infrequency of low depression score profiles among low-ability girls (see Table 54). Possibly it is better to say that absence of symptoms of depression is characteristic of high-ability girls. The trend does not extend so far as to result in many low-ability girls having depression as a chief high point (see Table 52).

English Usage Test and Personality (Tables 55–58)

There is considerable correlation between the Cooperative English test and the group tests for academic ability that provided the data in Tables 51–54. These correlations are .80 and .82 for 50 random boys and 50 random girls. It is consistent that scale 5, particularly for boys, shows a sharp relationship to these test scores: the upper English score group has more feminine boys. The trend among girls is also clear and consistent: the low scale 5 frequencies of Table 58 indicate that the more feminine direction of interests is associated with high English scores.

Poor English usage scores for both boys and girls appear with the schizoid component in personality. This is mainly apparent at the lowest ability level, although even in the middle group there are fewer high scale 8 profiles than expected. These data have been discussed above relative to the personality characteristics of low intelligence test scores (Tables 51–54).

High English ability scores from boys have a positive relationship to scale 3. This agrees with previous findings that, in recent times, hysteroid persons are more frequent at the higher ability levels. Among the girls a similar trend might be inferred from the absence of low 3 for those in the high English score group (see Table 58).

English test scores, like intelligence scores, differentiate boys by the fact that a good English test level is associated with low code 9. Good English scores also go with low code 0. Low scale 9 can be interpreted as symptomatic of a relatively lower energy output and less tendency to develop active enthusiasms; the low scale 0 is somewhat contrastingly indicative of social extroversion. Summarizing the evidence, one would say from Tables 55 and 57 that boys who get good English usage scores are less likely to be energetic and enthusiastic and yet more likely to exhibit social extroversion than low-scoring boys. The social extroversion relationship is clear for both boys and girls. The relationship between these personality traits and English ability tends to link social facility and hysteroid traits with language skill. To a definite degree, verbal aptitude is demonstrated as a positive value in adapting to our culture.

Profiles with no low point, meaning profiles in which no scale shows a value much below average, are far more common among girls with low English scores than among those with high scores. Indirectly this could be interpreted to say that girls with less ability to express themselves are likely to admit having an average or great number of complaints in every maladjustment area among the MMPI scales.

High School Rank and Personality (Tables 59–62)

Since high school rank is some kind of outcome of ability, motivation, and other aspects of personality that relate to grades and teacher acceptance, it is not surprising that large personality differences are reflected in Tables 59–62. In part, the tables increase the evidence on the points that have been made relative to the intelligence and English usage tests. For example, the upper high school grade ranks contain about twice as many boys with feminine interests as are predicted (see Table 59). Perhaps the small number of high scale 5 boys in the lower school grade group is of greater significance. Among the masculine boys of Table 61 the effect is more sharply evident. Boys with scale 5 as the lowest point of their profiles are in great preponderance below the 40th percentile high school rank.

In Table 62 the girls who get good grades are also more often feminine in interests. The relationship here is even stronger than was true when girls were grouped by the intelligence or English usage measures. Whatever MMPI scale 5 may otherwise measure, it does certainly express something significant for academic achievement.

High school rank, with even greater intensity than intelligence, shows variation of high scale 8 for both boys and girls. Corresponding with many clinical evidences, the finding here is that those adolescents with schizophrenic symptoms as a dominant feature of their MMPI profiles are definitely inferior in scholastic achievement.

Social conformity, if that is an interpretation of high scale 3, shows some increase with high academic rank, particularly among boys; among girls, and in less degree among boys, scale 3 as a low point is associated with low grades. That there should be a conformity factor associated with grade level seems reasonable. If one speaks of conformity as the key in these data, it should probably be stressed that conformity is very complex. At the moderate levels suggested by these code 3 profiles, the trait is not associated with inhibiting conformity but rather with enthusiastic conformity. Conforming to the value system of teachers suggests cooperation, attention, and a vigorous protest of self-reliance and other desirable qualities.

Low scale 9 can be interpreted to indicate that the person is not under pressure from energy and enthusiasm. Both boys and girls with 9 lowest in the profile are clearly likely to get good grades. The evidence from these data and those on high 3 profiles can be said to show that good grades are given to students who sit still, do what they are told, and are not readily or easily distracted. These personality factors go also with the intelligence (see Tables 51–54).

Conduct and Adjustment Ratings and Personality (Tables 63–70)

Three years after the ninth-grade testing, sets of ratings on conduct and adjustment were made by the field workers who collected the follow-up data. The source of these ratings was comments the field workers got from the people who talked about the subjects. A worker did not necessarily ask about conduct and achievement; instead the person giving information was led to respond broadly regarding the teen-ager's behavior in and out of school, using any terms he chose, and this information was then rated arbitrarily by the worker on a five-point scale from 0 through 4 for both adjustment and conduct, with the special rating 5 on the conduct scale for girls known to have had an illegitimate pregnancy or a forced marriage. This latter rating was quite valid when assigned, but some illegitimate pregnancies were not discovered. The ratings for severe conduct or adjustment problems were infrequent enough so that levels three and four are combined in the tables. The value of the data lies in the ways in which the personality test variables were expressed in the adjustment or conduct of the boys and girls as described by the teachers and others who knew them.

On both adjustment and conduct, those with high scale 4 profiles were given the severe ratings 2, 3, and 4 more often than others. Psychiatrists and psychologists in classifying young people who become delinquent or develop other forms of bad conduct regularly place certain of them in the diagnostic groups named psychopathic deviate or identified by some related terms. The ratings shown in these tables, like all other appropriate comparisons, confirm that scale 4 type adolescents are similar in behavior to the cases that are known professionally.

Scale 5 also shows the usual trend. Boys with masculine interests are more often rated as having bad conduct and boys with aesthetic and cultural interests are more often rated as good, that is, well behaved. This cultural rejection of the boys with low 5 scale scores should be evaluated along with the fact that such boys have a high rate of delinquency. This group of boys may represent a neglected area for development. Schools and most present-day vocational outlets possibly provide for too little expression of the interests of the low 5 boy, leaving him frustrated and low in self-esteem.

The most consistent trend of personality, related to both adjustment and conduct ratings for both boys and girls, is measured by the low-point frequencies on scale 9 shown in Tables 65, 66, 69, and 70. Low scale 9 suggests passivity and low expression of energetic interest. Such persons are rarely seen as bad in adjustment or conduct. In some degree this trend can mean that the unobtrusive child in school simply does not get rated. One may entirely miss the fact that some quiet child is maladjusted.

Scale 6 also provides some interesting data in these ratings. When the paranoid elements of the scale are not at abnormally high levels, it is customary to think of the scale as an indicator that the person is sensitive to criticism and, more generally, sensitive in interpersonal relationships. Tables 64 and 68 show that high 6 girls infrequently get an adverse rating for either adjustment or conduct.

These ratings significantly fail to differentiate the scale 8 profiles. Although this scale has been closely related to low intelligence and low scholastic achievement in the earlier tables, it does not seem to be pertinent in the ratings of adjustment or conduct. Thus, one of the most pervasive scale indicators of maladjustment appears not related to what the observers describe as maladjustment or bad conduct. There is a suggestion here that some of the really threatening adjustment problems in adolescents are not readily perceived. This may be an area where test data would be most effective in identifying those with problems who would otherwise be overlooked.

The rather small group of girls rated in the special category 5 is of interest because it is here studied in a more natural sample than are samples from maternity homes, agencies, and the like. The data in Tables 68 and 70 imply that these girls with illegitimate pregnancy have no personality traits that distinguish them from girls in general. The only item of any size at all appears in Table 70 — an infrequent low 9. Low 9 girls may be described as not so restlessly active as many of their peers. It may be surprising that high 4 girls are not represented with significant frequency among the illegitimately pregnant girls.

There have been many studies of the unmarried pregnant girl. So far as we are aware, this sample is the only one of any size in which the personality testing occurred before the pregnancy. Studies that have used girls already pregnant compared to a control group of girls have reported personality differences. For example, with the CPI scale of socialization (related to MMPI scale 4) Vincent (30) reported an average difference, pregnant girls being less well socialized. If there is a true contrast in these data, then it may be that, like delinquency, illegitimate pregnancy has a measurable effect upon the personality structure so that only longitudinal studies can analyze the predisposing personality factors. It is also possible that there would have been more difference if this study had been done around 1935, before cultural changes resulted in earlier marriages and the population rate increase.

Teacher Predictions and Personality (Tables 71–74)

At the time of MMPI testing the teachers were asked to name some boys and girls whom they expected would get into trouble with the law or develop emotional maladjustments. We refer to these as the teacher prediction groups. It is of interest to see which MMPI personality scales have the closest relationships to the teachers' choices (see also Chapter 8).

In predicting delinquency, the teachers undoubtedly knew of the existing records of some of their pupils (see Tables 105 and 106). In any case, they chose heavily from among those with psychopathic symptoms as shown by high scale 4. This was especially true for the boys and the girls who were listed by a teacher in both of the categories (see the "Both" column of Tables 71 and 72). Schizoid boys were also seen as likely to get into trouble with the law. Very few girls were chosen as likely delinquents, and the data on girls are not reliable except for the high scale 4 cases.

Obsessive-compulsive adolescents (high scale 7) and those socially introverted (high scale 0) are less often seen as probably delinquent. In accord with many other data, the teachers choose masculine boys (low scale 5) as likely to be delinquent (see Table 73).

Except for girls with no-low-point codes, there was not much relationship between the teacher choices for emotional trouble and the personality variables. What trend there is seems well accounted for by stating that the girls the teachers selected seemed to have more general symptoms than other girls. This statement is indicated by the no-low-point data. Another generality might be that those seen as likely to develop emotional problems were more diverse than were those expected to become delinquent.

PERSONALITY RELATED TO
THE VARIABLES

THIS section reviews with a fresh approach the findings presented in Tables 34–74 concerning the association between the MMPI scales and the variables by abstracting for each high-point and low-point personality class the most significant data on environment and behavior. As the emphasis in Chapter 5 was on the variables — what personality patterns are found to be characteristic of each group classified by some environmental or behavior criterion — here it is on the personality class — which environmental or behavioral items help us better to understand the dimensions of MMPI personality types. Although the items we list are statistically reliable, undoubtedly some are not so meaningfully reliable as others. For checks on this and for additional information not included here, all readers are urged to study for themselves the evidence in the full tables. The brief interpretative discussions for each scale that follow are deliberately loose and provocative; we intend only to point to some significant leads. Our interpretations of the data are often not rigorously established and we have no doubt overlooked many trends that are interesting.

In the abstracts that follow, the left-hand column shows the items associated with the given scale as the highest profile point and the right-hand column shows like data for classes determined by the low point of the profile. A plus means that observed values are larger than expected and a minus means the observed values are lower than expected. A plus can be read as "many," a minus as "few." For example, the first item of the first abstract below may be read as "Many boys with scale 1 as the highest profile point are rated as having poor school conduct."

Scale 1 Profiles

The items of scale 1 consist of complaints of poor health or physical lack of energy. In some degree the scale contains "true" symptoms that occur naturally with the physical symptoms of "organic" illnesses, but only patients with complex systemic physical disorders get high scores unless a neurotic element is also present, for a considerable number and variety of complaints are required to produce a high score on the scale.

As might be expected, profiles featuring high 1 are relatively unusual among the ninth-graders. Only 89 boys and 21 girls out of the 10,104 valid profiles of the

1 as Highest Scale	*1 as Lowest Scale*
+ poor school conduct (Table 67)	— urban residence (Table 36)

1 as Highest Scale	*1 as Lowest Scale*
	+ medium intelligence (Table 54)
	— high intelligence (Table 54)
	+ medium Cooperative English score (Table 58)

statewide sample were high 1. A larger number of profiles were classed as low 1, but few trends are evident in the tables. Study of the individual cases would undoubtedly support a few definitive items.

As the summary shows, only one cell seemed at all significant in occurrence of high 1 profiles and that could be a random finding. It suggests that boys with neurotic physical complaints tend to be rated as having bad school conduct.

Low scores on scale 1 occurred infrequently among the urban boys. Low-point profiles have more significance among the girls. Those girls with average school ability often are characterized by unusually few physical symptoms.

Scale 2 Profiles

The items of scale 2 are suggestive of depression. Admission of frequent crying, feelings of hopelessness, and loneliness will result in a high score. Like the other neurosis-related scales, 1 and 3, high scale 2 is an unusual pattern among adolescent subjects.

There are few places in the tables where the number of high scale 2 cases is sufficient for statistical reliability. The number of observed high 2 profiles did

2 as Highest Scale	*2 as Lowest Scale*
	+ high intelligence (Table 53)
	— low Cooperative English score (Table 57)
	— school dropout (Table 132)

2 as Highest Scale	*2 as Lowest Scale*
	— urban residence (Table 37)
	— low intelligence (Table 54)
	+ high intelligence (Table 54)
	— low Cooperative English score (Table 58)
	— high school rank low (Table 62)
	+ high school rank high (Table 62)

not differ significantly from the expected in any cell of the tables. Low 2 profiles, indicating a marked absence of depression, are clearly related among the boys to high intelligence test scores. Among the girls, low 2 also occurred with high scholarship, but it was infrequent among those living in urban centers.

In summary, absence of depressive concern and presence of a carefree attitude toward life characterize adolescents who have high ability and get good grades.

Scale 3 Profiles

Scale 3 was derived from criterion patient groups who combined physical complaints with the protest that they were not neurotic. The clinical prototype was conversion hysteria. Clinical evidence suggests that there is usually a psychological problem-solving aspect to the physical complaints. The complaint

BOYS

3 as Highest Scale	*3 as Lowest Scale*
+ professional and semiprofessional socioeconomic status (Table 39)	+ high school rank low (Table 61)
− day-laborer socioeconomic status (Table 39)	− high school rank high (Table 61)
− low intelligence (Table 51)	
+ high intelligence (Table 51)	
− low Cooperative English score (Table 55)	
+ high Cooperative English score (Table 55)	
− high school rank low (Table 59)	
+ high school rank high (Table 59)	
− school dropout (Table 130)	
+ good school adjustment (Table 63)	

GIRLS

3 as Highest Scale	*3 as Lowest Scale*
− low intelligence (Table 52)	− urban residence (Table 37)
+ high intelligence (Table 52)	+ residence on farm (Table 37)
− low Cooperative English score (Table 56)	− professional and semiprofessional socioeconomic status (Table 42)
− high school rank low (Table 60)	+ farmer socioeconomic status (Table 42)
	+ day-laborer socioeconomic status (Table 42)
	+ low intelligence (Table 54)
	− high intelligence (Table 54)
	+ low Cooperative English score (Table 58)
	− high Cooperative English score (Table 58)
	+ high school rank low (Table 62)
	− high school rank high (Table 62)

system excuses such a patient from some onerous situation. They differ from scale 1 patients in that their physical symptoms tend to be more circumscribed — paralysis, blindness, or the syndromes of appendicitis, cardiac malfunction, and the like. The patients employed for derivation of scale 3 were less tense than those for scale 1 and they were more often described as apparently indifferent to the severity of their disability. These patients also tended to be younger and less complicated psychologically than scale 1 patients. For patients with symptoms of conversion hysteria, there is typically a V shape in the MMPI profile formed with scales 1, 2, and 3 by a relatively low score on scale 2 and higher scales 1 and 3, with 3 higher. This is termed the "conversion V." Among the ninth-graders, high scale 3 profiles occurred more often than did high scale 1 or 2 profiles. Hysteria is classically a chief neurotic type for young people.

Children who play sick or who are episodically sick as a method of getting their way with parents or other persons would be expected to show high scale 3. Elevation of this scale in children or adults is often associated with the descriptive term "immature." There is, however, considerable evidence suggesting that the pressure for conformity in Western culture develops the scale 3 psychology, so that one might expect the trait at moderate levels among well-behaved and intelligent children. It expresses middle-class social conformity.

The high scale 3 profile boys bear out the generalized descriptive points about scale 3. High intelligence and achievement, with school dropout unlikely, are the findings; the data on the girls are similar. The boys especially were characterized by high intelligence, by good achievement in school, and by families at the professional level.

Low scale 3 profiles seem to indicate that there is a continuity of the scale meaning into scores below average to suggest opposite characteristics to those for high scores. Low 3 profile subjects had low grades, low ability, and a lower socioeconomic background than those with high 3. Only the girls show many statistically reliable differences, but the trend is the same for the boys.

In summary, the tables provide evidence that high scale 3 indicates a pattern of acceptance of middle-class values. One may loosely generalize about high scale 3 adolescents by saying they are intelligent and strive for achievement, and their parents are in the professional class.

Scale 4 Profiles

Scale 4 was derived from predominantly youthful groups of patients who showed little evidence of neuroticism but who were in some sort of trouble due to misbehavior, temper tantrums, and the like. The scale suggests self-centered immaturity. Usually these patients were rebellious against family or society. They often seemed asocial rather than antisocial. Although their defective character led frequently to some form of delinquency, not all the high scale 4 cases were known for delinquency or other antisocial behavior. But any delinquent group would be likely to contain young people of the high scale 4 type. It is probably important for counselors to distinguish the scale 4 boys and girls among the varieties of delinquents, others of whom are more neurotic and sensitive. Those with high scale 4 are hard to help by use of interpersonal relationship or appeals to cultural values and loyalties. They are likely to be attractive in personality and to promise improvement, and hence the counselor is often led to use treatment approaches that are ineffective with them.

This profile pattern is dominantly frequent among adolescents, even more among girls than boys. Adolescent girls are either more resistant to adult con-

---

BOYS

4 as Highest Scale	*4 as Lowest Scale*
+ urban residence (Table 34)	— school dropout (Table 132)
— residence on farm (Table 34)	— poor school adjustment (Table 65)
— farmer socioeconomic status (Table 39)	— poor school conduct (Table 69)
+ separated or divorced parents (Table 43)	+ good school conduct (Table 69)
+ school dropout (Table 130)	— delinquency ratings 3 and 4 (Table 114)
+ poor school adjustment (Table 63)	— teacher-predicted delinquency (Table 73)
— good school adjustment (Table 63)	
+ poor school conduct (Table 67)	
— good school conduct (Table 67)	
+ delinquency ratings 2, 3, 4 (Table 112)	
— nondelinquent (Table 112)	
+ teacher-predicted delinquency and emotional problems (Table 71)	
— no teacher prediction (Table 71)	

GIRLS

4 as Highest Scale	*4 as Lowest Scale*
+ urban residence (Table 35)	+ residence on farm (Table 37)
— residence on farm (Table 35)	— school dropout (Table 133)
— farmer socioeconomic status (Table 40)	
+ semiskilled and slightly skilled socioeconomic status (Table 40)	
+ separated or divorced parents (Table 44)	
— low Cooperative English score (Table 56)	
+ school dropout (Table 131)	
+ poor school adjustment (Table 64)	
+ poor school conduct (Table 68)	
— good school conduct (Table 68)	
+ delinquency ratings 2, 3, 4 (Table 113)	
+ teacher-predicted delinquency and emotional problems (Table 72)	

trols or react more strongly than do boys to other requirements of the transition period into adulthood. By age 21, for both sexes a great part of this phase of negative reaction is apparently over, and the pattern is much less often a feature of mature persons. Either a more relaxed acceptance of cultural norms or development of the more frequent adult neurotic patterns of scales 1, 2, and 3 seems to replace the high scale 4. Among older people there is a reversal and men show greater frequency of high 4 than do women.

The frequency of scale 4 profiles increases from a low rate in rural districts to a high rate in urban areas. A considerable number of variables are positively correlated with high scale 4; for example, delinquency, school dropout, and poor school conduct and adjustment ratings occur among boys and girls. Within the delinquency variable, the rate of high 4 profiles increases with the severity of delinquency. Tests given to the rural eleventh-graders suggest that their highest rate of high scale 4 profiles occurs a year or two later than among city youngsters. Perhaps, as indicated earlier, when our data are analyzed to develop the times of delinquent acts within the follow-up period, we shall find a peak for delinquency that is later among rural adolescents than among those living in urban areas. Broken homes have an association with high 4 profiles for both boys and girls.

In summary, adolescents with high 4 profiles are prone to a considerable number of troubles. These troubles are more reminiscent of character defect than of neuroticism. Apparently, urban life and broken homes contribute to the reaction.

Scale 5 Profiles

In developing scale 5, emphasis was placed upon the contrast of feminine men who have interests similar to those of women with presumably more masculine men in general. Clinical evaluations of high scale 5 men mention homosexuality as a frequent problem. The generalized interpretation of high scores includes positive appreciation of art, literature, and music, and acceptance of education, nonviolence, and cultural stability as ideals. These qualities are all endorsed more strongly by women than by men. Low scores by men indicate independent masculinity which is at times expressed as uncouth physical aggressiveness.

For women, high scores on scale 5 presumably indicate masculinity of interests. A value system favoring careers like those of men and a degree of aggressive independence express some of the high scale 5 meanings. Low scores from women suggest passive femininity.

The general interpretative significance of high scale 5 for boys is well supported by its relationships to other variables. A high socioeconomic status of the family, high intelligence and scholarship, continued education, and a low delinquency rate are the rule with high 5.

Boys with low scale 5 profiles contrast in nearly all ways with those having high 5 profiles. This variety of masculinity is associated with school underachievement, school dropout, and delinquency. Low scale 5 boys tend to get bad behavior ratings.

Girls with high scale 5 are more likely to live on farms, feminine girls in the city. The high scale 5 girls are not so intelligent or such good students as low 5 girls, but they do not get bad behavior ratings.

Girls with low scale 5 are rather like the boys with feminine scores. They are intelligent and get good grades, and their parents frequently have a clerical rating for socioeconomic status.

In summary, high scale 5 boys are probably considered to be sissies by at least the low scale 5 boys. They come from good homes, are intelligent, well behaved, and liked by teachers. Boys with low scale 5 are not so gentlemanly and are more aggressively obstreperous, and less conforming. The patterns for girls are less clear. To some extent their high scores are like low scores for boys. Farm girls get more high scores and often may be tomboys. Low-scoring feminine girls are brighter and are better students than high scorers.

BOYS

5 as Highest Scale	*5 as Lowest Scale*
+ professional and semiprofessional socioeconomic status (Table 39)	− professional and semiprofessional socioeconomic status (Table 41)
+ clerical socioeconomic status (Table 39)	+ low intelligence (Table 53)
− low intelligence (Table 51)	− high intelligence (Table 53)
+ high intelligence (Table 51)	+ low Cooperative English score (Table 57)
− low Cooperative English score (Table 55)	− high Cooperative English score (Table 57)
+ high Cooperative English score (Table 55)	+ high school rank low (Table 61)
− high school rank low (Table 59)	− high school rank high (Table 61)
+ high school rank high (Table 59)	+ school dropout (Table 132)
− school dropout (Table 130)	+ delinquency rating 2 (Table 114)
+ good school adjustment (Table 63)	+ teacher-predicted delinquency (Table 73)
− delinquency ratings 2, 3, 4 (Table 112)	
− teacher-predicted delinquency and emotional problems (Table 71)	

GIRLS

5 as Highest Scale	*5 as Lowest Scale*
− urban residence (Table 35)	− residence on farm (Table 37)
+ residence on farm (Table 35)	+ clerical socioeconomic status (Table 42)
+ farmer socioeconomic status (Table 40)	− low intelligence (Table 54)
− high intelligence (Table 52)	+ high intelligence (Table 54)
+ low Cooperative English score (Table 56)	− low Cooperative English score (Table 58)
− high Cooperative English score (Table 56)	+ high Cooperative English score (Table 58)
− poor school conduct (Table 68)	− high school rank low (Table 62)
− teacher-predicted delinquency and emotional problems (Table 72)	+ high school rank high (Table 62)

Scale 6 Profiles

The items of scale 6 were selected from the responses made by patients considered paranoid. The pattern of items in scale 6 suggests feelings of grandiosity and persecution. Moderately elevated scores on scale 6 are interpreted to suggest an oversensitivity to remarks and inferred attitudes of others. Some adolescents with behavior problems get high scores on scale 6 because their responses reflect the feeling that a parent, probation or parole officer, or teacher supervises them too closely. Moderately high scores can, however, be a favorable sign. Some persons are better companions because they have interpersonal sensitivity, and if their feelings are not hurt too easily, they can be responsive in social integration.

BOYS	
6 as Highest Scale	*6 as Lowest Scale*
+ residence on farm (Table 34)	
— medium intelligence (Table 51)	
+ early school dropout (Table 130)	

GIRLS	
6 as Highest Scale	*6 as Lowest Scale*
+ high intelligence (Table 52)	+ low intelligence (Table 54)
+ high Cooperative English score (Table 56)	— high intelligence (Table 54)
	— high Cooperative English score (Table 58)
+ high school rank high (Table 60)	
— poor school adjustment (Table 64)	+ high school rank low (Table 62)

Fewer clear differentiations appear among high 6 profile boys than among girls. Boys who do have a high 6 are more likely to drop out of school than boys with other high points on their profiles. Possibly the school environment becomes too painfully personal. Residence on a farm increases the probability of high 6 profiles.

Girls with high 6 tend to have high intelligence and to get good grades. High 6 girls are also likely to be considered well adjusted by others. Often these girls are very popular. Possibly the personal sensitivity leads to overcompensation in social contacts.

A summary of the implications from these tables and from the high 6 case histories in *An Atlas of Juvenile MMPI Profiles* (17) makes moderate elevation of scale 6 appear to be an asset for girls. Responsible and intelligent, the girls seem to make a special effort to be liked and appreciated. Boys with high 6 are not so successful, possibly because they are more aggressive.

Scale 7 Profiles

Scale 7 items came from the responses of persons who were clinically judged to be handicapped by fears, timidity, feelings of inadequacy, or related symptoms. Feelings of inferiority, personal or social, are most central in the personalities of persons with high scores. Depression, as measured by scale 2, is a clinically important modifier on the high scale 7 syndrome. Profiles with 27 ... or 72 ... codes indicate anxiety.

BOYS

7 as Highest Scale	*7 as Lowest Scale*
+ day-laborer socioeconomic status (Table 39)	
− high intelligence (Table 51)	

GIRLS

7 as Highest Scale	*7 as Lowest Scale*

Like the neurotic elements of scales 1, 2, and 3, the basic component of high scale 7 is a more common factor in later life than in adolescence; unlike scales 1, 2, and 3, scale 7 is, however, relatively frequent as a high profile in the ninth grade. Since only a few significant differences appear against other variables among the boys and none among the girls, the scale does not seem to be contributing much for general interpretation. Some clinicians consider the scale to measure a rigidity of personality that causes little trouble in youth but is a precursor of later mental handicap such as involutional depression. If so, these children must grow older and develop depression before trouble will be evident. It will be thirty more years before the high 7 adolescents will be at an age when the development of involutional depression or other undesirable outcomes might be in store for them.

Scale 8 Profiles

Schizophrenia is a ubiquitous diagnosis in mental illness and scale 8 was developed to aid in recognition of the syndrome. One diagnostic item in the characteristic pattern of schizophrenia is the early age at which the illness may first occur. The symptomatic description of schizophrenia patients is not easy. Poor contact with reality, inappropriate emotional responses, poor ability in social relations with unusual or erroneous perceptions of the motives and mental content of other people are salient descriptive characteristics. A common associated scale in young men is scale 6. The usual diagnosis for patients with 86 ... is paranoid schizophrenia.

Boys are more likely than girls to have profiles with high scale 8. Both boys and girls who have high 8 are likely to appear deficient among their companions. Low in intellect, low in achievement, and, among girls especially, likely to drop out of school, the high 8 youth seems to bear out the clinical interpretation of the scale.

The adolescents of the sample will need to be older before the majority of those who will develop schizophrenia can be diagnosed. Possibly, when the data are available, these boys and girls who had high 8 in the ninth grade will contribute the major proportion of the cases.

Unfortunately, this study does not provide evidence about the psychological

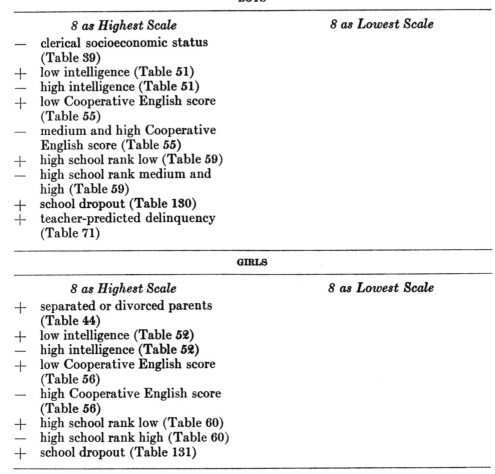

BOYS

8 as Highest Scale	*8 as Lowest Scale*
— clerical socioeconomic status (Table 39)	
+ low intelligence (Table 51)	
— high intelligence (Table 51)	
+ low Cooperative English score (Table 55)	
— medium and high Cooperative English score (Table 55)	
+ high school rank low (Table 59)	
— high school rank medium and high (Table 59)	
+ school dropout (Table 130)	
+ teacher-predicted delinquency (Table 71)	

GIRLS

8 as Highest Scale	*8 as Lowest Scale*
+ separated or divorced parents (Table 44)	
+ low intelligence (Table 52)	
— high intelligence (Table 52)	
+ low Cooperative English score (Table 56)	
— high Cooperative English score (Table 56)	
+ high school rank low (Table 60)	
— high school rank high (Table 60)	
+ school dropout (Table 131)	

relationships within the family. The data do not, however, suggest as much relationship to broken home life as might be expected from some current theories about the causes of schizophrenia.

Scale 9 Profiles

The clinical origins of scale 9 relate to hypomanic patients. These persons, many of them young, are characterized by overactivity, enthusiasm, and an optimism that contrasts with depression. When the symptoms are controlled in extent and nature, such patients can be exceedingly successful; they get things done. Some of them are subject to periods when they shift to depression. It is probably an indication of normal adjustment when youths have moderately high scores on scale 9.

The distribution of those with high 9 profiles suggests a positive relationship to urban life. This is in contrast to the occurrence of the high 8 profiles which are frequent in rural areas. Manic-depressive mental disorders have been reported to have a different ecological distribution from schizophrenic disorders and

BOYS

9 as Highest Scale	*9 as Lowest Scale*
— residence on farm (Table 34)	— low intelligence (Table 53)
— farmer socioeconomic status (Table 39)	+ high intelligence (Table 53)
— low intelligence (Table 51)	— low Cooperative English score (Table 57)
+ medium Cooperative English score (Table 55)	+ high Cooperative English score (Table 57)
+ high school rank medium (Table 59)	— high school rank low (Table 61)
— school dropout (Table 130)	+ high school rank high (Table 61)
	— school dropout (Table 132)
	— poor school adjustment (Table 65)
	+ good school adjustment (Table 65)
	— poor school conduct (Table 69)
	+ good school conduct (Table 69)
	— delinquency ratings 2, 3, 4 (Table 114)
	+ nondelinquent (Table 114)
	— teacher-predicted delinquency and emotional problems (Table 73)

GIRLS

9 as Highest Scale	*9 as Lowest Scale*
+ urban residence (Table 35)	+ residence on farm (Table 37)
— residence on farm (Table 35)	— clerical socioeconomic status (Table 42)
+ clerical socioeconomic status (Table 40)	+ farmer socioeconomic status (Table 42)
— farmer socioeconomic status (Table 40)	— high school rank low (Table 62)
	+ high school rank high (Table 62)
	— school dropout (Table 133)
	— illegitimate pregnancy (Table 70)
	+ good school conduct (Table 70)
	— delinquency ratings 2, 3, 4 (Table 115)

the present data are consistent with these findings. The occurrence of the high profiles among the middle achievement and the middle socioeconomic levels suggests that average ability and middle-class environment are conducive to this optimism and confidence.

Scale 9 as the lowest scale is a powerful predictor of good behavior for both boys and girls. The boys are generally interpretable as quiet and well behaved. Low 9 girls, frequently coming from farms, are also often bright and well behaved.

In general summary, high-scoring boys and girls are not sharply characterized, but profiles with scale 9 lowest are rather strongly predictive of the absence of bad items. Other data we have suggest that the combination 49 . . . is an indication of bad behavior, but the key to this behavior lies more with the high 4 than with high 9.

Scale 0 Profiles

Scale 0 was derived from female college students who were socially introverted in contrast to those who were socially extroverted. High 0 appears to be indicative not only of a failure to be active in social affairs but also of feelings of social inadequacy.

Low scores on scale 0 are interpretable in direct contrast to high scores. They suggest social participation and confidence.

BOYS

0 as Highest Scale	*0 as Lowest Scale*
— urban residence (Table 34)	+ urban residence (Table 36)
+ residence on farm (Table 34)	— residence on farm (Table 36)
— professional and semiprofessional socioeconomic status (Table 39)	+ professional and semiprofessional socioeconomic status (Table 41)
+ farmer socioeconomic status (Table 39)	+ clerical socioeconomic status (Table 41)
— divorced or separated parents (Table 43)	— farmer socioeconomic status (Table 41)
— school dropout (Table 130)	— day-laborer socioeconomic status (Table 41)
— poor school adjustment (Table 63)	— low intelligence (Table 53)
— poor school conduct (Table 67)	+ high intelligence (Table 53)
+ good school conduct (Table 67)	— low Cooperative English score (Table 57)
— delinquency ratings (Table 112)	+ high Cooperative English score (Table 57)
+ nondelinquent (Table 112)	— high school rank low (Table 61)
— teacher-predicted delinquency and emotional problems (Table 71)	— school dropout (Table 132)
+ no teacher prediction (Table 71)	

GIRLS

0 as Highest Scale	*0 as Lowest Scale*
— urban residence (Table 35)	+ urban residence (Table 37)
+ residence on farm (Table 35)	— residence on farm (Table 37)
— clerical socioeconomic status (Table 40)	+ professional and semiprofessional socioeconomic status (Table 42)
+ farmer socioeconomic status (Table 40)	— farmer socioeconomic status (Table 42)
— high school rank low (Table 60)	— low intelligence (Table 54)
— school dropout (Table 131)	+ high intelligence (Table 54)
— bad school conduct (Table 68)	— low Cooperative English score (Table 58)
— delinquency ratings 2, 3, 4 (Table 113)	+ high Cooperative English score (Table 58)
— teacher-predicted delinquency and emotional problems (Table 72)	— high school rank low (Table 62)

It is to be expected that scale 0 high and low profiles will relate to many variables in the tables. Socialization is one of the chief problem areas of the ninth-grade boy or girl.

Apparently feelings of great social inferiority strongly inhibit delinquency or other undesirable behavior. Despite the worry produced in parents and teachers by the child who is not socially active or confident, adolescents with high 0 profiles are infrequent among those receiving adverse behavior ratings.

Social introversion is a frequent pattern among boys and girls from farms. By contrast, social extroversion is frequent among those from professional families. Low scale 0 profiles are also associated with high ability but not with an appropriately high achievement. This supports the idea that there is some conflict between a child's social success and his academic success.

Profiles without Coded Points

When a profile has no coded high point, it means that the subject has answered all scale items with such low frequencies of significant responses that the T scores are near or below average. Presumably these profiles are produced by very well adjusted subjects or they are the result of successful attempts to hide a real or imagined abnormality.

Boys from farm families and girls from day-laborer families show more no-high-point (normal) profiles than expected. As one might expect, no-high-point profiles are common among girls who are bright and who get good grades.

When there is no coded low point for a profile, the profile usually shows several coded high points. In a way, no coded low point is a measure of the general elevation of the profile. To this extent, a no-low-point profile means simply that the profile deviated toward general maladjustment.

The tables show many variables that are related to profiles with no coded low points. No-low-point profiles do seem to suggest maladjustment. Teachers and others give adverse ratings on emotionality to no-low-point children and the girls are prone to be delinquent. Those with no-low-point profiles are more likely than others to drop out of school. Relatively few adolescents from middle-class families or with high scholastic ability have profiles with no low point.

BOYS

No Coded High Point	*No Coded Low Point*
+ farmer socioeconomic status (Table 39)	— clerical socioeconomic status (Table 41)
	+ low intelligence (Table 53)
	— high intelligence (Table 53)
	+ low Cooperative English score (Table 57)
	— medium and high Cooperative English score (Table 57)
	— high school rank low (Table 61)
	+ high school rank high (Table 61)
	+ school dropout (Table 132)

GIRLS

No Coded High Point		*No Coded Low Point*	
+	day-laborer socioeconomic status (Table 40)	+	urban residence (Table 37)
—	low intelligence (Table 52)	—	professional and semiprofessional socioeconomic status (Table 42)
+	high intelligence (Table 52)	+	low intelligence (Table 54)
+	high Cooperative English score (Table 56)	—	high intelligence (Table 54)
+	high school rank high (Table 60)	+	low Cooperative English score (Table 58)
		—	high Cooperative English score (Table 58)
		+	high school rank low (Table 62)
		—	high school rank high (Table 62)
		+	school dropout (Table 133)
		—	good school adjustment (Table 66)
		+	poor school conduct (Table 70)
		+	delinquency ratings 2, 3, 4 (Table 115)
		+	teacher-predicted delinquency and emotional problems (Table 74)

PERSONALITY IN TRANSITION

PERSONALITY, however one views it, is changeable. If in no other way, it changes with maturation of the nervous system during childhood and with deterioration of the cerebral cortex due to age, disease, or injury. We assume also that we can change the personalities of others or of ourselves. Psychotherapy, punishment, counseling, and other activities designed to treat or educate people are based on the assumption that personality can be modified. Occasionally dramatic personality changes follow the occurrence of critical events in the environment of the person: getting a very special teacher; succeeding or failing in sports, in school study, or in social relationships will sometimes produce a marked personality change in a child or even in an adult. Boys or girls occasionally change from socially retiring to aggressively social persons within a few weeks. Most shifts in personality among young people tend toward better adjustment, but undesirable changes were not uncommon among the boys and girls in our samples.

For the present study, the significance of individual shifts in personality lies in the fact that a personality test of a juvenile will frequently reflect a transient organization of the personality. Tested again, even within a few months, some fifteen-year-olds should have a different profile if the test is properly sensitive. The possibility of personality changes sets limits on the apparent usefulness and validity of a personality test, especially if the test is intended to be used predictively. A boy prone to delinquency and rebellious against society at a given age can sharply reverse his attitude and acquire a new personality, and if his behavior is evaluated at this later time he would be found obedient and acceptable. The boy's first test profile should show the then-current rebellious nature. Comparison of the later behavior to the earlier test profile would make it seem that the test missed in prediction.

It should be apparent, therefore, that a longitudinal study emphasizing relationships of later behavior to earlier test profiles cannot be expected to predict effectively for subjects whose personalities are in transition during the interval. For our data, the initial test with the MMPI preceded outcome evaluation by two to four years. This outcome evaluation was based on what informants remembered over the whole period and upon public records dated within the whole period. It was clear that there was a tendency to emphasize the subject's most recent behavior in the follow-up evaluation. If a boy had been a troublemaker at the time of testing but later seemed to have become much better adjusted, those who evaluated him tended not to mention his bad behavior in the ninth grade.

Our research was chiefly intended to provide an estimate of the predictive power of ninth-grade personality tests and to determine how helpful the test scores might be to those concerned with guidance programs. But in part we also wanted to estimate objectively the extent of the changes of personality over the same period. These two purposes contrast in that we were attempting in one to estimate the stable relationship of the ninth-grade test to the outcome behavior and in the other to estimate the instability of MMPI codes and of early and late personality ratings which, disregarding errors of measurement and of outcome ratings, express the characteristic changes in adolescent personality during the late teens. In keeping with the first objective, most of our data are presented with chief emphasis on the MMPI constancy from ninth to twelfth grade and on the closeness of relationships of ninth-grade MMPI scores to behavior in the follow-up period. For evidence on the second objective, this chapter will stress data on changes in the MMPI profiles of individuals as these appear with successive tests.

It may be appropriate at this point to present some data illustrating the significance of the dual purposes of our research and the implications of the interdependence of purposes of the research. Since we have established that those boys with ninth-grade test profiles coded high 4 will have a higher delinquency rate than other boys, we may profitably analyze a sample of high 4 boys for whom test results in both the ninth and twelfth grades are available. Table 75 presents the results of the analysis.

Let us assume for the moment that the test is perfectly reliable. The data in the table show that the significant personality configuration high 4 among ninth-graders persists to the twelfth grade at a rate of 37 per cent. (Table 77, however, shows that 60 per cent continue with scale 4 in either the first or the second place in the code.) Since most of the behavior that correlates with the high 4 pattern is not desirable, it is comforting to see that the majority of adolescents who have this pattern in the ninth grade do change. The rate of delinquency for those who change is only 31 per cent, but those who continue to score highest on scale 4 in the twelfth grade have a delinquency rate of 47 per cent. Further analysis of the patterns of change would no doubt show that some of the changes would still leave unfavorable profiles, such as those with 4 in second place and 6 or 9 high instead of the original 4. If we were to separate these unfavorable change cases from the cases who changed to favorable patterns, the latter group would show a still lower rate of delinquency. If, however, one wants evidence that adolescents are flexible and may be helped, then it is encouraging to find that so many of them do change. The table also shows how our delinquency rates covering a period of time average out. The over-all rate of 311 boys is, of course, intermediate at 38 per cent.

Test-Retest Data (Table 76)

Table 76 shows the correlations between ninth- and twelfth-grade test scores (from valid profiles only) and the comparable means and standard deviations for the two sets of scores. Our conservative criterion for defining valid profiles and the loss of dropout cases attenuate the correlations and reduce the test score variance so that the given correlation values are probably minimal.

If these correlations were valid measures of the degree of personality stability from the ninth to the twelfth grade, one would have to stress the inconstancy reflected. It is clear that predictions from the individual MMPI scales should be made with caution if the prediction period is to cover several years. Scale 0 is the most stable, and possibly most counselors would expect this. Feelings of social awkwardness and rejection have a tendency to persist, as does the social behavior of the extrovert. Similarly, the defensiveness-candidness attitudes represented by the K scale are relatively stable. By contrast, scales 4 and 6 have the lowest correlations. It seems reasonable to expect that youthful revolt, as suggested by these two scales, particularly fluctuates in intensity during the high school period.

Nearly all average T scores for the scales are larger than those of the standardization adult groups (T score 50); see also the general sample data in Table 22. At face value, these juvenile samples were more badly adjusted than were the adults used to establish the norms. Whatever this general elevation in score may represent, its amount is not greatly reduced by the time the individual is in the twelfth grade. Several of the differences between the means and the standard deviations are statistically reliable, but they are insignificant in magnitude.

The means and test-retest correlations of Table 76 do not properly represent the stability of profile shapes. The organization of personality is better expressed by profile codes; individual scale scores can change considerably without a shift in the coded pattern.

Ninth- to Twelfth-Grade Code Stability (Tables 77 and 78)

The ninth-grade code of each subject was compared to his own twelfth-grade code. Tables 77 and 78 summarize the data for these comparisons in three categories: the percentage frequency of each code as a high point in the ninth grade, the frequency with which the ninth-grade high point was maintained as one of the two highest codes on the twelfth-grade test, and the frequency with which the first high point in the ninth-grade code changed to a low point in the twelfth.

The main point to be noted in the tables is that there is appreciably more stability of profile when the T scores are equal to or greater than 70 ($\geqq$70). High 4 is relatively stable for both boys and girls. More than half of the high 4's continue to have 4 as one of the first two scales of the second profile. No boy with a high 4 in the ninth grade changes so much from that pattern as to have a code with low 4 in the twelfth grade. The more neurotic indicators, scales 1 and 2, are contrastingly changeable, moving frequently from high to low. Half of the boys who appear feminine in the ninth grade by obtaining a high 5 continue to show this pattern, but the extreme shift to a masculine low 5 is one of the most common changes. Among girls, the interest pattern changes even more frequently, but from masculine, as indicated by high scale 5, toward feminine. These scale 5 data support the hypothesis, also suggested in other tables, that in the high school years there is an active differentiation of sex role. The shift for girls is rather more clear, and we believe that averaged data over other life periods would show that both boys and girls are most masculine during their teens.

Ninth- to Twelfth-Grade Item Stability (Tables 79 and 80)

Table 79 lists the MMPI items on which there was more than a 17 per cent change between ninth- and twelfth-grade responses by a random sample of boys and girls. Such differences are statistically significant and are also large enough to be interesting. The items give an idea of the areas and character of change by teen-agers toward adult roles and mores (see also Chapter 4 and Tables 27 and 29).

Starred items are common to both sexes. One pair is interesting — the subjects admit less attraction to members of their own sex and more to the opposite sex after three years. Freedom from family rule increases, as does tolerance toward taking alcohol. Belief that people seem to require argument to be convinced decreases, and there is less avoidance of sexy shows.

Changes in boys include more interest in love and in flirting and dancing. They also come to worry more over disease and general health. The girls most markedly appear to become more tolerant and to feel better rapport with others. For example, they do not so much feel that people are jealous of them; neither do they so much dislike doing favors for people, or misunderstand them so much. There is less self-consciousness about blushing.

Many other interesting statements are prompted by these items, and the reader should look through the lists for himself.

Table 80 lists items with the greatest instability over the period. The actual frequency of "True" responses to these items was not much different in the ninth and twelfth grades, but 18 per cent or more of the individual students changed their answers from "True" in the ninth grade to "False" in the twelfth and vice versa. Changes of this sort are partly a result of item unreliability, but they also represent the shifting of personality that characterizes the high school period. Presumably the items tap ways in which change is occurring but this change is not consistent in direction. The content of a majority of the items refers to interpersonal behavior. It is rather hard to characterize the items generally. None appears on both the list for boys and that for girls, but there is some commonality in that many of the items concern introspective reports. Boys and girls both appear more likely to change the direction of response when an item speaks of personal judgments. An example from the boys' list is "Once in a while I think of things too bad to talk about."

Personality Change and Social Change (Tables 81 and 82)

As children grow older, some of the observed changes in personality may be a function of general changes in the social structure as these impinge upon and modify personality. One way to estimate this effect is to study MMPI scale averages on presumably comparable groups at different points in time.

In the course of our studies, the ninth-grade students of one school in a small city were tested in 1947; in 1954 the test was again administered under similar conditions to the ninth-graders of that school. The first test, given about the time of collection of our Minneapolis data, occurred in the immediate postwar period. Tables 81 and 82 give the comparative average results. The boys appear to reflect greater change than the girls. The differences among the boys for scales 1, 2, 3, 4, and 8 are significant. The averages of scales 1, 2, and 4 differ by more than half a standard deviation value. Less neuroticism and less behavioral revolt on the part of the 1954 sample are suggested by the data. Scale 2 also changes greatly for the girls, although the trend is not as strong as it is for the boys. All the findings support a generalization that the 1954 sample is psychologically more secure and the boys less rebellious than the 1947 group. The change in scale 4 could mean that, in general, boys are conforming with less resistance to the restraints of the social order. One could conclude that there is less evidence of reaction to stress in the later samples.

Comparisons of Twins (Table 83)

Still another aspect of the stability of personality may be illustrated by the data from twins who were in our samples. Our information was limited to the fact that there were children of like or unlike sex with the same birth date living in the same house. We have compared like-sex twins, unlike-sex twins, and randomly associated pairs of the same sex. One would expect like-sex twins to show the greatest effect of similar environment and heredity; twins of unlike sex should be somewhat similar in heredity and in home environment but unlike in the areas where the sex difference would modify personality; and, finally, like-sex random pairs should be similar only in general social milieu and in the contribution of sex to similarity. Some independent data for evaluation of the twin data are provided by the correlations between ninth- and twelfth-grade scores which show the average similarity of adolescents to themselves across a time interval.

Table 83 shows the symmetrical surface correlations among the three groups of twins in comparison to the test-retest correlations (see Table 76). Some twin correlations are not appreciably different from the test-retest correlations of ninth and twelfth grade. Every test-retest correlation for the boys is at least a few points higher than correlation values for male twins; this is not quite so consistent among the girls. There is a moderate tendency for like-sex twins to be more similar than unlike-sex twins with two significant exceptions. First, scale 9 reverses the trend: level of activity correlates reliably better between unlike-sex pairs. Social extroversion-introversion, scale 0, and degree of defensiveness, scale K, correlate reliably higher between like-sex twins. Second, the significant correlations on scale 5 indicate that there is a consistent trend for twins, whether of the same sex or of unlike sex, to have similar interest patterns, be they masculine or feminine. It must be remembered that the scoring of scale 5 is reversed so that, for example, in accord with the negative correlation of unlike-sex twins, boys with low scores have masculine interests and girls with high scores have masculine interests. If these findings prove stable, we shall need to think of sex role influence in a family as either masculinizing or feminizing, with these influences operating indiscriminately upon boys and girls alike.

We have no satisfactory explanation for the high correlations on the validity scales for female twins. At face value, test-taking sets, such as are measured by L, F, and K, are similarly derived by twin girls. Presumably the source would be the family, specifically the mother. Boys, however, seem to derive these sets from diverse sources that permit them greater individuality. This sex difference is seen even in the test-retest figures.

Data on twin resemblances can also be derived from the study of responses to items. The comparative frequencies of identical responses by twins and by randomly paired subjects to each item provide an opportunity to judge what kinds of item show twin similarity. The percentage of identical responses of random pairs of persons to an item is obviously a function of the base rate of item response. For example, the response to the item "I have convulsions" shows high agreement between all pairs since nearly everyone responds with "False." Minimum average frequency of agreement will occur on items having a normative "True" response of about 50 per cent. From purely parametric expectation, one can predict that two randomly selected persons will agree on such items with a most probable frequency of 50 per cent; in contrast, an item having a standard "True" frequency of 90 per cent should show random agreement at the rate of 82 per cent. For the twin data, we empirically established the base rates of pair agreement from standard frequencies on samples of randomly paired boys and randomly paired girls. We were then able to determine which items evoked responses from twins markedly more similar than those from randomly paired boys or girls. The following were the items on which the male twins agreed with at least a 25 per cent greater frequency than the randomly paired boys:

> Once in a while I feel hate toward members of my family whom I usually love.
> At times I have very much wanted to leave home.
> I am inclined to take things hard.
> I have very few quarrels with members of my family.
> I have often lost out on things because I couldn't make up my mind soon enough.
> It makes me angry to have people hurry me.
> I like to keep people guessing what I'm going to do next.
> I like to know some important people because it makes me feel important.
> I have very few fears compared to my friends.
> I like to cook.
> I think Lincoln was greater than Washington.
> I go to church almost every week.
> I am against giving money to beggars.
> I don't blame anyone for trying to grab everything he can get in this world.
> I am bothered by people outside, on streetcars, in stores, etc., watching me.
> I never attend a sexy show if I can avoid it.
> Sometimes I am sure that other people can tell what I am thinking.
> I feel uneasy indoors.
> Once in a while I think of things too bad to talk about.
> I love to go to dances.
> I used to like drop-the-handkerchief.
> I like or have liked fishing very much.
> I like to read newspaper editorials.
> I like to attend lectures on serious subjects.
> Everything is turning out just like the prophets in the Bible said it would.
> I know who is responsible for most of my troubles.

The comparable items for the girls were these:

> I find it hard to make talk when I meet new people.
> When in a group of people I have trouble thinking of the right things to talk about.
> I shrink from facing a crisis or difficulty.

I do not like everyone I know.

My way of doing things is apt to be misunderstood by others.

When I was a child, I belonged to a crowd or gang that tried to stick together through thick and thin.

I have often had to take orders from someone who did not know as much as I did.

I used to have imaginary companions.

I am inclined to take things hard.

If given the chance I would make a good leader of people.

At times I feel like swearing.

I sometimes feel that I am about to go to pieces.

I am often said to be hotheaded.

I have never vomited blood or coughed up blood.

I am made nervous by certain animals.

A windstorm terrifies me.

I worry quite a bit over possible misfortunes.

I am afraid to be alone in the dark.

I usually "lay my cards on the table" with people that I am trying to correct or improve.

I believe women ought to have as much sexual freedom as men.

I read in the Bible several times a week.

That similarity of environment and heredity produces more agreements between twins than between random pairs is again reasonably well supported by the item data. The reader will find many implications in the items. We have found it difficult to generalize. Some items seem obviously to depend upon the common environment of twins, but there are also items that appear to represent temperament and private experience.

Gottesman (12), also using the MMPI, has provided more rigorous analysis of the meaning of twin resemblances. Although the separation of genetic and environmental influence in such data cannot be complete, some of the personality aspects measured in MMPI scales appear to have appreciable variance attributable to heredity. Gottesman found social introversion (scale 0), psychopathic deviancy (scale 4), and depression (scale 2) to be most determined by heredity. By contrast, psychasthenia (scale 7), schizophrenia (scale 8), and hypomania (scale 9) appeared more determined by environment.

DELINQUENCY

THE significance of research findings such as those presented in this chapter depends heavily upon the method used in establishing delinquency ratings. We have outlined in Chapter 2 the basis upon which our ratings were made. Starting with level 1, which was assigned when there was contact enough with authorities so that a record of the fact was found or it was reliably reported, ratings progressed to level 4, which signified unmistakably delinquent behavior. The ratings were made by the field workers on the basis of all the data they had and were not automatically determined by public records alone. This procedure was deliberately adopted to correct at least in part for variations in recording practices of law-enforcing authorities — variations reflected in most available delinquency studies. A shift from a "soft" to a "tough" policy toward sex offenders, traffic-law violators, or shoplifters can materially alter delinquency rates based on public records. Similarly, the policies that guide the treatment of juveniles often are not uniform among counties or even among regions of a city. We do not intend to be critical of other ways of determining delinquency rates; but for the present study we wanted the judgments made concerning degree of delinquency to depend uniformly upon the personal acts of the subjects. Therefore some individuals were rated as delinquent even though nothing about them got into public records, and others received a low rating where an unmodified evaluation of the public record would have resulted in higher ratings.

We attempted to train the field workers to rate alike and to be consistent. We are not certain that this program resulted in the level of accuracy we could wish for. We did assure ourselves that raters were fairly reliable when tested against each other or by successive ratings. Unfortunately this kind of rater agreement does not assure that ratings are valid. Rater reliability is a necessary but not a sufficient condition of validity.

We have met with contrasting reactions to the delinquency rates we report. Some persons have emphasized the minor social significance of level 1 delinquency and dismiss the over-all rates that include it by saying deprecatingly that everyone gets traffic tickets or that all adolescents should be expected to get into some trouble. There is no doubt that the adult world must tolerate a considerable amount of misbehavior by boys and girls. It is equally true, however, that there are upper limits on how much mischief is tolerable.

Another point we emphasize concerning the level 1 delinquents is that they differ from adolescents with a 0 rating on nearly every variable correlated with delinquency. We consider this fact to be evidence that the power of the complex of traits disposing to delinquency varies continuously in strength from weak, in persons with almost completely acceptable social behavior, to strong, in persons who show severe criminal behavior. It is interesting to note here that the continuity of the probability variable for delinquency does not force us to assume that every personality trait that contributes to the probability of delinquency is continuous. We assume only that the average complex of numerous personal and environmental factors that contribute to the probability of delinquency appears as a single continuous variable.

Some persons have been shocked at our delinquency rates, believing that they express an alarming trend. If our data do suggest a high rate, it must be remembered that we have tried to account for all of the cases, including those who usually escape mention in reports on delinquency. Therefore the data we present cannot always be directly related to other existent data. As an example of this fact, the San Francisco Social Planning Committee (29) after reviewing this problem reported: "The obvious conclusion to be drawn in this case is, then, simply that statistics on juvenile delinquency are not readily comparable from city to city, from county to county, or from state to state. We get some idea of the weight of the problem by comparing numbers of cases; we get some idea of the relative seriousness of the problem in terms of resources by comparing rates."

Delinquency is a socially derived term. A person cannot be delinquent if he is socially isolated. A society that has no rules governing behavior will have no delinquency, and one that has many rules will have a high delinquency rate. High population density forces us to have rules, and with the present steady population increase the control of individual behavior becomes ever more difficult. The gradually increased controls operating on the juvenile as he grows older are likely to induce him to resist. We also note a lessening of parental responsibility for the training of children. With more rules and more complex social demands and less parental or other clearly defined responsibility there is bound to be an increasing delinquency rate. Finally, we should note that Western culture both encourages individual initiative and rewards conformity. There are many contradictions in our culture, and children are increasingly left without general guidelines for deciding when individuality must give way to conformity.

Although we speak of an individual's proneness to delinquency, our actual data are on the occurrence of delinquency. Behind the act of delinquency, however, lies the construct "proneness." Proneness can be thought of as a kind of aptitude to become delinquent which is measured by estimates of the probability that an individual will become delinquent if he is exposed to reasonably standard temptation and opportunity. The proneness construct is developed from the numerous probabilities of delinquency as these are inferred from studies relating classificatory data on individuals to frequencies of delinquency for the classes. When items of information place an adolescent into a class for which a rate has been established, then a proneness statement can be made. He may be considered highly prone if the class or classes into which he falls have been observed to exhibit a high delinquency rate. If fewer than average among the class become delinquent, the individual has little proneness. As is usual with such constructs, one can never fully establish the value of the proneness, nor can one clearly define its psychological nature.

One may think of highly delinquency-prone children as being among the first to appear on a delinquency record as they are exposed to societal rules. These boys and girls, from whatever they derive their proneness, contribute most to the delinquency rate data; they will tend to remain delinquent even under the most extreme measures of suppression. By contrast, those low in delinquency proneness become delinquent only under the most provocative situations. This is the group most amenable to programs of delinquency prevention.

What we mean by the construct "delinquency-proneness" will be further developed by our data. For the moment we wish merely to re-emphasize that no amount of proneness to delinquency alone determines that a child will become delinquent. Because environmental factors must contribute temptation and opportunity in order for the behavior to appear, it is surprising to find the degree to which certain personality variables are predictive of delinquency. This accuracy may be accounted for by the fact that there exist abundant social opportunities favoring the occurrence of delinquency. It is our hope that more complete knowledge of the personality of the delinquency-prone child will make our efforts more efficient both in modifying the cultural milieu by reducing the opportunity for delinquency and in developing better training programs designed to lessen or compensate for delinquency-proneness.

In many of our analyses we have been forced to use the level 1 delinquency rating along with levels 2, 3, and 4. Without the level 1 cases the numbers would not have been large enough to ensure the statistical stability of the analysis. Here again, it is apparent that the study samples should have been at least twice as large as they are. The problem of sample size is especially vexing in the case of girls, for whom the delinquency rate is only about one-third that for boys.

Delinquency and Age

The data permit only a rough estimation of the relationship between delinquency rates and age. Tables 18 and 20 present our data, and Wirt and Briggs (34) can be consulted for related data. The trend revealed suggests that the delinquency rate decreases as the subjects approach age nineteen. The rate for the sixteen-year-old group reflects an increase in number of traffic offenses since these boys and girls had now reached the legal age for driving automobiles. This, however, does not account for all of the increase.

In assessing the significance of these data, it should be remembered that the rates are based on the number of persons who committed offenses and that they represent only the number of separate individuals who were involved over the three- or four-year interval of the follow-up study. Minneapolis statistics (5) show that about 50 per cent of offending boys and about 37 per cent of girls are recidivist. It is assumed that these rates can be applied to our cases and in this aspect our figures inadequately express the community problem.

Delinquency and the Other Variables (Table 84)

Table 84 gives some general data on the distribution of the delinquent 2, 3, or 4 boys and the 1, 2, 3, or 4 girls. The percentage of all delinquents falling into each variable category is given first and then the rate of delinquency for each group. Thus, among the whole sample of delinquent boys, 46.5 per cent are from semiskilled homes, and these homes provided delinquents at a rate of 26.6 per cent. Contrastingly, day-laborer homes provided only 10.7 per cent of all delinquents although the rate was 30.5 per cent. Professional and semiprofessional homes provided nearly as many of the total delinquents as did the day-laborer group, but their delinquency rate was a little lower. About one-third of all delinquent boys came from the upper socioeconomic levels. Apparently the effect of socioeconomic status upon girls is greater than it is upon boys because the rates vary from a low of 5.7 to a high of 18.0 compared to a low of 12.7 and a high of 30.5 for boys.

The relation between school dropout and delinquency is illustrated dramatically by the fact that about one-third of the delinquent boys and nearly half the delinquent girls leave school before graduation. Also, 39 per cent of the boys who drop out are delinquent and 31 per cent of the girls, against base rates of 24.0 and 10.4. Delinquency of the girls is very closely related to dropout (see Chapter 9).

Only about one in ten boys and one in seven girls of the delinquent samples come from broken homes. These proportions are small despite the fact that the delinquency rates for children from broken homes stand second in size among all rates.

The rates of delinquency for boys at all intelligence levels are rather constant. The rates for girls vary more, but the small size of the sample makes the finding unreliable. A variable markedly related to delinquency is high school rank. It is necessary to remember that high school rank data were only available for those near to graduation from high school, and the true relationship would be even greater if there had been no dropout. Despite the close relationship, it is notable that among graduates 38 per cent of the delinquent boys and over half the delinquent girls still ranked above the fortieth percentile in school achievement.

The pages that follow provide only a highly simplified summary of the data in chi-square Tables 86–106, on the relation of the separate variables to delinquency. The summaries are intended to indicate the largest differences as shown by comparison of the table margin predictions to the observed population of each cell (see page 43 for an explanation of the table arrangement). It is fully recognized that this simplified overview is inadequate to develop the complex relationships found in these tables. The questions that we could ask were found to be so numerous that there seemed to be no practical alternative to this simplified approach. We are acutely aware of the fact that tables providing three or more dimensions of the data, with variance and factor analyses, would be valuable. It is obvious, for example, that the variables of school dropout, intelligence, and delinquency affect one another. But at this point we are forced to leave further analysis of such data for later publications.

Delinquency and Community Size (Tables 86–87)

Whatever may be the cause, delinquency rates vary with community size. Possibly this variable is better called population density. The lowest rate is found for farm children. It should be noted that field workers were instructed to be especially thorough in rural districts since it is often claimed that delinquent behavior is not well recorded by rural authorities. There is reason to believe, therefore, that the rates we show are a good estimate of the actual situation. City and suburban rates are generally about one-third larger than the expected rate and the rural rate is similarly about one-third less than the expected rate.

Possibly one can say that the delinquency rate of the girls is less affected by population density, although the trends are similar to those for boys (Table 87). One point is a little more clear. The rate of severe delinquency among suburban girls is not more than expected although minor trouble among them is relatively common. The obvious possibility presented is that the suburbs, although dense in population, do not so adversely affect girls as boys.

MMPI data in other of the tables show that the rural boys and girls also differ from urban adolescents in the frequencies for certain personality codes. These codes — high 4 is an example — interact differentially with the delinquency rates presented in Table 84; high 4 profiles are more common in cities and delinquency is more common with high 4 boys.

Delinquency and Socioeconomic Status (Tables 85 and 88–89)

In Chapter 2 we described the selection of two schools in the best neighborhoods and three schools in the poorest neighborhoods among the fifteen Minneapolis schools. Table 85 shows the observed comparative delinquency rates for these highly contrasting school areas. The best schools have a severe delinquency rate of three per hundred boys and the poorest schools fourteen per hundred with similar records. (The "severe" delinquency used here is comparable to levels 3 and 4 as used elsewhere.) It is obvious that appreciable severe delinquency occurs in the best neighborhoods, yet not at the rate of the poor neighborhoods.

If one looks at the frequencies for lesser offenses, the rates for the two regions are not greatly different. Improvement of poor neighborhoods does not appear to promise a marked decrease of delinquency when one keeps in mind the fact that families likely to include delinquent children move into poor neighborhoods from elsewhere and are in one sense not properly counted as products of the neighborhood. These mobile families might even be a chronic product of good neighborhoods from which they migrate.

Boys and girls from lower socioeconomic status homes in the statewide sample are more likely to be delinquent than those from higher status homes. The rural variable is strong enough to reverse the trend. (The delinquency rates of the three socioeconomic levels of farmer vary only slightly, and we combined them for these tables.) Delinquency among professional and semiprofessional families does not differ markedly from the general average except that there are fewer level 1 girls than expected from such homes. Most of the variance seems to be accounted for by the differences between farmers and the lower socioeconomic status categories. An interesting comparison of boys and girls can be seen in the groups from clerical homes, where more boys but fewer girls are delinquent at levels 2, 3, and 4 than is expected.

Comparison of these tables with Tables 86–87 will suggest that density of population is not so powerful a factor as is the occupation level when one evaluates the difference between those adolescents who live on farms and those whose fathers are farmers. Obviously these groups overlap one another to a large extent but, in spite of the overlap, the probability of delinquency for children of farmers is less than the probability for children who live on a farm. The chief difference between the groups is due to the fathers who work in towns but live in a farm house.

Delinquency and Parents' Marital Status (Tables 90–94)

Broken homes do relate to the frequency of delinquency. Further, if a home is broken, a child living with the mother is more likely to be delinquent than one for whom other arrangements are made. In the case of girls, even living with neither parent is less related to higher delinquency than is living with the mother.

Data for study of ordinal birth position and delinquency are unavailable, but we found little relationship between the delinquency rate for boys and the number of siblings in the family (Table 94).

Delinquency and Intelligence, Grades, and School Dropout (Tables 95–100)

The data show that there exists little relationship between delinquency and scores on intelligence tests for boys. This, however, is not so true of the girls. There may be a higher rate among girls just below average intelligence. The really close relationship is that between high school grades and delinquency. Some common source of these two outcomes seems indicated, but our data do not support the hypothesis that school ability as measured with intelligence tests is the contributing factor. The data clearly show that intelligence test scores will not identify all the children who will get poor grades. It is obviously indicated that prediction of school grades would be improved if one could have a test of delinquency proneness to combine with intelligence test scores.

The close association between school dropout and delinquency, especially with girls, follows very reasonably from the data on school achievement. We feel that such data must be very cautiously interpreted. The issue's complexity is illustrated in the data of Table 116 and the discussion on pages 96–98. Clearly the personality types, when separated into smaller groups, do not indicate an identical contribution to dropout and to delinquency. Despite the close general association, some personalities are much more prone to dropout than to delinquency and the reverse is true of other personalities.

To prevent school dropout forcibly, for example, might increase delinquency through the adolescent's reaction to the frustrations of being forced to continue in a school situation where he is unsuccessful and unhappy. If dropouts could move to a placement as satisfactory to them as is school for the good students who like it, then possibly the delinquency rate would fall. We favor this hypothesis, but we do not have good evidence for its support. One more point that must be kept in mind is that, although school dropouts have one of our highest rates of delinquency, they are a minority in the general population of these ages and so they contribute only about 31 per cent of all our delinquent group (Table 84).

Delinquency and Conduct Ratings (Tables 101–102)

The follow-up workers made a rating that represented their impressions of the general conduct and emotional adjustment of the cases. These ratings depended upon teachers and others whose reports were integrated arbitrarily by the follow-up rater.

A close relationship between delinquency and bad conduct ratings was inevitable (Tables 101 and 102, ratings 3 and 4). The failure to give all delinquents a bad conduct rating probably provides a measure of the fact that delinquent behavior by a certain juvenile can be partly excused by those who know the case. For both boys and girls, relatively many more good conduct ratings than bad conduct ratings are given to delinquents. These ratings also express the tendency of adults around a child to rate him favorably despite behavior that is objectively quite bad.

Delinquency and Adjustment Ratings (Tables 103–104)

The adjustment ratings, like the conduct ratings, came from the follow-up workers. It is not at all clear what these ratings express. They may be found to be related to mental illness if studies are done on the cases when they become adults.

A very interesting fact comes out when the distributions of the delinquent boys and girls are compared over the four tables (Tables 101–104). Many more of these delinquent cases are given bad adjustment ratings than are given bad conduct ratings. Among other interpretations, it may be that those evaluating the delinquents find it much more easy to call them badly adjusted than to rate them as having bad conduct. It is also possible that a considerable portion of the delinquents show themselves in school contacts as maladjusted but in the community they express this through antisocial acts.

Delinquency and Teacher Predictions (Tables 105–108)

When, at the time the original testing was done, the teachers were asked to name the pupils who seemed likely to get into trouble with the law or to develop emotional problems, or both, no effort was made to provide the teachers with more explicit definitions of terms. They could have interpreted "trouble with the law" to mean delinquency, crime, or minor difficulties. Although some subjects were named by several teachers, most of them were named by only one. All the pupils who were named once or more were placed in the teacher prediction groups. There were 790 boys and 280 girls in the delinquency prediction group for whom delinquency or both delinquency and emotional problems were predicted. These groups were, respectively, 13.9 and 5.0 per cent of the whole statewide samples of boys and girls.

As Tables 105 and 106 show, the teacher predictions were significantly related to the occurrence of delinquency. Even those for whom emotional trouble was predicted became delinquent reliably more frequently than expected. These tables also show what happened when those known to be delinquent before the time of teacher selection were eliminated. Although it seems that the teachers must have known and named some of these already delinquent children, their removal from the tables has little effect upon teacher accuracy.

Tables 107 and 108 show some data on the groups selected by the teachers. For this analysis the definition of delinquency for boys included delinquency levels 2, 3, and 4, and for girls levels 1, 2, 3, and 4. Level 1 was included for girls because of their low delinquency rate. In each table the data describe the pupils selected by teachers in relation to the variables. For example, column 1 of Table 107 shows that the teachers, in naming potential delinquents, selected 11.5 per cent of their boys from the day-laborer socioeconomic category and only 4.9 per cent from the professional and semiprofessional category. In column 2 these percentages are divided by the actual percentages of the total sample that are in each socioeconomic category. If the teachers had made a strictly proportional selection, the value in column 2 would be 1.00. For the day-laborer group, the value 1.46 means that the teachers expected 46 per cent more boys from this group to be delinquent than would be expected on the basis of proportion that this category is of the whole sample. For the professional and semiprofessional group the teacher selections were underrepresentative, with only 64 per cent of the proportional number.

Column 3 shows the teacher selection rates adjusted for actual delinquency rate. Since the delinquency rate is larger for the boys in the day-laborer category, a good prediction of delinquency would, therefore, choose more of these boys, as was the case. Column 3 should show the value 1.00 when the rate of column 2 is in proper proportion to the observed delinquency rate for the category. As column 3 for the boys and especially for the girls shows, teachers choose too freely from the farmer group even when this correction is made for the actual delinquency rate of the category. The teacher rate is 18 per cent larger than it should be for boys and 82 per cent larger than it should be for girls. The most marked selection discrepancy for boys occurs at the high end of the socioeconomic series where the figure .45 indicates the underrating by the teachers of delinquency among the professional group. Only among the boys from day-laborer and semiskilled and slightly skilled homes is the figure near 1.00, meaning that the prediction rate was comparable to the actual rate.

Column 4 shows the accuracy of the predictions made for each category of the variables. From the data in this column it can be seen that when the teachers do select boys from the professional and semiprofessional group, they are 54 per cent accurate. In contrast, when they select from among farm boys, they have only a 30 per cent accuracy. Although the methods of teacher prediction differed, there is a remarkably close agreement of our figure for over-all teacher accuracy, 45 per cent for boys, with that of the Cambridge-Somerville study, 42 per cent for boys (26).

The remaining data of these tables interpret similarly. There are many points of interest to be found in the tables. Teachers appear to be markedly influenced by high school grade rank in their choice of boys and girls who appear likely to be delinquent. They are reluctant to predict delinquency for a boy or girl who makes good grades, and their predictions are inaccurate when they do choose one. In contrast, 40.8 per cent of the boys chosen by teachers drop out of school and

10.7 per cent come from broken homes. Although the predictions of delinquency are quite accurate in predicting dropouts for boys and girls, the expected rates are greatly overestimated for boys; among the girls, however, this is not true, for the rate is near 1.00. Overestimation of rates for both boys and girls occurs for those from broken homes. For the girls not only do the teachers select too infrequently from the professional category, but they are also more inaccurate than with the boys in prediction of delinquency. Intelligence seems to be highly involved in teacher judgment of girls. Despite the fact that intelligence as measured by the ACE or IQ has little effect on the delinquency rate for boys and only a moderate effect for girls, and that fewer delinquents came from the lowest intelligence group than from any other level, teachers drew 20 per cent of their nominations from these groups. Their nominations are even more heavily loaded with boys and girls of low scholarship. Clearly the teachers tend to relate poor school ability and achievement to delinquency.

Predictions by the MMPI (Tables 109–110)

To provide some basis for judging the accuracy of teacher predictions these predictions were compared with MMPI code predictions. For comparable MMPI groups we selected boys and girls from the statewide sample by using cases with profiles known to relate to the frequency of delinquency. Using our Minneapolis findings to suggest code classes that should show a high delinquency rate, we drew codes and delinquency frequencies from the statewide rates of delinquency levels 2, 3, and 4 to form an MMPI delinquency prediction sample. The code selection was governed by the presence of what we called excitatory scales in our earlier report (15). The codes were dominated by high-point scales 4, 8, and 6 in the permutation forms 48, 49, and 46 mainly, but to adjust the number of cases, we used several code classes with underscoring that included one or two other scales. To establish a cutting point comparable to the teacher groups the MMPI codes from the statewide sample were selected to form a group approximately equal in number to the teacher groups. There were 795 boys and 253 girls.

In developing the MMPI prediction group we used a table like Table 116 except that it showed rates for delinquency levels 2, 3, and 4 instead of 1, 2, 3, and 4. Table 116 is given here because the larger delinquency rates improve the reliabilities of the rates. To illustrate the procedure or to find other cutting points, Tables 24 and 116 may be used. One draws on the tabled numbers giving the frequencies of each code class (Table 24) and those giving the percentage delinquent (Table 116). This continues until the separate percentages add up to the required percentage cutting point. The following example shows this procedure. Assume we want a sample with a high delinquency rate. From Table 116 we can see that code 48 . . . has a delinquency rate of .50. Table 24 shows the frequency of this code to be 3.7 per cent. Another class with a high delinquency rate in Table 116 has code 49 . . ., for which the rate is .54. Table 24 gives the frequency of this code as 4.1 per cent. Using only these two, we would have a way of selecting 3.7 plus 4.1 or 7.8 per cent of boys from the general population for whom the delinquency rate will be between .50 and .54. Other groups can be similarly added. It is well, of course, to avoid the classes that contain very few cases (classes marked with daggers).

Tables 109 and 110 show the categorical data on the adolescents selected by the MMPI. The columns are similar to those of the teacher prediction tables with which the data of these tables should be compared. Column 4, MMPI accuracy, for the girls shows only the over-all rate since there were too few cases in the subdivisions.

A general difference between the MMPI and teacher groups is that the MMPI tended to select predicted delinquents in proportion to the observed general base rates. The values in column 2 cluster closer to 1.00 than in Tables 107 and 108. This means that MMPI predictions are better representative of the group as a whole. The MMPI is not much influenced by high school rank; its predictions were freer of bias related to low scholarship than were those of the teachers. Also it does not choose so disproportionately from boys who will drop out of school, but its accuracy in selection of dropouts is higher than that of the teachers. In this connection, the high delinquency rate for school dropouts reflects the fact that some delinquents were encouraged or required to drop out by events related to their delinquency.

The base rates for delinquency levels 2, 3, and 4 for all boys is 24.0 per cent (Table 19). The corresponding delinquency rate among the boys predicted to be delinquent by teachers was 45 per cent, about twice the base rate. The delinquency rate for the MMPI-predicted boys was 37 per cent, which was about 82 per cent as accurate as the teacher predictions.

As was true for other analyses, the base delinquency rate for girls was so low that we were forced to use all four levels of delinquency rating. Consequently the data on accuracy of predictions for girls cannot be compared with those for boys. The general base rate of delinquency levels 1, 2, 3, and 4 for girls was 10.4 per cent. The delinquency 1, 2, 3, or 4 rate for the teacher-predicted group was 38 per cent and that of the MMPI-predicted group was 26 per cent, which is 68 per cent as accurate as the teacher predictions.

For both boys and girls, then, teachers predicted with more over-all accuracy than did the MMPI, despite the fact that the MMPI predicted groups in better proportion to their observed contribution to the make-up of the whole delinquent group. Teachers do not seem to have been able to heighten their accuracy from prior knowledge of delinquent acts by some of the subjects. MMPI predictions were also only slightly contaminated by previous delinquency even if the adolescent had been in repeated trouble. In any case the MMPI profile approach emphasizes the role of the individual personality organization in the occurrence of delinquency without directly allowing for the school and socioeconomic status data that are often available to teachers and which the tables show to influence their selections. Many children with personality patterns likely to lead to delinquency are protected by favorable environmental forces such as a good family or good organizational affiliations. Teachers frequently also knew facts of this sort. One hears such statements as "He'd probably get into trouble if he didn't have the stabilizing influence of his older brother who watches him and is close to him."

Whenever one is considering tests or other predictions of delinquency, it is important to look at the population base rates for delinquency. For example, the base rate of delinquency (at the 2, 3, or 4 level of severity) that we give for boys is 24 per cent. If one simply predicted that no boys would be delinquent, the accuracy would be 76 per cent. Since this prediction is of little value to programs directed at treating only a part of the population of boys, we are interested in predicting delinquency rather than in being accurate by assuming that no one will be delinquent. From this approach, a randomly picked sample of boys who are to be treated would be correctly assumed to need the treatment at the base rate 24 per cent. Now, if one were to have picked the group of boys nominated by the teachers, the accuracy of prediction would be 45 per cent. This still means that the prediction is more often wrong than right, but it is about twice as often right as would be the case with random selection. Obviously, the actual rate of being correct would vary with the cutting point used in a practical situation. By manipulating the number of boys to be selected for treatment from a population one might greatly improve the percentage of accuracy. This will be especially true if one needs to choose only a small percentage among all boys. Comparisons of accuracy for various prediction devices have to be based on comparable cutting points applied to comparable populations. This is why we equated the cutting points in the comparison data of Tables 107–108 and 109–110.

For further consideration of MMPI prediction of delinquency, see the discussion below relative to the scale for measuring delinquency proneness.

Delinquency and Personality (Tables 111–117)

Some data on the personality of the delinquent adolescent as revealed by MMPI studies have been reported (15, 34). Such results may be considered from two points of view: prediction and analysis. By prediction we mean the attempt to discover signs, test scores, or any other indicators that precede delinquent acts and can be used to reduce the base rate error in prediction of delinquency. Until practical methods of prediction are found, prevention programs cannot be highly efficient. We developed in an earlier chapter some general ideas about such predictions (Chapter 1), and we have given data on prediction in this chapter. By analysis we mean the study of predelinquents and delinquents to develop personality descriptions of them. Such description could lead to the discovery or imply the existence of causes and provide knowledge for better understanding of the psychology of delinquency. The following discussion and data are devoted to analysis.

The MMPI scale means and standard deviations of delinquent and nondelinquent boys from the Minneapolis sample are presented in Table 111. If one assumes that these MMPI scales are valid indicators of personality disturbance, then the results provide evidence that delinquents are a more disturbed group than are the nondelinquents. Conversely, if one begins with the assumption that delinquents are disturbed, then these scale data suggest where the main psychological areas of abnormality lie. The delinquent boys are more often psychopathic, schizoid, or hypomanic than nondelinquents. These abnormal patterns can occur singly or in combination. The delinquent girls show the same general differences. We do not wish to go any further in interpretation of the general data in Table 111, since we believe that differences in average scale values are of little aid in analyzing and predicting delinquency. The overlap between groups is too great for practical application.

Tables 112–115 show the single-high-point and single-low-point code frequencies against the levels of delinquency. These data are too coarsely grouped for many clear relationships to appear.

It is at once apparent that high scale 4 is related to delinquency, as many other evidences have established. Scale 0 is likewise related for boys and girls in that social introversion does not go with delinquency. Although high scale 9 does not predict delinquency, absence of the factor measured by scale 9 does predict a lower rate of delinquency (Tables 114–115). All these gross trends are complicated by the fact that the tables come from only the highest or lowest points on the profiles. The effect of high 9 is likely to be obscured by the fact that high 9 followed by 4 in the code of a profile suggests a relatively higher delinquency rate, but a high 9 followed by a 2 suggests a relatively lower delinquency rate.

The use of two-point codes is a much better way of studying the relationship between MMPI personality profiles and delinquency. Table 116 is a compilation of frequency data on the relation of codes to delinquency and school dropout. To provide large enough numbers, delinquency is defined to include all four levels. School dropout rates are included in Table 116 so that these may be compared readily with the delinquency rates. With a few important exceptions, there appear to be different degrees of relationship between personality and delinquency than between personality and school dropout. The problem of dropout is discussed in Chapter 9.

Table 116 begins with the delinquency rates for the various types of invalid profiles. For example, 86 per 1000 boys had high F profiles (45 plus 41). Of these, more than 40 per cent became delinquent. Without using any other indicator, one could therefore find as many as eight in every 100 boys in a similar school system on whom a delinquency prevention program could be tested with confidence that the work was being directed at a large number needing help.

High F does not provide enough information for analyzing the personality make-up of the delinquent. More meaningful material is available from valid profile codes. The data of Table 116 reveal points of interest too numerous to discuss in detail. Among the more striking items, however, are those for profile types 46 . . ., 48 . . ., and 49 . . . — boys with the personalities suggested by these profiles reach or exceed a delinquency rate of 50 per cent. Such uses of Table 116 have been more completely described above relative to prediction.

Knowing in general what scales 4, 6, 8, and 9 measure suggests analytical statements to relate personality and delinquency. Scale 4 was intended to measure the pattern clinically known as sociopathic character, a striking syndrome of adolescence and adulthood. This syndrome was formerly referred to as constitutional psychopath or asocial, amoral psychopath. It is characterized by an absence of the usual moral restraints. Viewed from the standpoint of the clinical symptoms of neurosis, high 4 persons appear super-normal, nearly immune to the punishing feelings of shame or embarrassment.

Scale 8, by contrast, was developed to identify the symptomatic pattern of schizophrenia. When scale 8 is scored high on persons who are not mentally ill, it appears to suggest a "lone wolf," bizarre, faulty orientation to the social world. Persons of both sociopathic and schizophrenic character types are clinically known to have difficulty in adapting to the usual controls and demands of society. On the basis of clinical experience with sociopathic and schizophrenic adult patients, one would expect that there would be a difference in kind between the delinquent acts of high 4 and high 8 boys. The schizophrenic component in the personality of delinquent boys would be expected to be associated with more persistent and bizarre misbehavior. We have collected some preliminary evidence to support this expectation, and we plan to publish this in the future.

It may be assumed that if these test-deviant boys and girls could be treated in some way so as to lower their scores on scales 8 and 4, the rate of delinquency among them would correspondingly decrease. Unfortunately, the data do not demonstrate that the personality patterns can be modified. To answer the question posed, one would need to undertake a study involving both control and experimental groups. We do know, however, that the test profiles of a great many of these adolescents change as they grow older (see Chapter 7), and we know that delinquency rates decrease with age.

One of the striking generalities that may be drawn from Table 116 is the fact that boys and girls are similar in their code types and delinquency rates. Usually those personality patterns associated with higher delinquency rates of boys are the same as those associated with higher rates of girls. If we select all code types in the statewide sample that had at least 30 cases — 34 different code types — the correlation between delinquency rates of boys paired with those of girls of the same type is .71 (N = 34). A similar correlation on the Minneapolis sample was .53, but the Minneapolis data were unreliable because of the small sample size.

Another interesting feature of the data in these tables is the fact that some personality types predict no delinquency about as accurately as others predict delinquency. For no-high-point profiles the delinquency rate drops from base rate 34 to 28 per cent. The neurotic features expressed in scales 2, 3, 7, 0, and 5 are also predictive of lower rates.

We have previously reported (15) that certain of the MMPI's variables can be classed as excitatory and others as inhibitory for the occurrence of delinquency. The role of an excitatory variable is indicated by the fact that the delinquency rate shows a definite increase as the T-score value of the scale increases. The reverse is true of the inhibitory scales, where a T-score increase is related to a decrease in the delinquency rate. Using this criterion, scale 4 is found to be a strongly excitatory scale. Thus the total 4 rate for boys is 40 per cent delinquency (Table 116) for profiles with the highest point less than 70 and 51 per cent delinquency when scale 4 is higher than T score 70. In sharp contrast, the delinquency rate for total high 2 boys when scores are above 70 is only 23, 33 for those with scale 2 scores below 70. Boys who react with depression seem relatively unlikely to be delinquent. Scale 7 shows the same inhibitory phenomenon: the clinical import of this scale, like scale 2, suggests neurotic tendencies. Generally, when inhibitory scales occur with excitatory scales in profiles, the stronger effect seems to be exerted by the excitatory scales. Thus for boys with codes 24... and 42..., the effect of depression seems largely canceled out by scale 4 — these codes suggest 39 per cent delinquency, which is greater than the general rate. Unfortunately, the numbers of delinquents are too small to permit extensive analysis of the effect of higher and lower scores. It seems safe, however, to suggest that a counselor should be aware of these general trends when advising or working with youngsters whose profiles are unusually deviant.

Considerable effort was spent on an attempt to derive a useful scale from the MMPI items for selecting predelinquent boys. The best scale developed is given below in the list of items found to discriminate boys who later became de-

DELINQUENCY SCALE

Item	Delinquent Response
At times I have very much wanted to leave home.	True
When someone does me a wrong I feel I should pay him back if I can, just for the principle of the thing.	True
During one period when I was a youngster I engaged in petty thievery.	True
As a youngster I was suspended from school one or more times for cutting up.	True
I believe women ought to have as much sexual freedom as men.	True
In school I was sometimes sent to the principal for cutting up.	True
Most people will use somewhat unfair means to gain profit or an advantage rather than to lose it.	True
I do not worry about catching diseases.	True
When I was a child, I belonged to a crowd or gang that tried to stick together through thick and thin.	True
I have the wanderlust and am never happy unless I am roaming or traveling about.	True
I am afraid when I look down from a high place.	False
I liked school.	False
I like to flirt.	True
I very much like hunting.	True
My parents have often objected to the kind of people I went around with.	True
I don't blame anyone for trying to grab everything he can get in this world.	True
I am entirely self-confident.	True
When in a group of people I have trouble thinking of the right things to talk about.	False
I can easily make other people afraid of me, and sometimes do for the fun of it.	True
At times I have been so entertained by the cleverness of a crook that I have hoped he would get by with it.	True
I have never been in trouble with the law.	False
If several people find themselves in trouble, the best thing for them to do is to agree upon a story and stick to it.	True
At times I have very much wanted to leave home.	True
I have had very peculiar and strange experiences.	True
I am often said to be hotheaded.	True
I played hooky from school quite often as a youngster.	True
I am attracted by members of the opposite sex.	True
I would like to be an auto racer.	True
It is all right to get around the law if you don't actually break it.	True
If I were in trouble with several friends who were equally to blame, I would rather take the whole blame than to give them away.	True

linquent from those who remained nondelinquent. This scale is a refined version of an earlier one (16). When this later scale was checked on cross-validation, we were dissatisfied with its power to separate delinquents from nondelinquents. Part of the evidence on which we rejected use of this De scale is given in Table 117 where one can assess the power of the scale against other methods. Table 117 shows the scores on the scale for 224 boys randomly selected except that the percentage of delinquency was stratified so that the rates for all levels corresponded to the general population rate and the base rate for the sample approximated the total sample base rate of 24 per cent. Delinquency levels 2, 3, and 4 made up 22 per cent of the 224 boys of Table 117. It appears reasonably accurate to refer to Table 117 as a standard sample.

If, now, we take the data used for the discussion of teacher prediction accuracy, it is possible to check the De scale. The teacher prediction group cut the population at about 13.9 per cent. Teacher prediction at this cut was 45 per cent accurate. Cutting the data of Table 117 at this level, one needs 31 cases. This number does not happen to occur in the accumulated frequency column. A cut at score 18 includes 34 cases of whom 10 are delinquent, an accuracy of only 29 per cent. Cutting at score 20 includes 13 cases of whom 5 are delinquent, an accuracy of 38 per cent. Teacher prediction appears clearly better.

Similarly, MMPI prediction accuracy shown in Table 109 was 37 per cent. Compared to the De scale accuracy, this also is as good or better. Finally, the overlapping of delinquency scores as shown in Table 117 is extreme. Three delinquent boys got scores below 10, a score well below the mean.

The De scale not only fails to differentiate well but it also fails in providing the analytical information that is given by using codes for prediction. The codes subdivide the probably delinquent group into smaller samples that are indicated to have differing personality characteristics. No single scale can express this information.

We could not compare the power of our scale with other scales that have been published, with the exception of scales similarly drawn from MMPI items. But we are not aware of any scale derivations or tests of scale power from any source which, like ours, came from longitudinally collected data and were checked by cross-validation cases similarly derived. We derived and tested the scale on predelinquent boys. It appears likely that the facts of delinquency and of being identified as a delinquent change group test responses to make it easier to show differences between delinquent and nondelinquent groups of boys.

In any event, we have satisfied ourselves that we could not find a single dimension, measurable with available items, which could be effectively used as a delinquency proneness scale. The personality patterns of the delinquency-prone adolescent are diverse, not monotonic. One boy can differ markedly from the next in personality and yet the two can have the same proneness to become delinquent. For example, it does not appear likely that a boy who steals to help get food for his family would have the same score on a scale of delinquency proneness as would a boy who steals because he wants to buy a motorcycle for racing.

The rates of delinquency with the various codes of Table 116 remain quite similar for the statewide and the Minneapolis samples in spite of the undoubtedly large differences introduced by placing the town and the farm subjects together in the statewide sample. The statewide-Minneapolis correlation between delinquency rates among the male code types with populations of more than 15 persons is .43 (N = 31). Although this is not large, it does establish the existence of a general agreement between the code personalities and delinquency rates of the two samples. It is interesting to note that this correlation is much smaller than the similar correlation of .71 (N = 34) between statewide boys and girls. Probably one may conclude that these two samples of boys are more different than are the sample of boys and girls who had similar backgrounds and were tested in the same year. This correlation supports the assumption that the personality types predicting delinquency are similar for boys and girls.

⑨

SCHOOL DROPOUT

ALMOST as significant as delinquency because of its social impact, school dropout, like delinquency, has many background conditions. While our data show the great importance of lack of interest in school and possibly of the appeal of the early independence that comes with a job, other factors obviously also contribute.

In part, school dropout represents a loss to society, especially if students of high ability drop out before finishing high school. But we find that the majority of potential dropouts do poorly in school, whatever the reason, and it does not appear desirable to hold these teen-agers in school forceably. Their being kept in school possibly impairs the general level of instruction to those who like school and who wish to do well.

Our data show a considerable overlap between the students who drop out and those who are delinquent. But when we break the two groups down in an attempt to analyze the particular personality contributions to dropout and delinquency, there appear to be real differences. The general nature of the personality patterns suggesting a high dropout rate seems to us to justify the conclusion that a considerable percentage of dropouts are unhappy with school discipline, school values, or the kind of work that school requires. If this is true, school dropout in such cases would not be so directly related to the appeals of other activities as to a rejection of school activities.

Such considerations lead us to some preliminary generalizations. Certain potential dropouts should be kept in school. We believe that efforts toward this end should take the direction of modifications in the school atmosphere and program — offering alternative courses of study, for example, or providing an extension of vocational school opportunities — so that school will be more appealing rather than aimed at stiffening of laws or other coercive attendance measures. We might illustrate by taking the case of boys and girls who find the school subjects in an "academic" or "pre-college" course too scholarly, too lacking in current application. Our personality data suggest to us the hypothesis that the current popular pressures on schools, asking for reinstatement of compulsory classical subjects and drill methods, might force out still more students of this kind. This may not be merely because of an increased work load but because the work demanded is less attractive, seems less viable, to the student.

A second general point may be made about the difference in personality between dropouts and delinquents. Neurotic, socially introverted, and schizoid adolescents are relatively more likely to drop out than they are to be delinquent. The function of school counseling might emphasize the personal and group adjustment of such students in order to keep them in school.

Finally, it is apparent that many girls are school dropouts because of early marriage. Some high schools still exclude or discriminate against the married high school girl. If the present trend toward early marriage continues, we shall obviously need to adjust our thinking in this area. Some of these girls re-enter school in middle life, but it may not be desirable that marriage should so often delay high school graduation. Here again, however, the data point to personality factors. Apparently these girls do not value school highly, especially in competition with marriage and children. Merely accepting them as continuing students may not keep them in school.

The foregoing generalities are quite arbitrary. We advance them as an introduction to the data we have in order that the reader may check these or his own ideas on this significant problem. We are mostly convinced that study of the tables will suggest the value of new patterns of thinking, with special emphasis upon the individual child and his adjustment potential against the requirements of both school and society.

General Data on Dropout (Tables 118–120)

Tables 118 and 119 summarize dropout data that are presented in more expanded form in succeeding tables. The last two columns of percentages show the rates of dropout among those of the category and the percentage of all dropouts that fall into each category.

The highest percentage rates of these tables occur with children of day-laborer families and of broken families. More than one in three children of broken families drop out. Among the day-laborer families, 38 per cent of boys and 32 per cent of girls drop out. These rates contrast sharply with the boys and girls from professional families who drop out at a rate of only 5 per cent.

The dropout rate is higher for the last two school years, with only one exception: the farm residence boys and sons of farmers tend to drop out earlier.

There is surprisingly little sex difference among the rates. The one large difference lies in the rates for the farm residence children and children of farmers. Among these, the boys who live on farms have the rather high rate of 24 per cent, nearly one in every four boys. The corresponding rate for farm girls is a comparatively low 15 per cent. The rate for daughters of farmers is still lower at 11 per cent.

As one would expect, intelligence tests predict school dropout. Among boys and girls with the lower intelligence test scores, 29 per cent of boys and 21 per cent of girls drop out. Above the average level of intelligence the rates abruptly drop to 6 per cent among boys and 7 per cent among girls.

In Table 14 we listed the reasons for dropout along with the percentage that each reason contributed to the sample of dropouts for whom we had a dropout reason. These were statewide figures and would change if they could be distributed into the separate places of residence. Lack of interest was chief among the reasons for boys, accounting for one-third of all dropouts. Military service took about one in four of the boys and only about one in seven dropped out to work.

Fifty-three per cent of female dropouts were the result of marriage or illegitimate pregnancy. An additional 21 per cent were reported to have dropped out for lack of interest. No doubt a real reason behind many of the marriages was that the girl lacked interest in school. It seems fair to assume that lack of interest really accounts for proportionally the largest group of all dropouts.

Table 120 presents a final interesting breakdown of the data on reason for dropout. In this table, two groups of boys — those listed as dropping out from lack of interest and those said to have dropped out to go to work or into military service — are compared. It might be expected that these groups would show clear differences on the personality variables, but differences fail to show up at a reliable level. There are not even evidences of a trend. Of course, the numbers are small, and larger samples might develop differences.

Dropout and Community Size (Tables 121–122)

The dropout rates for boys are more affected by community size than are those of girls. This is especially true for boys at the earlier grade levels. Probably the real explanation lies with the farm boys who leave school early to work. Restrictions on work opportunities for young boys are lower in rural areas than urban. We do not have data to check the point, but it is probable that the older boys leave the farms for city work and increase the need for their younger brothers to stop school to work on the farm. There is no marked corresponding effect on the girls, and no other significant variations occur in the table showing the distribution of the girls.

Dropout and Socioeconomic Status (Tables 123–124)

The general summary data (Tables 118 and 119) showed the clear relationship of dropout rates to socioeconomic status. The effects are heavily centered in the families of day laborers. At every grade level these families show clearly larger observed numbers of dropouts than are expected. Even the sons of farmers do not show such large differences between observed and expected rates. As was true in other of our tables, it makes a difference whether the adolescents live on farms or have fathers who are farmers (compare Tables 121–122 to Tables 123–124). Table 123 again gives evidence on the early dropout of boys whose fathers are farmers. Observed dropouts exceed the expected numbers for younger boys and are slightly less than the expected numbers for boys in the last two grades.

The daughters of farmers contrast with the corresponding samples of boys in that they have rather low dropout rates.

Dropout and Parents' Marital Status (Tables 125 and 126)

As the general rate tables showed, children from broken families are more likely to drop out than those from intact families. The chief new data in Tables 125 and 126 show that the effect is observable at all ages but that the older boys are possibly relatively less affected in this way than are the older girls. For the last two years, Table 125 shows there are 51 male dropouts observed against 33 expected. Corresponding data in Table 126 show 69 observed girls against

30 expected. The older girls thus drop out at a frequency over twice the expected rate.

Dropout and Intelligence (Tables 127 and 128)

The detailed figures on dropout and intelligence show very clearly how the lower scoring children drop out. The effect is sharply concentrated in the period before grade eleven. In the low intelligence group 251 boys drop out before this grade in contrast to an expected 143. The data for girls are comparable. These rates of dropout should be balanced against the fact that 71 per cent of the boys and 79 per cent of the girls among the low intelligence groups do not drop out at all despite their apparent handicap.

Dropout and Delinquency (Table 129)

In Table 84 we saw that about 39 per cent of boys and 31 per cent of girls who drop out have a delinquency rating. These percentages are not comparable since that for boys includes levels 2, 3, and 4 and that for girls also includes level 1 which raises the rate. The corresponding base rates (Table 19) were 24.0 and 10.4. The delinquency rate, at the levels given, is only 1.62 times the base rate for boys but is 2.98 times the base rate for girls. It seems that dropout and delinquency are more closely related for girls (see also Tables 99 and 100). Tables 99 and 100 also relate dropout to delinquency. The early years of high school have many more boy and girl delinquent dropouts than expected. It appears that remedial measures are needed at early school levels. Possibly the causes of dropout reach peak intensity in the eighth grade or earlier, and even more than for the problem of delinquency, the potential for dropout develops before our testing period in the ninth grade.

It will be recalled that the predictions of teachers asked to name children they thought would have trouble with the law or emotional problems were rather accurate when measured against the actual occurrence of delinquency, and, though they were not made with direct reference to dropout, they also predict dropout very well. Table 129 shows part of the data. Forty-six per cent of those boys on whom we had accurate school history information and for whom delinquency or delinquency and emotional trouble were predicted dropped out of school. Forty-five per cent of boys in the teacher prediction group actually were delinquent at the 2, 3, or 4 delinquency level (Table 107). Thirty-eight per cent of the girls for whom delinquency was predicted by teachers actually became delinquent at the 1, 2, 3, or 4 level (Table 108). However, 52 per cent of those girls predicted to become delinquent or to be delinquent and have emotional trouble dropped out of school.

If base rates of delinquency and dropout are different, then one cannot directly compare the accuracy rates given in Table 129. Base rates for the boys were 24.0 per cent delinquency (Table 19) and 17.6 per cent dropout (Table 13); for girls the delinquency base rate was 10.4 per cent (Table 19) and for dropout it was 14.5 per cent (Table 13). For comparison of the accuracy of prediction one must use an index arrived at by dividing the accuracy percentage by the base rate percentage. This index shows the relative concentration of the predicted group against the concentration in the general population. Dividing the 45 per cent male delinquent rate by the delinquency base rate 24.0 yields 1.88, which means that the delinquency rate of predicted cases was 88 per cent greater than the base rate. Dividing 46 by 17.6 yields a comparable dropout index of 2.41, larger than the index for prediction of delinquency. The prediction of male dropout is better than that for delinquency even when teachers are predicting delinquency. For girls the corresponding two indexes are 3.65 for delinquency and 3.59 for dropout. These relative accuracies are not much different.

The predictions that students will have emotional trouble are not so likely to indicate dropout. Only 27 per cent of boys and 24 per cent of girls were dropouts among those expected to develop emotional difficulty.

In summary, when teachers are naming students who are likely to get into trouble with the law, they are really doing as well or better at predicting which teen-agers will drop out of school. Our account of the accuracy of prediction of delinquency showed that these teacher predictions were also very closely related to poor schoolwork. It seems apparent that the teacher predictions elect those who are not doing well in several areas. It is quite likely that this aids the teachers to be more accurate, since boys and girls with problems in more than one area of behavior are, in a circular argument, those most likely to continue to be maladjusted. It would be interesting to study the individual delinquency or dropout cases elected by the teachers against those delinquent or dropout cases who were not named. The unnamed ones would probably be less complicated, more determined toward a particular area of maladjustment. If this is so, it could be that adolescents not recognized as potential delinquents or dropouts would be more rewarding targets for delinquency and dropout prevention programs than the generally maladjusted cases who are more likely to be named by teachers. Naturally this idea does not assume that the more maladjusted should not be included in prevention programs. It only suggests that such programs would perhaps appear more successful if they concentrated on the predelinquents and dropouts whose problems are less pervasive.

Dropout and Personality (Tables 116, 130–133)

We have pointed out that there are similarities between the characteristic personalities of delinquents and dropouts. That this is a gross difference rather than specific seems to be indicated by correlations between the dropout and delinquency rates. These correlations were obtained from Table 116. We went through the table using the pairs of percentages, percentage of delinquency and of dropout, for every code type that contained a population of twenty or more. The correlation for boys was .37 (N = 55) and that for girls was .26 (N = 54). These correlations are low, not large enough to exceed zero reliably. They seem to support the point that the two sets of percentages do not covary closely.

Some particular examples will illustrate the information in Table 116. To consider first the percentages of delinquency and dropout for boys, the base rates are 34 and 15 per cent. The rate of delinquency as defined here (level 1, 2, 3, 4) is about twice that of dropout. Now, we may choose a particular example where this two-to-one ratio does not hold; the total 3 category is a reliable case. The delinquency rate is nearly four times that of dropout. If scale 3 suggests conformity, the expression of it seems to inhibit dropout more than it does delinquency. Similar trends occur for scales 5 and 9. Scale 8 tends to show the opposite effect. One finds dropout rates that even reach the level of the delinquency rate. We have shown repeatedly that the schizoid symptoms of scale 8 are tied to school failure.

Among the girls, the base rates 10 and 14 for delinquency (1, 2, 3, and 4 level) and dropout are more nearly equal. Again scanning the table, we find that the total 1 girls show rates 12 and 26. For these girls who have physical complaints the dropout rate is more affected than the delinquency rate. The effect is even more apparent for depression, scale 2. There are many more examples of this trend to higher dropout rates. It appears that, although neurotic symptoms indicate low delinquency rates, they indicate high dropout rates.

Contrastingly, reversals in relative rate occur with some patterns. The rates for 49 . . . are 20 and 18, for example. The effect of the scale 4 excitatory influence toward delinquency appears to be somewhat specific against dropout. The reversal rates for 67 . . . are less understandable.

Tables 130–133 relate dropout and the time of dropout to the personality variables. Since the chi-square theory would not justify using the sum of all cells because the numbers are accumulative, this reliability check is applied only in the final two columns. We do give the usual numbers on all columns to be consistent with other tables. Scales 4, 8, and 0 are consistent among boys and girls as predictors of dropout. Scale 4 is also closely correlated with delinquency and other adverse behavior. One would expect these dropouts to be more clearly dependent upon rebellion against authority than upon personal patterns of interest. Scale 0 behaves in a surprising way. Both high scale 0 and low scale 0 profiles are relatively infrequent among dropout adolescents; neither social extroversion nor social introversion appears to be contributing to dropout. Scale 9 has a tendency to operate among boys, with both high and low scale 9 profiles related to low dropout rates.

Boys with high scale 8, boys who are schizoid in personality, are strongly prone to drop out of school. The trend is not present with the girls.

A very strong tendency emerges with no-low-point codes. When the MMPI profile has no score that falls much below average, the probability of dropout is much increased. Reversing this statement, we may say that it seems that a boy or girl whose profile suggests better than average adjustment in at least one area (at least one coded low point) will be likely to remain in school.

To relate further the personalities of dropouts to those of delinquents, Tables 112–115 may be compared to Tables 130–133. They may be studied in corresponding pairs with emphasis upon the 2, 3, and 4 delinquency level columns. Tables 112 and 130 added to Tables 114 and 132 show that the personality variables are much more generally related to dropout than to delinquency among boys. Most clear-cut are the effects of scales 8 and 9 on dropout. Schizoid and hypomanic symptom patterns are more characteristic of dropouts than of delinquents.

Tables 113 and 131 for girls show trends similar to those for boys, but the data are less reliable. Again, scale 8 is more closely related to dropout. Scale 0 is also significant, with socially introverted girls more probably dropping out.

In summary, as we have stated above, there are relationships between the personality patterns that suggest delinquency and dropout, but with closer analysis, these relationships are less apparent. Very generally, scale 4, with its implications of rebellion and immaturity, predicts delinquency a little better but relates to both outcomes. By contrast, the neurotic and schizoid traits of scales 1, 2, 3, and 8 are more indicative of school dropout.

CONCLUDING REMARKS

RESEARCH on social problems is difficult to execute with any appreciable precision. Most such research is inadequate because of the small size of the samples and the contamination of the variables that are studied. Variables based on data about family, economic status, housing, neighborhood, and many other environmental factors have been found to be associated with deviant personal or social behavior. But the identification of real causative sources among the many variables awaits better research methodology. We can only establish the existence of relationships and make inferences about which items are causes of others. In our studies we have used numerous variables, with the inevitable consequence that many of our conclusions are severely limited by the small numbers of individuals in subgroups.

The most accurate predictor of delinquency was teacher nomination; but these nominations were not helpful in differentiating personality patterns among those who were selected, and biases inconsistent with observed rates were shown to have influenced the teachers. They made, for example, too favorable judgments of children from professional families and too unfavorable judgments of children from low-income or broken families. Although predictions based on the MMPI were less accurate, they were more equitably distributed over the total sample and more clearly identified groups of children likely to have trouble than did predictions by teachers. No single MMPI code class dramatically predicted delinquency, however, and we seriously doubt that any one personality test pattern will be found to predict accurately that individual children will do things called delinquent by those about them.

Of course, such behavioral outcomes as delinquency and school dropout assume meaning and significance in the context of the cultural milieu in which they occur. What is and what is not called delinquent behavior varies with social values — even killing and pillage have been condoned in some cultures. Men in our culture have been called heroes for killing other men and for destruction of property when such acts were committed in conduct of a war. Acts like these are endemic in all cultures and even though we may deplore them, the fact remains that in our own society, policemen carry guns and shoot to kill, ardent proponents of causes may destroy property, and organized crime, if not officially accepted, at least gives a subcultural sanction to violence. Our teen-agers live with conflict and contrasts, and perhaps it should not be surprising that we found such high rates of delinquency as we report. There are many adults whose antisocial behavior provides examples for uncritical emulation by young people — behavior which is exciting and ambivalently presented by the press and in gossip but which is considered a mark of delinquency when circumstance exposes it to public evaluation. Often the family itself approves of behavior among its members that the surrounding society considers to be objectionable. It is impossible to say how much of the stealing, gross violation of traffic regulations, sexual misconduct, and other behavior that appeared in our sample of adolescents to label them delinquent was really in moral conflict with the family or peer group. The delinquent behavior for many of the youngsters studied probably occurred so naturally that no specifically characteristic personality pattern existed as a precursor.

Our data encourage what may be regarded as pessimistic conclusions. The sources of delinquent children are varied. The rates of delinquency are relatively comparable in all sources. The relationships between variables are so loose that elimination of no one background factor, even if it were causal, would result in a dramatic change of the total load. We think that our data contribute real evidence on why the few careful studies available (Cambridge-Somerville (26), for example) can be interpreted to imply that much of what is now being done by communities and individuals to control delinquency might be abandoned with no danger of appreciable increase in the size of the problem. Of course we do not recommend abandoning efforts to control delinquency. We do want to help put these efforts in proper perspective against our accumulated knowledge. It now appears wasteful to devote resources to certain of our community programs that are unlikely to achieve even their expressed goals. And some existing educational or action programs — aiming for stricter family discipline, more policemen, more and better training for correctional workers, tougher schools, and the like — may have reached or passed the point of development at which optimum results can be expected, and further expansion would yield scant return. Programs with holistic promises of radical prevention or treatment of delinquency and deviant behavior can sap strength from and delay the adoption of newer approaches emphasizing the individual personality of the child, approaches we believe to be currently most promising.

We think that our data, emphasizing as they do that the personality characteristics of delinquents and dropouts show individuality and contrast, suggest that efforts to control or prevent undesirable behavior should be designed for relatively homogeneous groups. The results point up the need to survey all children by methods that differentiate them in order to provide information to guide the development of programs of prevention or control. An important part of this guidance is the identification of children who are *unlikely* to get into trouble or to drop out of school.

The MMPI is far from wholly satisfactory in differentiating individual children or groups, but we are now recognizing that the test data do rather well in identifying some subgroups of children who may be considered difficulty-prone as well as some who are resistant to difficulty. In one such subgroup are those adolescents with high MMPI scale 4; their delinquency rate is well above the general base rate. The personality patterns associated with high 4 are well known in psychiatric and other literature and, although there is often justifiable pessimism about treatment, we have a rather good understanding of such children. It is known, for example, that most of them "grow out" of their adverseness and become acceptable citizens. We know too that treating them leniently and merely urging them to suppress their needs for excitement and revolt often has an effect opposite that desired. It does little good — may indeed provoke more mischief — to exhort them to settle down into school, home, and neighborhood like their well-behaved peers, since to them such a controlled life is intolerably boring and unrewarding. Schools and other agencies might well seek to provide outlets for acceptable expression of their exuberance and defiance, but those in charge of such programs would need to be more like this group in value system and temperament than are most school teachers and administrators.

We know that others of the boys and girls who get into trouble are schizoid, having high 8 profiles. This syndrome too is rather well known and understood. Professional workers would not expect such youngsters simply to grow out of their trouble as do most of those with high 4, nor can their problems be solved by encouraging drag racing and other exciting group activities. The schizoid and socially introverted children have interpersonal problems and experience difficulties in social relations which lead to further social isolation and arouse hostility and resentment in them. These adolescents tend toward senseless acts of vandalism and assault. Warm personal help is probably what they need. They might be encouraged to join organizations established to promote growth in self-respect and feelings of social confidence.

As a final example of the diagnostically recognizable children, there are a minority who are neurotic. These youngsters are often inarticulate. Contrasting sharply with the high scale 4 type, they are easily hurt by reprimands and the give and take of social life, and are often socially retiring. The disciplinary practices appropriate for most adolescents can do harm to this group. Like schizoid children but for different reasons, the neurotic children should receive a degree of protection and encouragement that would spoil an average youngster.

Dropout, like delinquency, is not always an abnormal or irrational act. Only in the context of our society's acute and growing need for technologically trained manpower does dropping out of school become a matter of intense public concern. The existence of a large percentage of unskilled workers in our society is generally regarded as a threat, since they swell the ranks of the unemployable and are a growing burden on our social security programs.

The dropouts have personalities suggestive of personal maladjustment in which poor school achievement and poor social adjustment are components. Delinquency itself often forces dropout; however, most of those children in our sample who dropped out did so because they did not like or fit the school. They apparently sought escape from an intolerable situation by going to work, into the armed services, or into marriage. Our data do not reveal clear-cut clues to why these boys and girls did not like school. Probably there were complex reasons. The school atmosphere with its interpersonal demands may have been of more importance in inducing dropouts than was dislike of schoolwork.

That the poor school record of those who drop out of school is related not only to level of intelligence but also to personality variables is not new, of course, but we have some direct evidence that helps us to analyze the nature of the personality variants contributing to good and bad grades. For boys, scale 8 was significantly related to poor grades. Contrastingly, scales 3 and 5 were related to good grades. If scale 3 is interpreted to indicate social conformity and scale 5 an interest in aesthetic and cultural values, then there exists support for the hypothesis that boys who conform receive good grades and are otherwise rewarded by teachers whose value standards stress these same interests.

There is a trend for girls who have low scale 9 or 5 or high scale 6 to get good grades. Low degrees of ebullient enthusiasm and, as with boys, femininity of interest as these traits are indicated by low 9 and 5 again are interpretable in terms of conformity. Even the high 6 girls can be looked upon as being motivated toward conformity, since they are above average in sensitivity to possible criticism and are likely not to risk any behavior which would call attention to themselves. However, for girls a high score on scale 8, even if it is regarded as symptomatic of nonconformity, does not appear to indicate problems.

Unfortunately the variety of personality types among dropouts makes it hard to predict accurately from the MMPI categories. To generalize from scale 8, which is most generally related to dropout for boys, some of these adolescents probably isolate themselves and are not very visible, appearing drab and uninteresting in contrast to their troublemaking and much more obstreperous classmates who are potential delinquents. Teachers attempting to pick future delinquents were found to be as good, if not better, in predicting instead which pupils would drop out of school. This was probably due in considerable degree to the fact that they knew the school grades and family status of their students. Of course, low school grades and a broken family suggested the likelihood of dropout. Such circumstances probably also contributed to the dropout's feelings of social inferiority and low personal worth, reflected by scale 8.

It would seem highly desirable to adopt some method of ensuring recognition of the fact that not all of the children who get poor grades or who are from broken homes drop out of school and thus counteract the understandable tendency of teachers and others to lump those with these handicaps indiscriminately into a group from whom nothing is expected. In any case, if teacher nominations were used to identify probable dropouts, a respectable number of the dropouts might be averted by attempts, guided by personality test results, to make school studies and the social life of the school more attractive to them. As with delinquency, the various personality patterns associated with high dropout rate suggest variations in treatment. In general, work with potential dropouts might be most effective if directed at the establishment of meaningful interpersonal contacts between students and teachers, counselors, or anyone else who would encourage a sense of personal worth and belonging.

One final word about treatment of potential delinquents and dropouts. Whatever the basis of efforts to achieve school and social conformity, we feel the contributions that nonconformists can make to society should not be sacrificed. It is only realistic to note, of course, that in view of the costs involved in developing diversified school programs, it may not be possible to provide the varying emphases to satisfy the varying needs of students; further the public is more receptive to supporting the old-fashioned, conventional programs. It is likely that the freer and more exciting programs appropriate for nonconforming youngsters would be offensive to the bulk of citizens who are themselves products and supporters of the conventional system. Obviously, there is a reciprocal effect in this. Those whose personality structures were compatible to the conventional system are the influential products of that system and understandably tend to perpetuate the procedures and values that seemed to have been good in their own development.

The reader of this report may be impressed by what appear to be high delinquency and dropout rates. What is, however, the most significant aspect of the data is the fact that the majority of the young people we studied were well enough adjusted and experienced few difficulties. When no specific information is available, it is absolutely more accurate to predict that any one child in the ninth grade will have little or no difficulty in adjusting than it is to predict otherwise. This is an important consideration when we come to evaluate broad, allinclusive programs created to prevent delinquency and school dropout. Thus even among the very small number of boys belonging to the groups having the highest rates of delinquency the probability of delinquency was only about one in two. It is true that significant rates of delinquency and dropout were found to exist in all the groups of adolescents no matter what variables were used to arrive at groupings, but of greatest significance is the fact that many of those even from broken and underprivileged families can be identified as belonging to groups in which the probability of getting into trouble is low. Blindly classing such children with their siblings and associates who show signs of trouble seems undesirable. Most of the boys and girls whose profile types were associated with a low delinquency rate and who did get into trouble were rated as having less severe problems than those in groups identified by codes predicting high delinquency rates. With more adequate numbers in the various groupings, we are confident that we could have better demonstrated that the average severity of delinquency among a subgrouping dropped as the delinquency rate of the group dropped. The necessity to combine delinquency levels due to the small sizes of many critical subgroupings tended to attenuate the relation of MMPI patterns to delinquency.

There is, as mentioned earlier, sporadic vigorous opposition to personality testing. Unfortunately, real breaches of professional responsibility in the application of personality tests to children do, no doubt, occur. Inexperienced or inadequately trained psychologists, counselors, and others occasionally do not provide suitable safeguards for confidential information. Often there is not a proper explanation of the testing so that the children and others can understand its purposes and what is to be done with test results. Sometimes permissions from parents are not obtained in cases where good practice requires them. Fortunately, the MMPI has largely escaped criticism. We have already noted that our 15,000 children, some in parochial schools, were tested without protests or other undesirable consequence. But we approached the task with trained personnel who were imbued with a sense of serious responsibility and dedicated to a research program aiming toward the betterment of individual children's lives.

Some among parents and the general public would wish to reserve the analytic evaluation of personality for unfortunately situated children or those already in trouble. However, we want to emphasize that the identification of healthy and strong children is one of our best contributions At the same time the MMPI results were often the only clue to potential difficulties. We found that nearly half of the boys and a fourth of the girls, many coming from the best of family backgrounds, showed some problem area. It is inconceivable to us that parents or others would oppose use of such tests as the MMPI when the information thereby acquired may offer a new hope of helping many youngsters. The results, reduced to discreet and reasonable interpretations by competent and responsible psychologists, provide invaluable individual information to the concerned parent, counselor, or teacher. Although MMPI data cannot be expected to detect all potential trouble areas in a child's psychology, the principles applied are similar to those accepted in the more developed medical area where physiological and physical tests are routinely directed to the early discovery of threatening body conditions. We must re-emphasize, however, that the MMPI is not a test to be used indiscriminately. Its use must be restricted to trained and responsible persons, competent and certified in service to those being tested. Critical vigilance is more appropriately directed toward those who apply personality tests than to the tests themselves.

In closing we must repeat once more that we are acutely aware of the limitations of our work. Ours is only one more study among numerous others dealing with the adolescent and his behavior. Thrasher, Shaw and McKay, Kvaraceus, the Gluecks, Cohen, Merrill, Nye and Short, the McCords, Powers and Witmer, Reckless, Gough, Miller, Cloward and Ohlin, to mention only some, have made distinguished contributions to our knowledge in this area. We gratefully recognize these contributions even though they are not extensively referred to in our **report.**

Appendixes

APPENDIXES

Appendix A. Procedures for Testers

1. Arrive at school at least a half an hour before the time scheduled for the test with ample materials.

2. Contact the principal and/or counselor to discuss plans for the administration of the test.

3. Distribute the Teacher Report forms to principal, counselor, all ninth-grade home room teachers, and to other ninth-grade teachers who know the pupils and are willing to complete the form.

4. If possible, distribute answer sheets and Personal Data sheets before the students come to the testing room.

5. If possible, meet with the teacher-proctors briefly to explain the program, test, and type of help they can give the students.

6. When the students are seated proceed without delay to complete the Personal Data Sheet and fill in the required information on the answer sheet. Use a public address system if possible or necessary.

7. Explain the purpose of the test, paraphrasing the following paragraph:

This is a test to study personality. The study is being made by people at the university and your records will be kept by them. No one will look at your answers to individual questions because the grades depend on counting up the marks only. The test has a great many statements about people, what they like, and what they think. It is used to aid in advising men and women about jobs and other problems. We want to see if it will be a help when taken by persons who are younger. So we are asking you to do it. You may find that some of the statements don't fit you at all, or they won't fit you until you are older. If you find any of these, answer them the best you can or leave them blank, but try to answer every statement. Work quickly but don't be careless. Some of the statements will be in the past tense; for example: "My father was a good man." Answer as though in the present if your father is living and you are with him.

8. Go through the directions for using the answer sheet.

9. Distribute the test booklets and have the students begin immediately.

10. The average time for the test is one and a half to two hours. Frequently the students have difficulty settling down and this may delay the test if allowed to continue. However, if the pupils have been prepared for the test ahead of time this situation is not so likely to occur. It is helpful to remind the pupils after an hour of writing that they should be at least half way through the test and to give them a slight break if conditions warrant it. Some malingerers will delay the test as long as possible to avoid going back to class.

11. Arrangements should be made to take care of those students who finish

early. It is better if they can leave the testing room and report to regular classes or study hall. If it is necessary that they remain until all are finished, they should have study materials with them.

12. The papers should be checked by the tester or teachers as they are turned in to make sure that each is complete. In small schools, the materials can be turned in in two piles; the test booklet on one and the Personal Data Sheet with the answer sheet on top on the other. In larger schools it is helpful to have the answer sheet and Personal Data Sheet placed in the test booklet and turned in by home rooms.

13. Leave tests for absentees if someone will be responsible for administering them.

14. On a summary sheet for the school the tester should note the following information:

1. Name of school. 2. Names of interested school personnel. 3. Number of students tested. 4. Number of tests left for absentees. 5. The facilities used for the testing. 6. The time used for the test. 7. The types of difficulties encountered. 8. Suggestions to facilitate future testing.

15. See the principal and/or counselor before leaving.

16. Suggestions: (1) Testing in home rooms by home room teachers seems to be the most satisfactory way of administering the MMPI to ninth-graders. However, study halls and other rooms utilizing desks also proved to be most satisfactory provided enough proctors were provided to assist the tester. (2) It is possible to delay the start of the test too long in taking care of the preliminaries. Where a strict time limit has been set it is advisable to get the students started as quickly as possible. By letting the students complete the Personal Data Sheet independently and then checking them during the time of the test, ten or fifteen minutes can be saved. One plan is to tell the students to ask any questions they might have independently after the test is started. This also helps to settle the group more quickly.

Appendix B. Personal Data Sheet

MALE _____
FEMALE _____

NAME _____
        Last   First   Middle

ADDRESS_____
            Street   City

AGE_____.   NUMBER OF BROTHERS_____.   NUMBER OF SISTERS_____.

FATHER LIVING?   MOTHER LIVING?   ARE YOUR PARENTS SEPARATED OR DIVORCED?

YES_____. NO_____.   YES_____. NO_____.   YES_____. NO_____.

WITH WHOM DO YOU LIVE: MOTHER_____.   FATHER_____.   NEITHER_____.   BOTH_____.

WHERE DO YOU LIVE: IN A CITY _____.   IN A SUBURB_____.   IN A TOWN_____.   ON A FARM_____.

DOES YOUR FAMILY OWN OR RENT YOUR HOME OR FARM: OWN_____.   RENT_____.

Appendix C. Teacher Report Form

Name of City	Homeroom or Name of Class	Number of Students

Name five students who are most likely to get into serious difficulties with the school authorities or the law within the next four years: 1_____. 2_____. 3_____. 4_____. 5_____.

Name five students who are most likely to show evidence of emotional maladjustment within the next four years: 1_____. 2_____. 3_____. 4_____. 5_____.

Tables 1–133

Table 1. Age of Subjects at Ninth-Grade Testing[a]

	Minneapolis Sample		Statewide Sample	
Age	Boys (N = 200)	Girls (N = 200)	Boys (N = 5701)	Girls (N = 5628)
18	0.0%	0.0%	0.1%	0.0%
17	1.5	0.0	0.8	0.3
16	24.5	9.5	7.0	3.0
15	58.0	65.5	42.0	36.0
14	15.5	25.0	49.0	60.0
13	0.5	0.0	1.0	1.0
Mean age	15.1	14.8	14.6 (15.1)	14.4 (14.9)

[a] The Minneapolis ages were obtained from birth dates and are tabulated to the nearest chronological year. The ages of the statewide group were reported in the usual fashion. This results in a different modal frequency. To make the means of this sample more accurately comparable to the Minneapolis sample, 0.5 year must be added, as shown by the figures in parentheses for mean age.

Table 2. Community Residence of Subjects

	Number of Subjects			Percentage	
Community	Boys	Girls	Total	All Subjects	Statewide Sample
Minneapolis	1958	2013	3971	26	
Duluth	679	657	1336	9	12
Suburb (Minneapolis and St. Paul)	1049	1010	2059	13	18
Town					
10,000–100,000	808	789	1597	10	14
5000–10,000	746	717	1463	10	13
2500–5000	219	256	475	3	4
1000–2500	203	201	404	3	4
500–1000	97	109	206	1	2
Less than 500	307	352	659	4	6
Farm	1593	1537	3130	20	28
Total	7659	7641	15,300	99	101

Table 3. Rent Level[a] of the Block in Which the Residence of Each Subject in the Minneapolis Sample Was Located

	Boys		Girls	
Rent Level	Number	Percentage	Number	Percentage
I (high)	209	10.7	238	11.8
II	589	30.1	544	27.0
III	696	35.5	763	37.9
IV (low)	376	19.2	377	18.7
Outside city limits	83	4.2	86	4.3
Unknown	5	0.3	5	0.2
Total	1958	100.0	2013	99.9

[a] Rent level is used as a very rough measure of socioeconomic status in the Minneapolis sample.

Table 4. Socioeconomic Status of Parent of Each Subject in the Statewide Sample

| | Boys | | Girls | |
Socioeconomic Status[a]	Number	Per-centage	Number	Per-centage
I: Professional	139	2.4	125	2.2
II: Semiprofessional	285	5.0	290	5.2
Classes I and II	(424)	(7.4)	(415)	(7.4)
III: Clerical	1128	19.8	1104	19.6
IVA: Farmer, high	179	3.1	183	3.3
IVB: Farmer, medium	761	13.4	778	13.8
IVC: Farmer, low	273	4.8	258	4.6
Classes IVA, B, C	(1213)	(21.3)	(1219)	(21.7)
V: Semiskilled	1278	22.4	1319	23.4
VI: Slightly skilled	1012	17.8	945	16.8
Classes V and VI	(2290)	(40.2)	(2264)	(40.2)
VII: Day laborer	436	7.7	410	7.3
Public assistance, mother working, unclassifiable	210	3.7	216	3.8
Total	5701	100.1	5628	100.0

[a] For these categories the occupation of the parent, usually the father, was used. If the data were insufficient, the father's level of schooling was used.

Table 5. Family Status of Subjects in the Minneapolis Sample

| | Boys | | Girls | |
Family Status[a]	Number	Per-centage	Number	Per-centage
Normal	1599	81.7	1605	79.7
Divorced parents	101	5.2	112	5.6
Separated parents	46	2.3	54	2.7
Father deceased	110	5.6	109	5.4
Mother deceased	28	1.4	36	1.8
Both parents deceased	10	0.5	7	0.3
Stepparent(s)	61	3.1	82	4.1
Foster parents	1	0.1	5	0.2
One parent unknown	0	0.0	2	0.1
Unknown	2	0.1	1	0.0
Total	1958	100.0	2013	99.9

[a] These classes were obtained from school records.

Table 6. Family Status of Subjects in the Statewide Sample, by Person Lived With

| | Boys | | Girls | |
Person(s) with Whom Subject Lived[a]	Number	Per-centage	Number	Per-centage
Both parents	4927	86.4	4830	85.8
Mother	436	7.7	460	8.2
Father	91	1.6	82	1.5
Stepparent(s)	129	2.3	136	2.4
Neither parent	118	2.1	117	2.1
Unknown	0	0.0	3	0.1
Total	5701	100.1	5628	100.1

[a] The Personal Data Sheet asked the student to indicate whom he lived with (see Appendix B).

Table 7. Family Status of Subjects in the Statewide
Sample, by Status of Parents

	Boys		Girls	
Status of Parents[a]	Number	Per-centage	Number	Per-centage
Father				
Living	5401	94.7	5309	94.3
Not living	300	5.3	319	5.7
Total	5701	100.0	5628	100.0
Mother				
Living	5591	98.1	5516	98.0
Not living	110	1.9	112	2.0
Total	5701	100.0	5628	100.0
Parents' marital status				
Separated or divorced	364	6.4	363	6.4
Not separated or divorced	5337	93.6	5265	93.6
Total	5701	100.0	5628	100.0

[a] The Personal Data Sheet asked the student to indicate the marital status of his
father and mother and whether they were living or not.

Table 8. Number of Siblings Reported by Subjects in the
Statewide Sample

	Boys		Girls	
Number of Siblings[a]	Number	Per-centage	Number	Per-centage
0	363	6.4	339	6.0
1	1216	21.3	1132	20.1
2	1259	22.0	1238	22.0
3	980	17.2	1027	18.2
4	686	12.0	660	11.7
5	405	7.1	399	7.1
6	261	4.6	287	5.1
7	164	2.9	191	3.4
8	133	2.3	131	2.3
9 or more	225	3.9	221	3.9
Unknown	9	0.2	3	0.1
Total	5701	99.9	5628	99.9

[a] Brothers and sisters were grouped for this table.

Table 9. IQ Scores[a] for Subjects in the Minneapolis Sample

	Boys		Girls	
IQ Score	Number	Per-centage	Number	Per-centage
Greater than 110	392	20.0	521	25.9
90–110	830	42.4	859	42.7
Less than 90	159	8.1	85	4.2
Unknown	577	29.5	548	27.2
Total	1958	100.0	2013	100.0

[a] These IQ readings on the Minneapolis sample were mostly taken from the
Otis Group Test.

Table 10. ACE Scores for Subjects in the Statewide Sample[a]

ACE Percentile Score	Boys		Girls	
	Number	Per-centage	Number	Per-centage
1–15	714	12.5	599	10.6
16–39	1404	24.6	1256	22.3
40–68	1600	28.0	1638	29.1
69–90	1241	21.8	1372	24.4
91–100	640	11.2	685	12.2
Unknown	102	1.8	78	1.4
Total	5701	99.9	5628	100.0

[a] These data (and those reported in Tables 11 and 12) were provided through the cooperation of the University of Minnesota Counseling Bureau's Statewide Testing Program. The ACE scores were mostly from the eleventh grade. Some were from the ninth grade, and some were derived from another intelligence test which was found in the school records and prorated to an equivalent ACE percentile.

Table 11. Cooperative English Test Scores (Eleventh Grade) for Subjects in the Statewide Sample

Cooperative English Test Percentile Score	Boys		Girls	
	Number	Per-centage	Number	Per-centage
1–15	940	16.5	281	5.0
16–36	1133	19.9	722	12.8
37–80	1794	31.5	2229	39.6
81–96	473	8.3	1122	19.9
97–100	102	1.8	345	6.1
Unknown	1259	22.1	929	16.5
Total	5701	100.1	5628	99.9

Table 12. High School Ranks for Subjects in the Statewide Sample

High School Rank Percentile[a]	Boys		Girls	
	Number	Per-centage	Number	Per-centage
1–19	1111	19.5	679	12.1
20–39	1059	18.6	729	13.0
40–69	1300	22.8	1441	25.6
70–89	650	11.4	1206	21.4
90–100	310	5.4	618	11.0
Dropout, transfer, unknown ...	1271	22.3	955	17.0
Total	5701	100.0	5628	100.1

[a] Most of these ranks are based on the eleventh-grade standing of the subject.

Table 13. School Status of Subjects in the Statewide Sample at the Time of the Follow-Up

School Status	Boys			Girls		
	Number	Per-centage	Cumula-tive Per-centage	Number	Per-centage	Cumula-tive Per-centage
Dropout[a]						
Ninth grade	140	2.5	2.5	75	1.3	1.3
Tenth grade	308	5.4	7.9	226	4.0	5.3
Eleventh grade	352	6.2	14.1	330	5.9	11.2
Twelfth grade	200	3.5	17.6	185	3.3	14.5
Transfer and status unknown	512	9.0	26.6	472	8.4	22.9
Attending twelfth grade	4189	73.5	100.1	4340	77.1	100.0

[a] The time of dropout depended partly upon the legal age at which students may leave school — in Minnesota, sixteen. Dropouts also included cases sent to institutions.

Table 14. Reasons for Dropout of Subjects in the Statewide Sample

Reason[a]	Boys		Girls	
	Number	Per-centage	Number	Per-centage
Failing school	96	11.7	36	5.4
Lack of interest	272	33.0	142	21.2
Poor health	10	1.2	11	1.6
Marriage or illegitimate pregnancy	22	2.7	357	53.2
Work	111	13.5	59	8.8
Institutionalization	30	3.6	8	1.2
Death	15	1.8	4	0.6
Military service	201	24.4	9	1.3
Other	67	8.1	45	6.7
Total	824	100.0	671	100.0

[a] The reason listed in each case was decided upon by the follow-up interviewer. The information usually came from teachers. Note the importance of marriage or illegitimate pregnancy among the girls.

Table 15. Teacher Predictions for Students in the Statewide Sample

Prediction[a]	Boys		Girls	
	Number	Per-centage	Number	Per-centage
No teacher prediction	4382	76.9	4842	86.0
Legal difficulties	462	8.1	119	2.1
Emotional difficulties	529	9.3	506	9.0
Both legal and emotional difficulties	328	5.8	161	2.9
Total	5701	100.1	5628	100.0

[a] These predictions by the teachers that certain students would be delinquent or emotionally maladjusted were obtained at the time of testing. There was little uniformity in the number named for each school.

Table 16. Follow-Up Ratings on Conduct in School of Subjects
in the Statewide Sample

Rating[a]	Boys		Girls	
	Number	Per-centage	Number	Per-centage
0	3512	64.7	4375	81.1
1	977	18.0	569	10.5
2	589	10.9	186	3.4
3	302	5.6	56	1.0
4	47	0.9	19	0.4
5			189	3.5
Total	5427	100.1	5394	99.9
Unknown	274		234	

[a] These ratings of school conduct were made by the follow-up interviewers. Ratings larger than 0 mean that it was judged that the student's bad
conduct increasingly interfered with school effectiveness. Girls illegitimately pregnant were arbitrarily given a rating of 5.

Table 17. Follow-Up Ratings on Adjustment in School of Subjects
in the Statewide Sample

Rating[a]	Boys		Girls	
	Number	Per-centage	Number	Per-centage
0	2429	44.6	3303	61.0
1	1487	27.3	1215	22.5
2	946	17.4	616	11.4
3	527	9.7	246	4.5
4	61	1.1	32	0.6
Total	5450	100.1	5412	100.0
Unknown	251		216	

[a] The adjustment ratings by follow-up interviewers emphasized irrita-
bility, anxiety, moodiness, insecurity, and the like. A rating of 0 signified
no appreciable trouble.

Table 18. The Accumulated Frequencies of Combined Delinquency Ratings 2,
3, and 4 at Different Modal Ages[a]

Modal Age	Boys		Girls	
	Number	Per-centage	Number	Per-centage
15				
Minneapolis sample	247	12.6	61	3.0
Statewide sample	282	5.0	75	1.4
17 (Minneapolis sample)	461	23.5	167	8.3
18 (statewide sample)	1345	23.6	343	6.2
19 (Minneapolis sample)	556	28.4	182	9.0

[a] Although the two samples are not strictly comparable either in case composition or in time of observation, the rates come to be nearly equal at the older
ages. Minneapolis sample size: boys, 1958, girls, 2013; statewide sample size:
boys, 5701, girls, 5628.

Table 19. The Frequencies of the Delinquency Rating Levels at Modal Age
Eighteen for the Statewide Sample

Delinquency Rating	Boys			Girls		
	Number	Percentage	Cumulative Percentage	Number	Percentage	Cumulative Percentage
4	136	2.4	2.4	37	0.7	0.7
3	352	6.3	8.7	74	1.3	2.0
2	857	15.3	24.0	232	4.2	6.2
1	591	10.6	34.6	232	4.2	10.4
0	3665	65.4	100.0	4945	89.6	100.0
Total	5601	100.0		5520	100.0	
Unknown	100			108		

Table 20. The Frequencies of Delinquency Levels 2, 3, and 4 Combined According to
the Time of Delinquency for the Boys in the Minneapolis Sample

Time of Delinquency [a]				Percentage of Minneapolis Delinquent Group of Boys	Percentage of Total Sample of Boys
Before 9th-Grade Test	After 9th Grade and before 12th Grade	12th Grade and After	Number		
+	+	+	18	3.2	0.9
+	+	0	20	3.6	1.2
+	0	0	161	29.0	8.2
+	0	+	48	8.6	2.5
0	+	+	81	14.6	4.1
0	0	+	85	15.3	4.3
0	+	0	143	25.7	7.3
			556	100.0	

[a] The plus signs show the period or periods in which each boy was delinquent. Thus, 18 boys were found to have been delinquent in each of the three periods, 20 in both the first and the second period, and so on. The first follow-up was carried out while the subjects were in the eleventh grade; the second period, then, runs from the time of the test in the ninth grade to the time of follow-up in the eleventh grade. The second follow-up came in the fall after completion of the twelfth grade. Each of the last two periods is roughly two years.

Table 21. Frequency of L and F Invalidity among Subjects
from Communities of Various Sizes

Community, with Total Number of Subjects from Each	High L	High F	UHF	Both L and F Invalid
BOYS				
Duluth (N = 679)	2.1%	4.7%	1.8%	0.4%
Suburb (N = 1049)	1.4	5.1	2.6	0.3
Town (N = 2380)	2.3	5.2	2.5	0.1
Farm (N = 1593)	3.8	6.6	4.0	0.5
Total sample (N = 5701)	2.5	5.5	2.9	0.3
GIRLS				
Duluth (N = 657)	1.7	3.3	0.8	0.5
Suburb (N = 1010)	1.6	1.2	0.5	0.2
Town (N = 2424)	1.7	2.9	0.6	0.2
Farm (N = 1537)	4.0	3.5	0.6	0.0
Total sample (N = 5628)	2.3	2.8	0.6	0.2

Table 22. Means and Standard Deviations of Scores on Each Scale for
the Minneapolis and Statewide Samples[a]

| | Minneapolis Sample | | | | Statewide Sample | | | |
| | Boys (N = 200) | | Girls (N = 200) | | Boys (N = 4944) | | Girls (N = 5207) | |
Scale	Mean	S.D.	Mean	S.D.	Mean	S.D.	Mean	S.D.
L	3.6	2.06	3.8	2.09	3.8	2.16	3.9	2.14
F	5.8	3.66	5.1	3.39	6.0	4.65	5.1	3.31
K	14.2	4.78	14.2	2.92	13.5	5.02	13.8	4.57
1 (+.5K)	50.4	8.51	48.3	7.54	49.8	9.19	48.1	8.55
2	52.0	9.88	48.1	7.72	51.6	10.71	48.8	8.81
3	51.7	7.51	50.9	8.00	51.7	8.44	51.7	8.48
4 (+.4K)	59.5	10.37	59.7	10.16	59.2	10.32	58.7	9.27
5	52.3	8.77	55.6	9.09	50.5	9.29	52.8	9.83
6	52.9	9.36	49.9	9.53	55.4	9.72	55.6	9.70
7 (+K)	56.2	9.84	54.4	7.92	58.3	10.01	56.7	8.32
8 (+K)	59.1	10.00	57.0	8.83	61.2	11.78	58.6	9.81
9 (+.2K)	59.5	10.30	56.9	10.83	59.1	11.50	56.7	11.68
0	51.4	7.96	52.9	7.77	54.2	8.87	54.7	9.30

[a] The statewide sample is the better source of standard scores. Not only are the Minneapolis data exclusively from urban cases but they also depend upon smaller random samples of 200, and they were obtained six years earlier than the statewide data. General adult norms for the MMPI use a mean T score of 50 and a standard deviation of 10.

Table 23. Intercorrelation Matrices of K-Corrected MMPI Variables for Samples
of 200 Minneapolis Boys and 200 Minneapolis Girls[a]

Scale	L	F	K	1	2	3	4	5	6	7	8	9	0
L		—.27	.52	.09	.12	.10	—.12	.08	—.14	—.11	—.12	—.25	—.18
F	—.19		—.44	.22	.16	.06	.36	—.12	.30	.41	.57	.44	.28
K	.44	—.42		.22	.07	.32	.11	.03	—.08	—.01	—.07	—.25	—.52
1	.26	.06	.45		.41	.69	.38	.03	.29	.43	.50	.08	.09
2	.22	.16	.08	.42		.44	.41	.24	.27	.40	.36	—.12	.43
3	.28	.03	.45	.73	.43		.39	.15	.31	.32	.38	—.04	—.01
4	.01	.29	.27	.38	.24	.40		—.09	.42	.46	.54	.33	.05
5	—.08	.04	—.05	.22	.31	.33	.15		.05	.09	—.06	—.23	.07
6	—.16	.39	—.14	.19	.23	.22	.26	.33		.42	.53	.18	.13
7	—.07	.29	.11	.46	.50	.42	.44	.25	.42		.75	.35	.37
8	—.10	.40	.08	.43	.29	.38	.44	.30	.49	.68		.50	.24
9	—.35	.30	—.23	—.11	—.19	—.06	.27	.08	.26	.09	.31		—.19
0	.07	.23	—.27	.04	.35	—.10	—.03	.10	.11	.32	.19	—.09	

[a] The italic correlation coefficients are for boys, the roman for girls.

TABLE 24   119

Table 24. Frequency of Two-Point Code Classes among the Statewide Sample[a]

Code Class	Rates per 1000[b] Boys				Rates per 1000[b] Girls			
	T < 70	T ≥ 70[c]	Total High	Total Low	T < 70	T ≥ 70[c]	Total High	Total Low
INVALID PROFILES								
L ≥ 10			26				23	
F = 16–21			56				29	
F ≥ 22			30				6	
? ≥ 40			8				5	
VALID PROFILES								
Indet.[d]	55	8	63	37	62	8	70	46
NHP	16	0	0	16	16	0	0	16
1–	0	0	0†	29	0	0	0†	41
12	1	0	1†	12	0	0	1†	21
13	2	1	4	33	0	0	1†	38
14	1	2	3	4	0	0	1†	5
15	0	0	0†	8	0	0	1†	13
16	1	1	1†	4	0	0	0†	9
17	1	1	2†	3	0	0	0†	3
18	1	3	4	3	0	0	1†	3
19	1	1	2†	3	0	0	0†	7
10	1	1	2†	3	0	0	0†	4
Total 1	9	9	18	103	2	2	4	144
2–	3	0	3	37	1	0	1†	48
21	1	1	2†	20	0	0	0†	31
23	1	1	2†	16	1	1	2†	18
24	4	4	8	5	1	1	2	4
25	1	1	2	22	0	0	0†	10
26	1	1	2†	7	1	0	1†	9
27	2	3	5	5	1	1	2†	6
28	1	4	5	1	1	1	2†	0
29	2	1	3	4	0	0	0†	5
20	4	4	9	19	3	2	5	36
Total 2	21	20	41	134	9	6	15	166
3–	3	0	3	25	3	0	3	22
31	2	1	3	20	1	2	3	25
32	2	0	2†	5	1	1	2	8
34	6	1	7	2	9	3	12	2
35	2	0	2†	6	2	0	3	2
36	3	0	3	3	4	0	4	4
37	2	1	3	1	2	1	3	1
38	2	0	2†	0	4	1	5	0
39	2	0	2	1	2	0	3	4
30	1	0	1†	1	1	0	1†	0
Total 3	25	2	27	64	30	9	39	69

[a] An asterisk (*) indicates the two-point code is among the fifteen most common for each sex; italics set off the corresponding rates. A dagger (†) is used to indicate that there are fewer than eleven in the total two-point code class.

[b] Rates per thousand rather than rates per hundred are used because of the small numbers that occur in many of the code classes. Since numbers are rounded off, the figure in the total high column is not always the sum of the figures in the preceding columns; nor does the figure for the one-point code class (Total 1, etc.) always equal the sum of the figures above. To obtain the actual observed number for the samples, multiply these rates by 4.9 for boys and by 5.2 for girls.

[c] The height of the first point only in each code class was considered.

[d] Included in the "indeterminate" class are all codes with underscoring on the first three or more high points. If underscoring occurred on the first two high points only, one-half a tally was assigned to the first high point and one-half a tally to the second high point.

Table 24 — continued

Code Class	Rates per 1000 Boys				Rates per 1000 Girls			
	T < 70	T ≧ 70	Total High	Total Low	T < 70	T ≧ 70	Total High	Total Low
4–	10	1	10	7	9	0	9	3
41	4	4	8	3	2	1	2	3
42	7	6	13	3	4	2	7	3
43*	14	6	20	3	14	8	22	2
45*	6	3	9	1	17	4	21	1
46*	10	9	19	1	14	15	28	1
47*	9	10	19	1	14	7	21	2
48*	15	22	37	1	17	17	34	0
49*	24	17	41	2	19	20	39	3
40	6	1	7	0	10	4	14	0
Total 4	105	77	182	23	120	79	199	20
5–	4	0	4	72	17	4	21	70
51	0	0	0†	11	1	0	1†	16
52	2	2	4	13	2	1	3	12
53	2	1	3	15	4	1	4	4
54*	6	2	8	2	14	7	21	2
56	4	2	6	11	5	4	9	3
57	3	1	4	3	5	1	6	1
58	3	3	6	1	9	5	14	1
59*	4	2	6	11	13	9	22	12
50	3	1	5	15	15	5	20	10
Total 5	33	13	47	154	84	36	120	131
6–	4	0	4	21	5	0	5	8
61	1	0	1†	5	0	0	0†	8
62	1	0	2†	4	1	0	2†	8
63	2	1	3	6	4	1	5	5
64	4	5	9	2	9	10	18	1
65	3	2	5	10	4	1	5	2
67	2	2	4	2	6	5	11	2
68	4	8	12	1	6	12	18	1
69	5	5	10	4	7	5	12	5
60	5	2	7	4	9	4	13	2
Total 6	32	26	58	59	51	38	89	52
7–	2	0	2†	2	3	0	3	3
71	1	0	1†	3	0	0	1†	1
72	2	3	5	3	1	1	2	2
73	2	1	3	1	2	0	2	1
74	5	5	10	1	5	2	7	1
75	2	1	3	2	3	0	3	0
76	3	2	5	1	3	2	5	2
78*	8	20	28	1	9	6	15	1
79	5	4	9	1	4	2	5	2
70	7	4	11	2	5	2	7	1
Total 7	37	40	77	17	36	16	52	12
8–	2	0	2	1	2	0	2	1
81	2	5	8	3	0	2	2†	1
82	1	6	7	0	1	1	2†	0
83	3	1	4	0	2	2	4	0
84*	10	20	30	0	8	6	14	0
85	3	2	5	1	5	3	8	0
86*	6	13	19	1	5	11	15	0
87*	11	43	54	1	10	13	23	0
89*	12	31	44	1	7	13	20	1
80	8	5	13	0	6	5	11	0
Total 8	59	127	186	8	46	56	102	4

Table 24 — continued

Code Class	Rates per 1000 Boys				Rates per 1000 Girls			
	T < 70	T ≧ 70	Total High	Total Low	T < 70	T ≧ 70	Total High	Total Low
9–*	18	2	21	44	8	1	9	48
91	2	1	3	4	0	1	1†	13
92	2	1	3	2	1	0	1†	6
93	6	2	8	2	3	2	5	6
94*	21	30	51	2	16	25	41	5
95*	6	6	13	11	15	12	27	12
96*	7	12	19	5	8	13	21	5
97*	7	10	18	2	8	7	15	4
98*	17	46	63	2	14	30	44	3
90	9	3	12	3	7	3	10	5
Total 9	96	114	210	77	81	93	174	107
0–	11	1	12	42	13	1	14	27
01	1	0	1†	3	1	0	1†	4
02	7	2	8	10	5	4	9	18
03	1	0	1†	1	2	0	3	1
04	5	1	6	0	9	4	13	0
05*	6	1	7	11	18	2	21	6
06	6	1	7	2	11	4	15	2
07*	8	4	12	2	15	6	21	1
08	9	3	12	0	11	6	17	0
09	8	1	8	5	6	1	7	3
Total 0	62	13	75	76	93	28	120	62

Table 25. Number of Boys and Girls in Each One-Point Code Class
(Actual Sample Sizes for Most of the Succeeding Analyses)[a]

Code Class	Total Number of Boys in Each Class		Total Number of Girls in Each Class	
	High	Low	High	Low
1	89	507	22	748
2	201	663	78	866
3	135	317	202	358
4	899	112	1034	101
5	230	761	628	684
6	286	291	462	273
7	382	84	271	64
8	922	40	529	18
9	1036	382	907	555
0	370	374	626	325
NHP	80		83	
NLP		1229		976

[a]The sums of the high and low columns are not identical because those profiles with more than the first two high or low points underscored were excluded (this is the class called "indeterminate" in Table 24).

Table 26. Frequency (in Percentage) of the Response "True" to Each MMPI Item by Random Samples of 100 Boys and 100 Girls from the Ninth-Grade Statewide Group

Booklet Item No.	Boys	Girls	Booklet Item No.	Boys	Girls	Booklet Item No.	Boys	Girls
1	83	11	44	2	7	87	16	42
2	94	99	45	75	68	88	96	96
3	69	81	46	85	72	89	63	47
4	4	47	47	9	11	90	93	96
5	31	25	48	0	6	91	48	29
6	65	64	49	8	1	92	1	55
7	91	84	50	8	12	93	43	28
8	89	85	51	85	90	94	39	49
9	87	89	52	12	14	95	75	90
10	5	2	53	12	14	96	70	57
11	13	16	54	89	95	97	34	34
12	79	78	55	79	74	98	72	75
13	10	9	56	8	2	99	75	67
14	6	4	57	76	74	100	61	74
15	62	45	58	50	51	101	74	47
16	4	7	59	55	46	102	39	49
17	90	94	60	96	96	103	85	81
18	78	75	61	17	5	104	9	5
19	37	38	62	20	36	105	82	92
20	90	93	63	88	82	106	20	21
21	37	40	64	41	38	107	93	98
22	13	24	65	95	95	108	8	8
23	5	2	66	14	11	109	62	63
24	8	13	67	49	55	110	22	17
25	24	44	68	84	82	111	47	60
26	56	40	69	50	34	112	83	77
27	26	21	70	38	77	113	94	95
28	36	28	71	82	72	114	8	8
29	2	6	72	4	8	115	84	89
30	76	73	73	18	10	116	29	16
31	8	11	74	7	70	117	40	35
32	20	24	75	96	99	118	32	8
33	36	37	76	4	4	119	62	72
34	3	13	77	17	87	120	91	85
35	8	6	78	17	44	121	1	7
36	61	57	79	74	38	122	81	83
37	87	88	80	55	45	123	5	2
38	29	11	81	76	29	124	64	49
39	48	45	82	16	17	125	2	6
40	21	32	83	99	99	126	36	73
41	25	22	84	48	44	127	43	43
42	5	4	85	1	5	128	76	70
43	7	7	86	23	25	129	63	69

TABLE 26   **123**

Table 26 — continued

Booklet Item No.	Boys	Girls	Booklet Item No.	Boys	Girls	Booklet Item No.	Boys	Girls
130	84	80	180	53	54	230	70	64
131	63	57	181	73	83	231	29	25
132	24	64	182	5	5	232	28	19
133	82	90	183	38	25	233	35	22
134	76	73	184	5	5	234	49	60
135	41	29	185	94	95	235	39	30
136	60	61	186	29	29	236	4	16
137	89	89	187	88	88	237	18	22
138	25	53	188	61	64	238	52	40
139	17	27	189	8	8	239	16	30
140	62	88	190	88	78	240	19	7
141	64	64	191	39	33	241	52	48
142	64	57	192	93	92	242	86	76
143	27	37	193	92	84	243	83	88
144	53	17	194	8	9	244	45	38
145	53	22	195	68	77	245	17	14
146	29	14	196	100	98	246	4	1
147	50	40	197	2	1	247	10	13
148	53	48	198	66	37	248	53	60
149	3	47	199	64	80	249	72	72
150	89	89	200	7	5	250	38	34
151	4	1	201	52	54	251	7	10
152	74	68	202	11	4	252	11	4
153	89	92	203	20	47	253	61	66
154	83	89	204	17	33	254	58	51
155	26	54	205	10	1	255	18	23
156	16	7	206	14	23	256	16	14
157	42	30	207	91	96	257	78	79
158	10	39	208	48	55	258	96	97
159	12	13	209	10	8	259	26	22
160	64	69	210	3	3	260	35	21
161	8	7	211	2	2	261	19	45
162	33	33	212	23	21	262	69	42
163	79	70	213	11	12	263	21	17
164	76	80	214	62	49	264	34	20
165	48	65	215	4	5	265	20	12
166	35	52	216	10	7	266	28	45
167	29	19	217	45	60	267	33	40
168	5	2	218	11	4	268	78	75
169	96	88	219	57	7	269	19	14
170	53	21	220	95	97	270	59	33
171	38	49	221	67	51	271	49	41
172	34	52	222	51	41	272	96	96
173	65	80	223	89	38	273	7	4
174	83	69	224	30	26	274	72	60
175	86	78	225	63	98	275	6	5
176	78	47	226	44	54	276	88	95
177	93	98	227	15	13	277	26	15
178	92	94	228	74	73	278	33	57
179	11	12	229	50	68	279	21	12

Table 26 — continued

Booklet Item No.	Boys	Girls	Booklet Item No.	Boys	Girls	Booklet Item No.	Boys	Girls
280	42	32	330	84	87	380	76	81
281	84	78	331	6	2	381	33	32
282	46	60	332	26	20	382	50	64
283	79	49	333	8	9	383	42	47
284	25	28	334	30	27	384	37	43
285	94	77	335	22	25	385	15	29
286	12	9	336	37	37	386	36	31
287	56	32	337	21	23	387	23	20
288	2	0	338	22	20	388	14	26
289	61	59	339	4	3	389	38	27
290	17	14	340	59	74	390	45	54
291	5	3	341	7	8	391	48	77
292	28	30	342	19	7	392	11	33
293	8	3	343	37	43	393	6	1
294	66	91	344	28	29	394	60	65
295	27	65	345	16	32	395	48	48
296	71	82	346	15	29	396	33	37
297	45	36	347	86	91	397	24	36
298	53	28	348	49	49	398	24	20
299	26	23	349	17	20	399	57	51
300	66	13	350	10	29	400	49	36
301	6	7	351	8	11	401	79	77
302	91	91	352	21	36	402	27	46
303	25	28	353	56	54	403	85	92
304	48	65	354	3	6	404	49	58
305	11	14	355	10	15	405	96	91
306	90	91	356	21	25	406	43	36
307	29	26	357	33	31	407	82	75
308	40	45	358	41	28	408	52	68
309	86	80	359	36	48	409	45	46
310	88	97	360	2	5	410	57	39
311	27	9	361	16	30	411	27	22
312	7	6	362	15	25	412	77	63
313	72	74	363	17	11	413	49	47
314	61	47	364	15	16	414	26	33
315	4	4	365	38	11	415	44	30
316	52	42	366	9	8	416	48	67
317	15	23	367	76	55	417	47	31
318	82	88	368	28	38	418	39	50
319	51	39	369	74	61	419	14	6
320	25	12	370	73	82	420	12	12
321	28	60	371	62	66	421	29	29
322	15	16	372	63	72	422	13	9
323	30	31	373	71	62	423	79	67
324	31	29	374	52	59	424	40	31
325	19	20	375	27	37	425	41	66
326	14	22	376	93	97	426	47	38
327	73	73	377	29	19	427	21	69
328	24	21	378	71	68	428	44	49
329	52	31	379	77	70	429	28	31

TABLE 26 125

Table 26 — continued

Booklet Item No.	Boys	Girls	Booklet Item No.	Boys	Girls	Booklet Item No.	Boys	Girls
430	65	74	480	15	32	530	32	53
431	26	32	481	54	55	531	27	41
432	31	13	482	57	32	532	85	84
433	18	21	483	80	88	533	76	79
434	50	11	484	26	26	534	67	43
435	15	54	485	36	28	535	8	5
436	74	72	486	84	75	536	57	60
437	52	51	487	23	33	537	63	24
438	51	50	488	53	82	538	3	50
439	28	46	489	33	53	539	93	53
440	85	78	490	19	36	540	94	91
441	16	44	491	18	19	541	18	11
442	24	32	492	42	78	542	81	80
443	39	44	493	53	58	543	15	11
444	32	43	494	12	22	544	28	22
445	88	93	495	62	47	545	27	33
446	34	11	496	79	73	546	53	38
447	51	45	497	93	92	547	75	92
448	24	37	498	69	60	548	53	63
449	60	82	499	46	83	549	14	39
450	79	94	500	59	58	550	64	16
451	88	86	501	59	62	551	34	53
452	21	15	502	67	69	552	68	42
453	40	20	503	44	60	553	12	18
454	50	24	504	43	35	554	24	59
455	52	38	505	43	29	555	16	27
456	24	15	506	13	18	556	68	93
457	47	42	507	30	29	557	13	72
458	29	17	508	88	97	558	76	64
459	19	11	509	29	32	559	16	30
460	76	83	510	13	21	560	25	36
461	44	39	511	27	33	561	80	85
462	82	89	512	5	4	562	54	79
463	38	91	513	59	53	563	88	27
464	75	81	514	19	5	564	57	56
465	56	59	515	85	97	565	12	11
466	86	89	516	51	61	566	28	77
467	17	31	517	9	4			
468	57	75	518	39	42			
469	39	29	519	8	1			
470	23	26	520	67	65			
471	25	8	521	59	47			
472	21	24	522	76	34			
473	18	11	523	46	20			
474	82	81	524	71	61			
475	53	53	525	29	39			
476	15	26	526	11	7			
477	48	44	527	88	91			
478	69	67	528	80	68			
479	85	82	529	41	68			

Table 27. Frequency of Occurrence (in Percentage) of Certain High-Point Code
Classes among Profiles of Adults as Contrasted to Profiles of
Minneapolis Ninth-Graders[a]

High-Point Code Class	Males		Females	
	9th-Graders (N = 1836)	Adults (N = 258)	9th-Graders (N = 1946)	Adults (N = 360)
NHP	4.6	23.6*	9.6	25.8*
Total 1	3.6	10.6*	0.8	8.7*
13	0.7	3.5*	0.3	3.9*
Total 2	6.0	6.7	2.5	12.5*
21	0.6	0.8	0.0	2.5*
27	1.0	0.8	0.3	3.3*
Total 3	3.6	7.1	3.8	7.7*
31	0.7	1.6	0.4	3.1*
Total 4	24.1*	11.6	26.0*	8.4
46	2.3*	0.0	3.9*	1.1
47	2.8*	0.4	3.1*	0.6
48	6.1*	1.9	5.2*	0.3
49	5.3*	1.9	5.7*	1.1
Total 8	16.7*	5.2	11.3*	6.2
87	4.5*	0.4	2.8	1.1
89	4.2*	0.4	2.4	1.1
Total 9	24.7*	17.6	22.7*	13.1
9–	4.0	9.3*	5.3	7.5
94	8.3*	4.3	7.2*	2.2
98	6.9*	0.8	5.9*	0.8

[a] An asterisk marks the larger of a pair of percentages yielding a difference reliable above the .01 level of confidence.

Table 28. MMPI Items on Which the Difference in Percentages of "True" Responses by Male
Adults and Adolescents Was 25 Points or More (Compared with the Percentages of
"True" Responses by Female Adults and Adolescents on the Same Items)

Item	Males			Females		
	Adults (N = 226)	Adolescents (N = 100)	Diff.	Adults (N = 315)	Adolescents (N = 100)	Diff.
I am neither gaining nor losing weight.	84%	26%	58%	74%	54%	20%
My relatives are nearly all in sympathy with me.	65	18	47	73	22	51
Sometimes at elections I vote for men about whom I know very little.	62	18	44	62	23	39
I would like to hunt lions in Africa.	20	63	43	22	24	2
I like poetry.	59	17	42	87	44	43
I worry over money and business.	53	15	38	58	16	42
I like to attend lectures on serious subjects.	62	28	34	57	31	26
I never worry about my looks.	52	19	33	42	7	35
I would like to be an auto racer.	17	50	33	1	11	10
Someone has been trying to influence my mind.	40	8	32	37	3	34
The one to whom I was most attached and whom I most						

TABLE 28   127

Table 28 — continued

Item	Males			Females		
	Adults (N = 226)	Adoles-cents (N = 100)	Diff.	Adults (N = 315)	Adoles-cents (N = 100)	Diff.
admired as a child was a woman. (Mother, sister, aunt, or other woman.)	85	54	31	64	79	15
I would like to wear expensive clothes.	72	41	31	97	68	29
I have been quite independent and free from family rule.	70	39	31	67	30	37
I have had periods in which I lost sleep over worry.	54	24	30	68	32	36
I prefer work which requires close attention, to work which allows me to be careless.	83	53	30	76	58	18
I enjoy reading love stories.	47	17	30	73	87	14
I go to church almost every week.	45	75	30	56	90	34
I like to read newspaper editorials.	73	44	29	76	49	27
I could be happy living all alone in a cabin in the woods or mountains.	21	50	29	14	24	10
At times I feel like picking a fist fight with someone.	24	53	29	17	22	5
I tend to be on my guard with people who are somewhat more friendly than I had expected. ..	78	49	29	69	49	20
I have often met people who were supposed to be experts who were no better than I.	71	43	28	56	36	20
I am entirely self-confident.	62	34	28	41	20	21
I dream frequently about things that are best kept to myself. ...	25	52	27	25	48	23
Children should be taught all the main facts of sex.	91	64	27	94	80	14
It is safer to trust nobody.	46	20	26	40	12	28
I think I would like the work of a building contractor.	31	57	26	9	7	2
I like movie love scenes.	54	28	26	81	77	4
I like to read about history.	78	53	25	64	38	26
It makes me nervous to have to wait.	53	28	25	65	46	19
Bad words, often terrible words, come into my mind and I cannot get rid of them.	16	41	25	14	28	14
I often think, "I wish I were a child again."	49	24	25	44	20	24

Table 29. MMPI Items on Which the Difference in Percentages of "True" Responses by Female Adults and Adolescents Was 25 Points or More (Compared with the Percentages of "True" Responses by Male Adults and Adolescents on the Same Items)

Item	Females			Males		
	Adults (N = 315)	Adoles-cents (N = 100)	Diff.	Adults (N = 226)	Adoles-cents (N = 100)	Diff.
My relatives are nearly all in sympathy with me.	73%	22%	51%	65%	18%	47%
I would like to be a private secretary.	21	72	51	13	13	0
Usually I would prefer to work with women.	6	54	48	17	15	2
I like poetry.	87	44	43	59	17	42
I worry over money and business.	58	16	42	53	15	38
I feel that it is certainly best to keep my mouth shut when I'm in trouble.	82	40	42	72	56	16
I have very few fears compared to my friends.	74	32	42	73	56	17
It does not bother me that I am not better looking.	83	42	41	89	69	20
When I get bored I like to stir up some excitement.	43	83	40	50	73	23
Dirt frightens or disgusts me.	61	21	40	34	13	21
Sometimes at elections I vote for men about whom I know very little.	62	23	39	62	18	44
I have been quite independent and free from family rule.	67	30	37	70	39	31
I have had periods in which I lost sleep over worry.	68	32	36	54	24	30
I practically never blush.	55	20	35	60	46	14
I never worry about my looks.	42	7	35	52	19	33
I think I would like the work of a dressmaker.	15	50	35	2	3	1
Once in a while I feel hate toward members of my family whom I usually love.	26	60	34	23	46	23
I like to read newspaper articles on crime.	30	64	34	50	65	15
I go to church almost every week.	56	90	34	45	75	30
I have no patience with people who believe there is only one true religion.	53	19	34	44	18	26
Someone has been trying to influence my mind.	37	3	34	40	8	32
I enjoy detective or mystery stories.	47	78	31	70	79	9
I like to flirt.	24	55	31	34	48	14
I have been inspired to a program of life based on duty which I have since carefully followed.	50	19	31	42	28	14
I daydream very little.	66	37	29	73	66	7
I would like to wear expensive clothes.	97	68	29	72	41	31
I like to go to parties and other affairs where there is lots of loud fun.	39	67	28	60	75	15

TABLE 29   **129**

Table 29 — continued

Item	Females			Males		
	Adults (N = 315)	Adolescents (N = 100)	Diff.	Adults (N = 226)	Adolescents (N = 100)	Diff.
Once a week or oftener I become very excited.	17	45	28	10	28	18
I have no fear of water.	49	77	28	70	79	9
At times I have worn myself out by undertaking too much.	74	46	28	57	45	12
I like tall women.	72	44	28	37	16	21
It is safer to trust nobody.	40	12	28	46	20	26
I usually "lay my cards on the table" with people that I am trying to correct or improve. ...	74	47	27	80	62	18
I am always disgusted with the law when a criminal is freed through the arguments of a smart lawyer.	86	59	27	77	61	16
What others think of me does not bother me.	48	21	27	60	53	7
I like adventure stories better than romantic stories.	54	27	27	78	88	10
I would like to be a nurse.	28	55	27	6	1	5
I like to read newspaper editorials.	76	49	27	73	44	29
I am inclined to take things hard.	57	30	27	38	16	22
I like to attend lectures on serious subjects.	57	31	26	62	28	34
I shrink from facing a crisis or difficulty.	13	39	26	30	14	16
I find it hard to set aside a task that I have undertaken, even for a short time.	65	39	26	67	44	23
I like to read about history.	64	38	26	78	53	25
I am often afraid that I am going to blush.	28	53	25	19	32	13
One or more members of my family is very nervous.	54	29	25	42	29	13
I should like to belong to several clubs or lodges.	43	68	25	54	50	4
I have met problems so full of possibilities that I have been unable to make up my mind about them.	49	74	25	57	61	4
I wish I were not bothered by thoughts about sex.	11	36	25	22	45	23

Table 30. Sex Differences in Frequency of High-Point Codes
from Valid Profiles of the Statewide Sample[a]

High-Point Code Class	Boys	Girls
04 and 40	1.3%	2.7%
05 and 50	1.2	4.1
06 and 60	1.4	2.8
1	1.8	0.4
2	4.1	1.5
45 and 54	1.7	4.2
5–	0.4	2.1
58	0.6	1.4
59 and 95	1.9	4.9
5	4.6	12.0
64	0.9	1.8
67	0.4	1.1
78 and 87	8.2	3.8
84	3.0	1.4
89	4.4	2.0

[a] Code classes are shown for which the ratio of frequency is two or more.

Table 31. MMPI Items on Which the Difference in Percentages of "True" Responses by
Boys and Girls of the Statewide Sample Was 25 Points or More

Item	Boys (N = 100)	Girls (N = 100)	Diff.
I like mechanics magazines.	83%	11%	72%
I enjoy reading love stories.	17	87	70
I have often wished I were a girl. (Or if you are a girl) I have never been sorry that I am a girl.	7	70	63
I like adventure stories better than romantic stories.	88	27	61
I would like to be a private secretary.	13	72	59
I would like to be a nurse.	1	55	54
There never was a time in my life when I liked to play with dolls. ...	66	13	53
I used to like hopscotch.	38	91	53
I very much like hunting.	89	38	51
I think I would like the work of a building contractor.	57	7	50
I like movie love scenes.	28	77	49
I am embarrassed by dirty stories.	21	69	48
I like repairing a door latch.	64	16	48
I think I would like the work of a dressmaker.	3	50	47
I think I would like the kind of work a forest ranger does.	76	29	47
I used to keep a diary.	3	47	44
I think I would like the work of a librarian.	4	47	43
I have no fear of spiders.	76	34	42
I like collecting flowers or growing house plants.	24	64	40
I am not afraid of mice.	93	53	40
I used to like drop-the-handkerchief.	38	77	39
I would like to be an auto racer.	50	11	39
Usually I would prefer to work with women.	15	54	39
I would like to hunt lions in Africa.	63	24	39
I liked "Alice in Wonderland" by Lewis Carroll.	27	65	38
I must admit that I have at times been worried beyond reason over something that really did not matter.	46	83	37
I like dramatics.	36	73	37
My feelings are not easily hurt.	74	38	36
I would like to be a soldier.	53	17	36

TABLE 31   **131**

Table 31 — continued

Item	Boys (N = 100)	Girls (N = 100)	Diff.
I dread the thought of an earthquake.	42	78	36
If I were an artist I would like to draw children.	24	59	35
I gossip a little at times.	63	98	35
I am easily embarrassed.	28	60	32
What others think of me does not bother me.	53	21	32
I do not have a great fear of snakes.	78	47	31
At times I feel like picking a fist fight with someone.	53	22	31
If I were a reporter I would very much like to report sporting news.	79	49	30
I cry easily.	10	39	29
I daydream very little.	66	37	29
I love to go to dances.	48	77	29
I pray several times every week.	53	82	29
Criticism or scolding hurts me terribly.	25	53	28
I am neither gaining nor losing weight.	26	54	28
I like tall women.	16	44	28
I like poetry.	17	44	27
I believe women ought to have as much sexual freedom as men.	74	47	27
If I were a reporter I would very much like to report news of the theater.	20	47	27
It does not bother me that I am not better looking.	69	42	27
I feel uneasy indoors.	38	11	27
I would like to wear expensive clothes.	41	68	27
I would like to be a florist.	16	42	26
I like to cook.	62	88	26
If I were an artist I would like to draw flowers.	19	45	26
When I leave home I do not worry about whether the door is locked and the windows closed.	59	33	26
I could be happy living all alone in a cabin in the woods or mountains.	50	24	26
I practically never blush.	46	20	26
I like to read about science.	68	42	26
I have never been in trouble with the law.	66	91	25
If several people find themselves in trouble, the best thing for them to do is to agree upon a story and stick to it.	53	28	25
I dream frequently.	41	66	25
While in trains, busses, etc., I often talk to strangers.	57	32	25
I shrink from facing a crisis or difficulty.	14	39	25
I am very careful about my manner of dress.	68	93	25
The one to whom I was most attached and whom I most admired as a child was a woman. (Mother, sister, aunt, or other woman.)	54	79	25

Table 32. Items Left Unanswered by Two or More Boys or
Girls of the Statewide Sample per 100

Item	Boys	Girls
Sometimes at elections I vote for men about whom I know very little.	6%	9%
Everything is turning out just like the prophets of the Bible said it would.	5	6
When I take a new job, I like to be tipped off on who should be gotten next to.	4	5
I believe women ought to have as much sexual freedom as men.	3	6
I am very strongly attracted by members of my own sex.	4	3
I believe in the second coming of Christ.	4	2
I am a special agent of God.	3	3
I think Lincoln was greater than Washington.	3	2
I have been inspired to a program of life based on duty which I have since carefully followed.	3	3
I have diarrhea once a month or more.	2	3
I am liked by most people who know me.	3	2
When a man is with a woman he is usually thinking about things related to her sex.	1	3
My sex life is satisfactory.	1	3
I have never noticed any blood in my urine.	1	3
I have had no difficulty starting or holding my urine.	2	2
I think that I feel more intensely than most people do.	3	1
I am a good mixer.	3	1
I believe there is a Devil and a Hell in afterlife.	2	2
A minister can cure disease by praying and putting his hand on your head.	1	2
I believe in a life hereafter.	2	1
I brood a great deal.	3	1
I have to urinate no more often than others.	0	3
The one to whom I was most attached and whom I most admired as a child was a woman. (Mother, sister, aunt, or other woman.)	2	0

TABLE 33   133

Table 33. Summary of Associations between Personality Patterns of Boys (M) and Girls (F) and Certain Variables (Based on the Extended Findings Presented in Tables 34–74)

Variable Category	Low Depression (Low 2)	Expansive; Optimistic; Enthusiastic (9)	Idealistic; Naive; Conforming (3)	Socially Active; Extrovert (Low 0)	Sensitive; Stubborn (6)	Serious; Self-Dissatisfied (2, 1, 7)	Social Inferiority (0)	Realistic; Unconforming (Low 3)	Low Energy and Enthusiasm (Low 9)	Rebellious; Selfish; Cynical (4)	Negative; Odd; Difficult (8)	Masculine; Rough; Aggressive (5)	Sensitive; Mannerly; Intellectual (5)
Place of residence													
Urban		F		MF						MF			
Rural					M	MF		F	F			F	
Broken home										MF	F		
Socioeconomic status													
Professional and semi-professional	M		M	MF		F							M
Clerical		F		M									MF
Farmer					M	MF		F	F			F	
Semiskilled and laborer					M			F		F			
Intelligence and school status													
School ability high	MF	MF	MF	F				M					MF
English ability high		M	MF	F				M					MF
Good school grades	F	M		F				MF					MF
School ability low									F		MF	M	
English ability low									F		MF	MF	
Poor school grades									MF		MF	M	
School dropout				M						MF	MF	M	
Adjustment													
Predicted delinquent										MF	M	M	
Rated conduct problem	M				M	F				MF		M	
Became delinquent										MF		M	
Predicted emotional problems										MF			
Rated badly adjusted										MF			

TABLES 34–74. RELATIONSHIPS BETWEEN ENVIRONMENTAL AND BEHAVIORAL
VARIABLES AND ADOLESCENT PERSONALITY

Personality is here categorized by the high-point or low-point scale on the MMPI profile. The reliability of the relationship in each cell is roughly suggested by a number that is derived from the difference between the observed number of subjects (o) and the statistically expected number of subjects (e). The derived number, a portion of χ^2, is obtained for each cell by the equation $(o - e)^2/e$. The sum of these numbers for each row and column makes up the χ^2 value. The χ^2 values are finally marked by asterisks if the values are large enough to support reliably the hypothesis that the observed data differ from margin expectations. The asterisks have the conventional meaning: * indicates significance at .05, ** at .01, *** at .001. A dagger (†) indicates that the observed number of cases in the cell probably differs significantly from the expected value. After computing the tables the numbers in the e column were rounded to the nearest whole number to facilitate reading; the precision lost is negligible.

Table 34. Community Size Related to High-Point Scale for the Boys

High Scale	Duluth and Suburbs		Towns		Farm		Total N	χ^2
	o	e	o	e	o	e		
1	23	22	25	30	22	19	70	
	.09		.77		.58			1.44
2	51	50	68	69	44	43	163	
	.00		.02		.00			.02
3	38	32	38	44	28	28	104	
	1.13		.87		.00			2.00
4	297	243	344	335	147	210	788	
	12.15†		.25		19.10†			31.50***
5	65	59	87	82	40	51	192	
	.59		.36		2.49			3.44
6	57	71	94	98	79	61	230	
	2.69		.15		5.04†			7.88*
7	82	94	127	129	95	81	304	
	1.44		.04		2.35			3.83
8	237	247	320	340	244	214	801	
	.38		1.22		4.24†			5.84
9	283	285	426	393	216	247	925	
	.01		2.75		3.89†			6.65*
0	73	99	132	137	117	86	322	
	6.92†		.18		11.17†			18.27***
NHP	20	25	32	34	29	22	81	
	.96		.17		2.54			3.67
Total N	1226		1693		1061		3980	
χ^2	26.36**		6.78		51.40***			84.54***

Table 35. Community Size Related to High-Point Scale for the Girls

High Scale	Duluth and Suburbs o	Duluth and Suburbs e	Towns o	Towns e	Farm o	Farm e	Total N	χ^2
1	2	4	7	6	5	4	14	
		1.15		.13		.54		1.82
2	19	18	21	26	19	15	59	
		.08		.93		.89		1.90
3	53	48	72	69	33	41	158	
		.61		.11		1.56		2.28
4	319	272	411	396	173	235	903	
		8.05†		.56		16.17†		24.78***
5	134	168	234	245	190	145	558	
		6.95†		.47		13.97†		21.39***
6	116	117	156	170	115	100	387	
		.00		1.11		2.09		3.20
7	45	58	98	84	49	50	192	
		2.87		2.26		.02		5.15
8	122	126	182	183	113	108	417	
		.11		.00		.20		.31
9	291	238	346	346	152	205	789	
		11.90†		.00		13.70†		25.60***
0	112	165	238	240	196	142	546	
		16.81†		.01		20.63†		37.45***
NHP	26	26	38	38	23	23	87	
		.00		.00		.01		.01
Total N	1239		1803		1068		4110	
χ^2	48.53***		5.58		69.78***			123.89***

Table 36. Community Size Related to Low-Point Scale for the Boys

Low Scale	Duluth and Suburbs o	Duluth and Suburbs e	Towns o	Towns e	Farm o	Farm e	Total N	χ^2
1	108	131	190	179	121	109	419	
		4.07†		.74		1.23		6.04*
2	171	184	279	251	139	154	589	
		.96		3.15		1.42		5.53
3	58	74	116	101	63	62	237	
		3.54		2.23		.02		5.79
4	27	29	31	39	33	24	91	
		.08		1.57		3.56		5.21
5	217	215	289	292	180	179	686	
		.02		.04		.00		0.06
6	84	77	98	105	65	65	247	
		.58		.49		.00		1.07
7	13	19	31	25	15	15	59	
		1.64		1.39		.01		3.04
8	10	8	11	12	6	7	27	
		.30		.02		.14		0.46
9	118	110	130	149	103	92	351	
		.61		2.54		1.42		4.57
0	137	101	144	138	43	85	324	
		12.50†		.26		20.46†		33.22***
NLP	391	386	497	525	345	322	1233	
		.07		1.51		1.66		3.24
Total N	1334		1816		1113		4263	
χ^2	24.37**		13.94		29.92***			68.23***

Table 37. Community Size Related to Low-Point Scale for the Girls

Low Scale	Duluth and Suburbs o	e	Towns o	e	Farm o	e	Total N	χ^2
1	167	178	277	260	156	162	600	
		.70		1.17		.24		2.11
2	189	222	350	324	210	203	749	
		5.04†		2.09		.28		7.41*
3	61	83	122	121	96	75	279	
		5.79†		.01		5.63†		11.43**
4	15	24	29	35	36	22	80	
		3.25		.91		9.60†		13.76**
5	205	181	268	263	136	165	609	
		3.21		.08		4.97†		8.26*
6	69	66	100	96	53	60	222	
		.15		.17		.82		1.14
7	17	15	18	21	14	13	49	
		.39		.48		.05		0.92
8	5	4	4	5	3	3	12	
		.54		.28		.01		0.83
9	129	148	197	216	173	135	499	
		2.49		1.65		10.76†		14.90***
0	104	77	121	113	36	71	261	
		9.06†		.58		16.88†		26.52***
NLP	329	292	393	425	261	266	983	
		4.69†		2.44		.08		7.21*
Total N	1290		1879		1174		4343	
χ^2	35.31***		9.86		49.32***			94.49***

Table 38. Neighborhood Related to High-Point Scale for the Minneapolis Boys

High Scale	"High" Neighborhood o	e	"Low" Neighborhood o	e	Total N	χ^2
1	13.5	10	6.5	10	20	2.31
		1.14		1.17		
2	5.5	10	15	10	20.5	4.69*
		2.31		2.38		
3	11	8	4	7	15	3.08
		1.52		1.56		
4	61	71	78.5	69	139.5	2.65
		1.31		1.34		
5	23	17	11.5	17	34.5	3.51
		1.73		1.78		
6	6	9	11	8	17	1.59
		.79		.80		
7	24.5	20	15	20	39.5	2.05
		1.01		1.04		
8	47.5	53	58	52	105.5	1.32
		.65		.67		
9	73.5	67	58.5	65	132	1.36
		.67		.69		
0	15.5	16	17	16	32.5	.10
		.05		.05		
NHP	9	9	8	8	17	.04
		.02		.02		
Total N	290		283		573	
χ^2	11.20		11.50			22.70*

Table 39. Socioeconomic Status Related to High-Point Scale for the Boys

High Scale	Professional and Semi-professional o	e	Clerical o	e	Farmer o	e	Semiskilled and Slightly Skilled o	e	Day Laborer o	e	Total N	χ²
1	6	5	13	14	20	14	20	28	8	5	67	7.01
	.09		.12		2.57		2.43		1.80			
2	13	12	30	33	28	33	68	66	17	12	156	3.50
	.03		.35		.65		.07		2.40			
3	16	8	24	21	17	21	40	42	2	7	99	13.37**
	8.31†		.37		.67		.08		3.94†			
4	65	60	171	162	111	158	354	320	57	57	758	18.43**
	.35		.48		14.08†		3.52		.00			
5	29	15	55	41	35	40	63	80	8	14	190	24.81***
	12.80†		5.02†		.56		3.73		2.70			
6	17	18	37	48	62	47	91	95	17	17	224	7.60
	.04		2.48		4.94†		.14		.00			
7	15	23	59	62	75	61	111	123	31	22	291	11.49*
	2.90		.17		3.37		1.17		3.88†			
8	48	61	139	164	183	160	332	324	65	58	767	11.34*
	2.81		3.84†		3.28		.43		.98			
9	83	71	203	191	151	186	390	377	64	67	891	10.03*
	2.03		.81		6.59†		.48		.12			
0	12	25	70	67	94	66	124	133	15	24	315	22.78***
	6.84†		.10		12.09†		.62		3.13			
NHP	2	7	2	18	26	17	27	36	4	6	84	11.73*
	3.30		1.42		4.13†		2.04		.84			
Total N	306		822		802		1624		288		3842	
χ²	39.50***		15.16		52.93***		14.71		19.79*			142.09***

Table 40. Socioeconomic Status Related to High-Point Scale for the Girls

High Scale	Professional and Semi-professional o	e	Clerical o	e	Farmer o	e	Semiskilled and Slightly Skilled o	e	Day Laborer o	e	Total N	χ²
1	2	1	1	3	4	3	5	6	2	1	14	3.54
	.74		1.33		.33		.14		1.00			
2	3	4	6	12	16	12	23	23	7	4	55	6.98
	.45		2.70		1.58		.00		2.25			
3	16	12	40	31	27	32	58	63	7	11	148	6.29
	1.49		2.48		.64		.34		1.34			
4	71	69	186	183	127	185	418	367	66	63	868	25.36***
	.04		.05		18.13†		7.03†		.11			
5	32	43	108	114	147	115	215	228	38	39	540	12.95*
	2.90		.31		8.90†		.79		.05			
6	40	30	87	79	89	80	139	159	21	27	376	9.01
	3.26		.75		.99		2.52		1.49			
7	23	15	37	40	42	40	75	80	12	14	189	4.94
	4.13†		.21		.07		.30		.23			
8	24	31	76	83	93	84	168	166	32	29	393	3.74
	1.74		.57		1.03		.02		.38			
9	71	61	192	161	109	163	337	323	54	56	763	25.90***
	1.64		5.97†		17.61†		.63		.05			
0	30	42	77	111	173	113	210	223	38	39	528	47.49***
	3.53		10.62†		32.54†		.79		.01			
NHP	5	7	25	18	16	18	26	36	12	6	84	11.89*
	.43		3.01		.20		2.54		5.71†			
Total N	317		835		843		1674		289		3958	
χ²	20.35*		28.00**		82.02***		15.10		12.62			158.09***

Table 41. Socioeconomic Status Related to Low-Point Scale for the Boys

Low Scale	Professional and Semi-professional o	e	Clerical o	e	Farmer o	e	Semiskilled and Slightly Skilled o	e	Day Laborer o	e	Total N	χ^2
1	38	34	80	89	87	85	173	170	31	32	409	
	.42		.82		.07		.05		.01			1.37
2	62	48	126	125	106	119	249	240	33	44	576	
	3.95†		.02		1.44		.36		2.93			8.70
3	15	19	54	49	46	46	87	94	23	17	225	
	.77		.58		.01		.47		1.88			3.71
4	5	7	17	19	29	18	32	37	5	7	88	
	.78		.21		6.41†		.58		.48			8.46
5	27	56	150	144	139	138	298	277	51	51	665	
	14.71†		.26		.01		1.64		.00			16.62**
6	14	20	57	51	50	49	95	99	21	18	237	
	1.70		.63		.02		.13		.40			2.88
7	6	5	14	13	12	12	19	24	7	5	58	
	.30		.18		.00		1.08		1.39			2.95
8	3	2	6	6	2	6	14	11	2	2	27	
	.21		.01		2.31		.70		.00			3.23
9	26	28	79	74	80	70	124	141	31	26	340	
	.20		.40		1.34		2.16		.88			4.98
0	55	27	92	69	32	66	125	132	13	24	317	
	30.65†		7.98†		17.21†		.36		5.33†			61.53***
NLP	93	98	215	253	268	242	496	488	100	90	1172	
	.26		5.85†		2.70		.14		1.04			9.99*
Total N	344		890		851		1712		317		4114	
χ^2	53.95***		16.94		31.52***		7.67		14.34			124.42***

Table 42. Socioeconomic Status Related to Low-Point Scale for the Girls

Low Scale	Professional and Semi-professional o	e	Clerical o	e	Farmer o	e	Semiskilled and Slightly Skilled o	e	Day Laborer o	e	Total N	χ^2
1	38	46	119	116	129	126	247	240	37	42	570	
	1.30		.07		.09		.20		.66			2.32
2	66	58	140	147	156	158	312	303	45	53	719	
	1.19		.30		.04		.27		1.29			3.09
3	9	22	46	55	77	60	100	114	38	20	270	
	7.43†		1.50		5.15†		1.65		16.20†			31.93***
4	7	6	9	16	26	17	28	33	8	6	78	
	.08		2.99		4.50†		.73		.83			9.13
5	54	47	142	120	112	130	248	248	34	44	590	
	.95		3.91†		2.52		.00		2.19			9.57*
6	14	17	44	43	44	47	100	89	10	16	212	
	.53		.01		.16		1.28		2.07			4.05
7	4	4	9	10	10	11	19	20	6	4	48	
	.00		.07		.03		.07		1.60			1.77
8	1	1	2	2	2	3	4	5	3	1	12	
	.00		.66		.14		.24		4.90			5.94
9	46	39	79	99	145	107	181	204	33	36	484	
	1.34		3.93†		13.75†		2.57		.23			21.82***
0	48	20	59	50	25	54	100	104	15	18	247	
	40.16†		1.47		15.97†		.15		.60			58.35***
NLP	47	75	200	190	192	206	415	393	80	69	934	
	10.39†		.48		.94		1.19		1.65			14.65**
Total N	334		849		918		1754		309		4164	
χ^2	63.37***		15.39		43.29***		8.35		32.22***			162.62***

Table 43. Parents' Marital Status Related to High-Point Scale for the Boys

High Scale	Separated or Divorced		Not Separated or Divorced		Total N	χ^2
	o	e	o	e		
1	3	4	67	66	70	
		.39		.03		.42
2	11	10	152	153	163	
		.12		.01		.13
3	5	6	97	96	102	
		.23		.02		.25
4	64	48	722	738	786	
		5.41†		.35		5.76*
5	14	12	179	181	193	
		.41		.03		.44
6	13	14	216	215	229	
		.07		.00		.07
7	11	19	293	285	304	
		3.04		.20		3.24
8	52	49	750	753	802	
		.20		.01		.21
9	60	56	863	867	923	
		.24		.02		.26
0	9	20	311	300	320	
		5.65†		.37		6.02*
NHP	2	5	85	82	87	
		2.05		.13		2.18
Total N	244		3735		3979	
χ^2	17.81		1.17			18.98*

Table 44. Parents' Marital Status Related to High-Point Scale for the Girls

High Scale	Separated or Divorced		Not Separated or Divorced		Total N	χ^2
	o	e	o	e		
1	0	1	14	13	14	
		.90		.06		.96
2	4	4	55	55	59	
		.01		.00		.01
3	7	10	150	147	157	
		1.00		.07		1.07
4	77	59	827	845	904	
		5.63†		.39		6.02*
5	29	36	530	523	559	
		1.47		.10		1.57
6	24	25	362	361	386	
		.05		.00		.05
7	9	13	183	179	192	
		.98		.07		1.05
8	42	27	375	390	417	
		8.19†		.57		8.76**
9	44	51	745	738	789	
		1.04		.07		1.11
0	24	36	522	510	546	
		3.73		.26		3.99*
NHP	5	6	80	79	85	
		.05		.00		.05
Total N	265		3843		4108	
χ^2	23.05*		1.59			24.64**

Table 45. Parents' Marital Status Related to Low-Point Scale for the Boys

Low Scale	Separated or Divorced		Not Separated or Divorced		Total N	χ²
	o	e	o	e		
1	32	27	387	392	419	
		.81		.06		.87
2	40	38	549	551	589	
		.07		.00		.07
3	14	16	223	221	237	
		.15		.01		.16
4	3	6	88	85	91	
		1.43		.10		1.53
5	38	45	648	641	686	
		1.00		.07		1.07
6	15	16	232	231	247	
		.08		.01		.09
7	5	4	54	55	59	
		.38		.03		.41
8	4	2	23	25	27	
		2.69		.19		2.88
9	12	23	339	328	351	
		5.19		.36		5.55
0	24	21	300	303	324	
		.40		.03		.43
NLP	91	80	1142	1153	1233	
		1.40		.10		1.50
Total N	278		3985		4263	
χ²	13.60		.96			14.56

Table 46. Parents' Marital Status Related to Low-Point Scale for the Girls

Low Scale	Separated or Divorced		Not Separated or Divorced		Total N	χ²
	o	e	o	e		
1	44	38	554	560	598	
		1.05		.07		1.12
2	43	47	709	705	752	
		.41		.03		.44
3	19	18	260	261	279	
		.11		.01		.12
4	1	5	79	75	80	
		3.20		.21		3.41
5	33	38	576	571	609	
		.76		.05		.81
6	14	14	208	208	222	
		.00		.00		.00
7	2	3	47	46	49	
		.39		.03		.42
8	0	1	12	11	12	
		.80		.06		.86
9	26	32	473	467	499	
		.96		.06		1.02
0	17	16	244	244	261	
		.02		.00		.02
NLP	75	62	908	921	983	
		2.73		.18		2.91
Total N	274		4070		4344	
χ²	10.43		.70			11.13

Table 47. The Person with Whom the Child Lives Related to High-Point Scale for the Boys

High Scale	Neither Parent o	e	χ²	Stepparent o	e	χ²	Mother o	e	χ²	Father o	e	χ²	Both Parents o	e	χ²	Total N	χ²
1	3	2	1.50	2	2	.05	5	5	.02	0	1	1.10	60	60	.00	70	2.67
2	2	4	.71	4	4	.00	11	12	.12	3	2	.15	143	141	.03	163	1.01
3	0	2	2.20	4	2	1.07	5	8	.95	2	1	.17	91	88	.10	102	4.49
4	22	17	1.28	19	19	.00	75	59	4.34	10	12	.27	660	679	.25	786	6.14
5	4	4	.01	7	5	1.25	18	15	.84	6	3	3.31	158	167	.46	193	5.87
6	7	5	.80	8	6	1.14	14	17	.60	2	3	.58	198	198	.00	229	3.12
7	7	7	.01	5	7	.72	22	23	.03	5	5	.03	265	263	.02	304	.81
8	15	18	.38	23	19	.75	57	60	.17	17	12	2.08	690	693	.01	802	3.39
9	20	20	.00	18	22	.79	70	69	.01	10	14	1.05	805	797	.07	923	1.92
0	4	7	1.29	4	8	1.78	20	24	.67	4	5	.13	288	277	.48	320	4.35
NHP	3	2	.64	1	2	.58	1	7	4.65	2	1	.38	80	75	.31	87	6.56
Total N	87			95			298			61			3438			3979	
χ²	8.82			8.13			12.40			9.25			1.73				40.33

Table 48. The Person with Whom the Child Lives Related to High-Point Scale for the Girls

High Scale	Neither Parent o	e	χ²	Stepparent o	e	χ²	Mother o	e	χ²	Father o	e	χ²	Both Parents o	e	χ²	Total N	χ²
1	0	0	.30	0	0	.40	0	1	1.20	0	0	.20	14	12	.33	14	2.43
2	0	1	1.20	2	1	.17	2	5	1.72	1	1	.05	54	51	.23	59	3.37
3	2	3	.39	7	4	2.46	14	13	.76	2	2	.02	132	135	.05	157	3.68
4	29	18	6.56	22	23	.00	81	75	.50	16	13	.92	755	775	.51	903	8.49
5	10	11	.13	9	14	1.79	46	46	.01	5	8	1.01	489	480	.18	559	3.12
6	8	8	.01	9	10	.05	25	32	1.53	4	5	.36	340	331	.23	386	2.18
7	1	4	2.06	3	5	.68	13	16	.53	2	3	.18	173	165	.42	192	3.87
8	14	8	3.92	14	10	1.25	39	35	.56	9	6	1.77	341	358	.79	417	8.29
9	11	16	1.46	23	20	.55	72	65	.67	14	11	.82	668	676	.10	788	3.60
0	7	11	1.40	9	14	1.61	43	45	.12	6	8	.34	481	468	.33	546	3.80
NHP	1	2	.29	3	2	.39	5	7	.62	0	1	1.20	76	73	.13	85	2.63
Total N	83			101			340			59			3523			4106	
χ²	17.72			9.35			8.22			6.87			3.30				45.46

Table 49. The Person with Whom the Child Lives Related to Low-Point Scale for the Boys

Low Scale	Neither Parent		Stepparent		Mother		Father		Both Parents		Total N	χ²
	o	e	o	e	o	e	o	e	o	e		
1	13	9	8	10	34	34	9	7	355	360	419	
	2.25		.33		.00		.87		.07			3.52
2	9	12	13	14	52	48	9	9	506	506	589	
	.75		.05		.37		.01		.00			1.18
3	6	5	5	6	21	19	3	4	201	203	236	
	.30		.05		.17		.13		.02			.67
4	2	2	2	2	3	7	0	1	84	78	91	
	.00		.00		2.62		1.40		.43			4.45
5	13	14	15	16	52	56	11	11	596	590	687	
	.07		.08		.26		.00		.06			.47
6	1	5	7	6	16	20	5	4	218	212	247	
	3.20		.25		.80		.31		.16			4.72
7	1	1	1	1	5	5	0	1	52	51	59	
	.04		.11		.00		.90		.03			1.08
8	1	1	4	1	3	2	0	0	19	23	27	
	.27		19.27		.29		.40		.76			20.99
9	3	7	8	8	22	29	4	6	314	302	351	
	2.45		.00		1.48		.41		.51			4.85
0	9	7	10	8	28	26	5	5	272	278	324	
	.87		.76		.11		.00		.15			1.89
NLP	29	25	27	29	110	100	21	19	1046	1060	1233	
	.57		.12		.98		.13		.17			1.97
Total N	87		100		346		67		3663		4263	
χ²	10.77		21.02		7.08		4.56		2.36			45.79

Table 50. The Person with Whom the Child Lives Related to Low-Point Scale for the Girls

Low Scale	Neither Parent		Stepparent		Mother		Father		Both Parents		Total N	χ²
	o	e	o	e	o	e	o	e	o	e		
1	12	12	18	15	49	49	14	9	505	514	598	
	.00		.84		.00		3.23		.15			4.22
2	17	15	16	18	57	61	10	11	649	644	749	
	.21		.24		.28		.07		.04			.84
3	5	6	10	7	23	23	4	4	236	239	278	
	.06		1.63		.00		.00		.04			1.73
4	1	2	2	2	6	7	0	1	71	69	80	
	.23		.01		.04		1.20		.07			1.55
5	9	12	15	15	44	50	9	9	533	524	610	
	.93		.00		.68		.00		.15			1.76
6	2	5	5	5	14	18	2	3	199	191	222	
	1.39		.03		.93		.45		.35			3.15
7	0	1	0	1	2	4	2	1	45	42	49	
	1.00		1.20		1.00		2.41		.20			5.81
8	1	0	0	0	1	1	0	0	10	10	12	
	3.20		.30		.00		.20		.01			3.71
9	6	10	8	12	40	41	4	7	441	429	499	
	1.66		1.39		.01		1.42		.35			4.83
0	6	5	4	6	26	21	3	4	222	224	261	
	.09		.84		1.04		.17		.02			2.16
NLP	29	20	27	24	92	80	15	14	819	844	982	
	4.16		.43		1.77		.03		.73			7.12
Total N	88		105		354		63		3730		4340	
χ²	12.93		6.91		5.75		9.18		2.11			36.88

Table 51. Intelligence[a] Related to High-Point Scale for the Boys

High Scale	Intelligence Percentile Score						Total N	χ²
	1–39		40–68		69–100			
	o	e	o	e	o	e		
1	26	24	20	21	23	24	69	
	.15		.02		.08			.25
2	68	56	41	48	51	56	160	
	2.67		.94		.54			4.15
3	25	36	23	30	54	36	102	
	3.18†		1.80		9.00†			13.98***
4	248	269	247	230	276	272	771	
	1.62		1.29		.05			2.96
5	33	66	43	56	113	67	189	
	16.42†		3.14		32.14†			51.70***
6	93	79	48	67	85	80	226	
	2.56		5.58†		.34			8.48*
7	107	104	106	89	85	105	298	
	.09		3.33		3.88†			7.30*
8	367	272	214	232	197	275	778	
	33.75†		1.38		21.98†			57.11***
9	281	319	304	272	329	323	914	
	4.48†		3.64		.12			8.24**
0	93	110	94	94	129	112	316	
	2.68		.00		2.71			5.39
NHP	22	30	25	25	38	30	85	
	1.95		.00		2.13			4.08
Total N	1363		1165		1380		3908	
χ²	69.55***		21.12*		72.97***			163.64***

[a] When necessary in Tables 51–54 IQ scores and ninth-grade ACE scores were equated to eleventh-grade ACE percentile scores in order to be included in this table.

Table 52. Intelligence Related to High-Point Scale for the Girls

High Scale	Intelligence Percentile Score						Total N	χ²
	1–39		40–68		69–100			
	o	e	o	e	o	e		
1	8	3	3	4	3	5	14	
	9.66		.30		1.07			11.03
2	21	19	22	17	15	22	58	
	.28		1.47		2.44			4.19
3	28	50	43	45	83	59	154	
	9.34†		.10		9.38†			18.82***
4	270	286	255	261	365	343	890	
	.92		.07		1.40			2.39
5	200	176	170	160	177	211	547	
	3.30		.59		5.42†			9.31**
6	104	123	106	112	172	149	382	
	2.88		.31		4.18†			7.37*
7	47	62	65	56	80	74	192	
	3.50		1.34		.49			5.33
8	192	131	103	120	114	158	409	
	27.83†		2.36		12.06†			42.25***
9	248	251	233	229	300	301	781	
	.04		.08		.00			.12
0	174	175	159	159	210	209	543	
	.00		.00		.00			.00
NHP	12	27	29	25	44	33	85	
	8.57†		.68		3.82†			13.07**
Total N	1304		1188		1563		4055	
χ²	66.32***		7.30		40.26***			113.88***

Table 53. Intelligence Related to Low-Point Scale for the Boys

Low Scale	Intelligence Percentile Score						Total N	χ²
	1–39		40–68		69–100			
	o	e	o	e	o	e		
1	105	120	134	123	138	134	377	
	1.92		.93		.15			3.00
2	146	170	170	175	218	189	534	
	3.47		.12		4.42†			8.01*
3	79	70	75	72	65	77	219	
	1.18		.16		2.02			3.36
4	33	27	22	27	28	29	83	
	1.59		.96		.07			2.62
5	240	182	193	187	139	203	572	
	18.19†		.19		19.91†			38.29***
6	61	69	84	70	70	76	215	
	.84		2.67		.49			4.00
7	12	19	22	19	25	21	59	
	2.46		.38		.80			3.64
8	6	9	12	9	9	9	27	
	.79		1.16		.04			1.99
9	64	99	100	102	147	110	311	
	12.49†		.03		12.37†			24.89***
0	38	93	83	96	171	103	292	
	32.61†		1.64		44.19†			78.44***
NLP	407	333	326	342	312	370	1045	
	16.30†		.72		9.09†			26.11***
Total N	1191		1221		1322		3734	
χ²	91.84***		8.96		93.55***			194.35***

Table 54. Intelligence Related to Low-Point Scale for the Girls

Low Scale	Intelligence Percentile Score						Total N	χ²
	1–39		40–68		69–100			
	o	e	o	e	o	e		
1	183	179	198	166	166	202	547	
	.09		5.96†		6.29†			12.34**
2	172	230	222	214	310	259	704	
	14.76†		.28		9.87†			24.91***
3	115	81	84	75	48	91	247	
	14.48†		1.03		20.32†			35.83***
4	28	24	20	23	27	28	75	
	.50		.34		.01			.85
5	105	180	165	168	281	203	551	
	31.38†		.04		29.97†			61.39***
6	81	65	65	61	53	73	199	
	3.88†		.32		5.62†			9.82**
7	13	14	8	13	23	16	44	
	.14		2.18		2.85			5.17
8	1	4	6	3	4	4	11	
	1.88		2.21		.00			4.09
9	138	150	134	140	187	169	459	
	.98		.23		1.89			3.10
0	50	76	62	70	119	85	231	
	8.67†		.98		13.50†			23.15***
NLP	392	274	225	255	222	309	839	
	50.40†		3.60		24.59†			78.59***
Total N	1278		1189		1440		3907	
χ²	127.16***		17.17		114.91***			259.24***

Table 55. Cooperative English Score Related to High-Point Scale for the Boys

High Scale	Cooperative English Percentile Score						Total N	χ²
	1–36		37–80		81–100			
	o	e	o	e	o	e		
1	29	24	20	23	6	8	55	
		.95		.47		.30		1.72
2	58	53	46	52	18	17	122	
		.36		.63		.10		1.09
3	24	38	39	36	23	12	86	
		5.04†		.19		10.63†		15.86***
4	235	253	266	244	75	79	576	
		1.32		1.98		.17		3.47
5	36	72	68	70	60	22	164	
		18.08†		.03		63.11†		81.22***
6	102	85	67	82	24	26	193	
		3.44		2.68		.22		6.34*
7	117	111	112	107	23	34	252	
		.35		.26		3.78		4.39
8	342	262	204	253	51	82	597	
		24.08†		9.46†		11.48†		45.02***
9	310	340	373	328	91	106	774	
		2.71		6.20†		2.07		10.98**
0	109	120	115	116	49	37	273	
		1.00		.00		3.67		4.67
NHP	28	30	29	29	12	9	69	
		.17		.00		.72		.89
Total N	1390		1339		432		3161	
χ²	57.50***		21.90*		96.25***			175.65***

Table 56. Cooperative English Score Related to High-Point Scale for the Girls

High Scale	Cooperative English Percentile Score						Total N	χ²
	1–36		37–80		81–100			
	o	e	o	e	o	e		
1	2	1	2	3	2	2	6	
		.53		.28		.01		.82
2	10	9	24	22	11	14	45	
		.14		.24		.80		1.18
3	9	27	70	65	56	43	135	
		11.73†		.38		3.72		15.83***
4	113	139	372	339	219	226	704	
		5.00†		3.23		.20		8.43*
5	119	97	247	236	125	157	491	
		4.89†		.48		6.67†		12.04**
6	61	68	148	165	133	110	342	
		.66		1.67		4.95†		7.28*
7	26	35	86	84	63	56	175	
		2.18		.04		.85		3.07
8	111	68	155	165	77	110	343	
		27.36†		.62		9.90†		37.88***
9	139	131	308	319	216	213	663	
		.45		.39		.05		.89
0	89	96	230	234	167	156	486	
		.54		.07		.81		1.42
NHP	9	17	30	40	45	27	84	
		3.48		2.68		12.18†		18.34***
Total N	688		1672		1114		3474	
χ²	56.96***		10.08		40.14***			107.18***

Table 57. Cooperative English Score Related to Low-Point Scale for the Boys

Low Scale	Cooperative English Percentile Score						Total N	χ^2
	1–36		37–80		81–100			
	o	e	o	e	o	e		
1	136	150	160	143	44	47	340	
	1.22		1.92		.20			3.34
2	189	221	233	212	81	70	503	
	4.66†		2.04		1.87			8.57*
3	97	87	79	83	21	27	197	
	1.25		.20		1.45			2.90
4	29	35	41	34	10	11	80	
	1.09		1.53		.11			2.73
5	284	218	183	210	30	69	497	
	19.64†		3.40		21.88†			44.92***
6	89	89	95	86	19	28	203	
	.00		1.03		2.95			3.98
7	17	22	22	21	11	7	50	
	1.14		.04		2.44			3.62
8	8	11	10	10	7	4	25	
	.82		.02		3.50			4.34
9	89	126	131	121	67	40	287	
	10.97†		.81		18.77†			30.55***
0	66	121	136	116	74	38	276	
	25.21†		3.30		33.55†			62.06***
NLP	482	405	336	389	104	128	922	
	14.51†		7.22†		4.40†			26.13***
Total N	1486		1426		468		3380	
χ^2	80.51***		21.51*		91.12***			193.14***

Table 58. Cooperative English Score Related to Low-Point Scale for the Girls

Low Scale	Cooperative English Percentile Score						Total N	χ^2
	1–36		37–80		81–100			
	o	e	o	e	o	e		
1	87	106	273	240	144	158	504	
	3.41		4.42†		1.17			9.00*
2	114	138	311	312	230	205	655	
	4.08†		.01		3.10			7.19*
3	75	48	111	109	42	71	228	
	15.33†		.04		12.04†			27.41***
4	18	15	26	34	27	22	71	
	.64		1.84		1.04			3.52
5	55	108	225	245	233	160	513	
	25.86†		1.59		32.86†			60.31***
6	42	39	103	88	39	57	184	
	.28		2.63		5.95†			8.86*
7	8	9	16	20	17	13	41	
	.04		.66		1.38			2.08
8	0	2	8	4	1	3	9	
	1.90		3.18		1.16			6.24
9	90	92	188	208	158	136	436	
	.03		1.92		3.45			5.40
0	26	46	103	105	91	69	220	
	8.83†		.03		7.16†			16.02***
NLP	246	160	363	362	150	237	759	
	46.77†		.00		32.12†			78.89***
Total N	761		1727		1132		3620	
χ^2	107.17***		16.32**		101.43***			224.92***

Table 59. High School Rank Related to High-Point Scale for the Boys

High Scale	High School Rank in Percentile						Total N	χ²
	1–39		40–69		70–100			
	o	e	o	e	o	e		
1	31	26	11	17	13	13	55	
		1.14		1.95		.01		3.10
2	51	56	37	36	32	28	120	
		.43		.01		.70		1.14
3	28	42	23	27	39	21	90	
		4.61†		.71		16.18†		21.50***
4	278	270	188	177	114	133	580	
		.23		.75		2.82		3.80
5	43	77	45	51	78	38	166	
		15.22†		.60		41.47†		57.29***
6	90	88	54	57	44	43	188	
		.07		.18		.01		.26
7	115	115	74	76	59	57	248	
		.00		.03		.07		.10
8	351	280	152	183	97	138	600	
		18.29†		5.10†		12.18†		35.57***
9	350	360	270	235	152	177	772	
		.26		5.24†		3.66		9.16*
0	108	127	87	83	78	63	273	
		2.90		.18		3.68		6.76*
NHP	28	33	21	21	21	16	70	
		.66		.00		1.49		2.15
Total N	1473		962		727		3162	
χ²	43.81***		14.75		82.27***			140.83***

Table 60. High School Rank Related to High-Point Scale for the Girls

High Scale	High School Rank in Percentile						Total N	χ²
	1–39		40–69		70–100			
	o	e	o	e	o	e		
1	3	2	2	3	3	3	8	
		.29		.10		.03		.42
2	13	13	17	14	16	19	46	
		.01		.51		.50		1.02
3	19	37	45	42	70	56	134	
		8.56†		.26		3.67		12.49**
4	179	190	230	217	287	289	696	
		.67		.83		.02		1.52
5	137	133	158	165	190	201	485	
		.15		.29		.65		1.09
6	81	92	88	105	167	140	336	
		1.29		2.63		5.38†		9.30**
7	39	47	50	54	83	71	172	
		1.36		.23		1.88		3.47
8	145	94	104	106	93	142	342	
		28.37†		.05		16.97†		45.39***
9	201	178	207	203	244	271	652	
		2.89		.08		2.65		5.62
0	108	134	151	153	231	204	490	
		5.04†		.01		3.72		8.77*
NHP	15	21	18	24	44	32	77	
		1.76		1.50		4.50†		7.76*
Total N	940		1070		1428		3438	
χ²	50.39***		6.49		39.97***			96.85***

Table 61. High School Rank Related to Low-Point Scale for the Boys

Low Scale	High School Rank in Percentile						Total N	χ^2
	1–39		40–69		70–100			
	o	e	o	e	o	e		
1 147	147		120	104	72	88	339	
	.00		2.43		2.98			5.41
2 218	215		146	152	132	129	496	
	.05		.26		.07			.38
3 101	83		57	59	33	50	191	
	4.10†		.04		5.61†			9.75**
4 30	34		25	24	23	20	78	
	.43		.04		.36			.83
5 301	218		134	155	69	131	504	
	31.51†		2.77		29.49†			63.77***
6 101	86		53	61	44	52	198	
	2.73		1.00		1.09			4.82
7 20	22		15	16	16	13	51	
	.20		.03		.55			.78
8 7	11		11	8	7	6	25	
	1.34		1.41		.35			3.10
9 97	128		90	91	108	77	295	
	7.34†		.00		12.68†			20.02***
0 93	122		103	86	85	73	281	
	6.73†		3.23		1.94			11.90**
NLP 335	386		275	274	283	232	893	
	6.84†		.00		11.02†			17.86***
Total N	1450		1029		872		3351	
χ^2	61.27***		11.21		66.14***			138.62***

Table 62. High School Rank Related to Low-Point Scale for the Girls

Low Scale	High School Rank in Percentile						Total N	χ^2
	1–39		40–69		70–100			
	o	e	o	e	o	e		
1 148	144		162	154	194	206	504	
	.09		.47		.72			1.28
2 150	185		197	196	298	264	645	
	6.55†		.00		4.43†			10.98**
3 91	64		77	68	54	91	222	
	11.80†		1.31		14.91†			28.02***
4 17	20		20	21	32	28	69	
	.40		.05		.51			.96
5 95	146		140	155	275	209	510	
	17.87†		1.51		21.14†			40.52***
6 70	54		56	57	61	76	187	
	5.02†		.00		3.14			8.16*
7 8	12		9	12	24	17	41	
	1.17		.98		3.09			5.24
8 2	2		4	2	2	3	8	
	.04		1.08		.51			1.63
9 100	125		114	133	222	178	436	
	4.96†		2.66		10.71†			18.33***
0 42	62		71	66	103	88	216	
	6.40†		.41		2.41			9.22**
NLP 310	220		248	234	210	314	768	
	36.82†		.86		34.50†			72.18***
Total N	1033		1098		1475		3606	
χ^2	91.12***		9.33		96.07***			196.52***

Table 63. Adjustment Rating Related to High-Point Scale for the Boys

High Scale	Adjustment Rating								Total N	χ²
	3 and 4		2		1		0			
	o	e	o	e	o	e	o	e		
1	7	7	14	11	18	18	27	30	66	
	.00		.82		.00		.34			1.16
2	15	16	26	25	34	40	74	68	149	
	.02		.05		.96		.49			1.52
3	5	10	9	16	21	27	63	45	98	
	2.73		3.34		1.14		7.30†			14.51**
4	110	78	146	125	196	201	294	342	746	
	12.83†		3.68		.14		6.66†			23.31***
5	12	19	22	31	48	50	103	85	185	
	2.82		2.56		.08		3.95†			9.41*
6	22	23	33	37	53	59	112	101	220	
	.05		.37		.69		1.24			2.35
7	24	31	46	49	86	80	140	136	296	
	1.62		.23		.47		.14			2.46
8	80	82	135	130	224	210	339	356	778	
	.04		.20		.92		.84			2.00
9	105	94	147	149	241	241	399	408	892	
	1.36		.03		.00		.22			1.61
0	16	33	43	52	92	85	163	144	314	
	8.76†		1.69		.61		2.56			13.62**
NHP	7	9	18	14	21	23	40	39	86	
	.44		.90		.21		.01			1.56
Total N	403		639		1034		1754		3830	
χ²	30.67***		13.87		5.22		23.75***			73.51***

Table 64. Adjustment Rating Related to High-Point Scale for the Girls

High Scale	Adjustment Rating								Total N	χ²
	3 and 4		2		1		0			
	o	e	o	e	o	e	o	e		
1	1	1	1	1	1	2	7	6	10	
	.50		.01		.73		.13			1.37
2	2	3	2	6	11	13	40	34	55	
	.14		2.76		.23		1.18			4.31
3	2	7	9	17	41	35	100	93	152	
	3.66		3.69		1.03		.50			8.88*
4	65	40	126	96	187	198	483	528	861	
	14.82†		9.67†		.61		3.80			28.90***
5	26	25	56	60	125	124	333	331	540	
	.01		.25		.01		.01			.28
6	11	18	27	42	83	87	256	231	377	
	2.54		5.24†		.16		2.68			10.62*
7	5	9	19	21	40	43	125	116	189	
	1.71		.19		.28		.71			2.89
8	18	19	58	45	92	93	236	248	404	
	.05		3.89†		.01		.55			4.50
9	27	35	94	88	177	172	451	459	749	
	1.91		1.43		.13		.14			3.61
0	28	25	40	59	129	123	336	327	533	
	.36		6.23†		.33		.26			7.18
NHP	1	4	5	9	21	19	54	50	81	
	2.06		1.78		.31		.37			4.52
Total N	186		437		907		2421		3951	
χ²	27.76		35.14***		3.83		10.33			77.06***

Table 65. Adjustment Rating Related to Low-Point Scale for the Boys

Low Scale	Adjustment Rating								Total N	χ^2
	3 and 4		2		1		0			
	o	e	o	e	o	e	o	e		
1	48	41	71	68	96	110	191	186	406	
	1.12		.11		1.76		.11			3.10
2	62	58	94	96	161	154	251	261	568	
	.32		.03		.34		.38			1.07
3	26	23	35	38	75	61	88	103	224	
	.48		.19		3.37		2.16			6.20
4	1	9	12	15	24	24	52	41	89	
	7.11†		.60		.00		3.01			10.72*
5	75	66	123	109	176	175	273	297	647	
	1.32		1.83		.00		1.97			5.12
6	18	24	41	40	67	64	110	108	236	
	1.50		.04		.15		.02			1.71
7	8	6	7	10	13	16	30	27	58	
	.75		.80		.46		.43			2.44
8	2	3	6	4	4	7	14	12	26	
	.14		.58		1.29		.37			2.38
9	14	34	38	56	91	90	191	153	334	
	11.68†		5.89†		.00		9.22†			26.79***
0	42	31	48	52	69	84	150	142	309	
	3.58		.31		2.58		.45			6.92
NLP	119	121	213	200	331	323	528	547	1191	
	.03		.79		.22		.67			1.71
Total N	415		688		1107		1878		4088	
χ^2	28.03**		11.17		10.17		18.79*			68.16***

Table 66. Adjustment Rating Related to Low-Point Scale for the Girls

Low Scale	Adjustment Rating								Total N	χ^2
	3 and 4		2		1		0			
	o	e	o	e	o	e	o	e		
1	30	27	72	65	139	131	344	362	585	
	.31		.78		.44		.86			2.39
2	25	34	77	80	153	163	470	448	725	
	2.16		.14		.59		1.06			3.95
3	16	12	34	30	61	60	157	166	268	
	1.05		.62		.01		.46			2.14
4	2	4	4	9	16	18	57	49	79	
	.78		2.62		.16		1.38			4.94
5	27	27	57	65	116	132	388	364	588	
	.00		1.03		1.94		1.65			4.62
6	9	10	25	24	51	49	131	133	216	
	.10		.04		.13		.05			.32
7	1	2	4	5	12	11	30	29	47	
	.65		.28		.18		.03			1.14
8	0	1	3	1	1	3	8	7	12	
	.60		2.22		1.07		.05			3.94
9	14	22	36	54	104	109	330	299	484	
	3.15		5.83†		.20		3.17			12.35**
0	9	12	28	28	53	56	161	155	251	
	.58		.00		.20		.22			1.00
NLP	60	42	123	102	231	206	504	568	918	
	7.31†		4.37†		3.01		7.11†			21.80***
Total N	193		463		937		2580		4173	
χ^2	16.69		17.93		7.93		16.04			58.59**

Table 67. Conduct Rating Related to High-Point Scale for the Boys

High Scale	3 and 4 o	e	χ²	2 o	e	χ²	1 o	e	χ²	0 o	e	χ²	Total N	χ²
1	5	4	.20	14	7	6.15†	15	12	1.00	32	43	2.81	66	10.16*
2	9	9	.01	12	17	1.23	20	26	1.55	109	98	1.28	150	4.07
3	2	6	2.67	5	11	3.04	14	17	.56	76	63	2.59	97	8.86*
4	76	46	19.39†	105	82	6.58†	148	131	2.23	415	485	10.13†	744	38.33***
5	5	11	3.67	15	20	1.43	24	33	2.27	141	121	3.45	185	10.82*
6	16	14	.42	19	24	1.08	37	38	.06	147	143	.12	219	1.68
7	12	18	2.23	27	33	.99	42	52	2.03	216	194	2.59	297	7.84
8	43	48	.54	85	85	.00	151	136	1.56	496	505	.17	775	2.27
9	59	55	.29	115	98	3.10	162	156	.22	551	578	1.29	887	4.90
0	7	19	7.93†	20	34	6.03†	42	55	3.11	244	204	7.80†	313	24.87***
NHP	4	5	.32	4	10	3.18	16	15	.05	62	56	.62	86	4.17
Total N	238			421			671			2489			3819	
χ²	37.67***			32.81***			14.64			32.85***				117.97***

Table 68. Conduct Rating Related to High-Point Scale for the Girls

High Scale	2, 3, 4 o	e	χ²	1 o	e	χ²	5 o	e	χ²	0 o	e	χ²	Total N	χ²
1	0	1	.50	1	1	.03	0	0	.40	10	9	.14	11	1.07
2	2	3	.10	7	6	.17	1	2	.50	46	46	.01	56	.78
3	4	7	1.22	21	17	1.23	5	5	.03	123	124	.01	153	2.49
4	71	39	27.20†	120	92	8.38†	31	30	.04	633	694	5.40†	855	41.02***
5	14	24	4.30†	46	58	2.41	16	19	.42	460	435	1.41	536	8.54*
6	12	17	1.47	23	41	7.63†	14	13	.05	328	306	1.57	377	10.72**
7	8	9	.03	16	20	.95	4	7	1.02	161	153	.38	189	2.38
8	20	18	.16	43	44	.01	16	14	.23	326	329	.02	405	.42
9	33	34	.07	106	80	8.37†	33	26	1.88	571	603	1.72	743	12.04**
0	13	24	5.11†	35	58	8.93†	12	19	2.40	475	434	3.79	535	20.23***
NHP	1	4	1.97	7	9	.33	6	3	3.66	67	66	.02	81	5.98
Total N	178			425			138			3200			3941	
χ²	42.13***			38.44***			10.63			14.47				105.67***

Table 69. Conduct Rating Related to Low-Point Scale for the Boys

Low Scale	Conduct Rating 3 and 4 o	e	2 o	e	1 o	e	0 o	e	Total N	χ²
1	24	24	45	42	72	74	261	262	402	
		.00		.23		.05		.01		.29
2	47	34	64	59	106	104	348	368	565	
		5.34†		.44		.03		1.14		6.95
3	14	13	20	23	35	41	154	145	223	
		.04		.47		.88		.51		1.90
4	0	5	2	9	10	17	78	59	90	
		5.40†		5.83†		2.62		6.35†		20.20***
5	51	38	75	67	127	119	392	421	645	
		4.13†		.88		.58		1.94		7.53
6	11	14	22	24	49	43	151	152	233	
		.61		.22		.87		.01		1.71
7	2	3	8	6	12	11	35	37	57	
		.58		.75		.21		.13		1.67
8	2	3	0	3	7	5	17	17	26	
		.17		2.70		1.01		.00		3.88
9	5	20	15	35	52	61	261	217	333	
		11.06†		11.18†		1.41		8.83†		32.48***
0	21	18	41	32	62	56	180	198	304	
		.46		2.73		.67		1.69		5.55
NLP	65	71	132	124	216	218	774	774	1187	
		.46		.54		.03		.00		1.03
Total N	242		424		748		2651		4065	
χ²	28.25**		25.97**		8.36		20.61*			83.19***

Table 70. Conduct Rating Related to Low-Point Scale for the Girls

Low Scale	Conduct Rating 2, 3, 4 o	e	1 o	e	5 o	e	0 o	e	Total N	χ²
1	21	27	63	61	21	20	477	474	582	
		1.41		.04		.10		.02		1.57
2	30	34	85	76	27	24	579	587	721	
		.39		1.04		.30		.11		1.84
3	10	13	18	28	11	9	228	217	267	
		.50		3.69		.44		.53		5.16
4	1	4	5	8	1	3	72	64	79	
		1.97		1.31		1.07		.92		5.27
5	23	27	62	62	23	20	476	475	584	
		.65		.09		.55		.00		1.29
6	6	10	38	23	8	7	164	176	216	
		1.66		10.13†		.07		.79		12.65**
7	0	2	7	5	2	2	37	37	46	
		2.10		.90		.17		.00		3.17
8	2	1	0	1	1	0	9	10	12	
		3.27		1.30		.90		.07		5.54
9	17	23	24	51	7	16	434	392	482	
		1.34		14.22†		5.22†		4.43†		25.21***
0	13	12	30	26	11	8	196	204	250	
		.14		.49		.80		.28		1.71
NLP	71	43	107	97	28	31	713	748	919	
		18.41†		1.03		.27		1.65		21.36***
Total N	194		439		140		3385		4158	
χ²	31.84***		34.24***		9.89		8.80			84.77***

Table 71. Teacher Prediction Related to High-Point Scale for the Boys

High Scale	Predicted Delinquency		Predicted Emotional Problems		Both		No Prediction		Total N	χ²
	o	e	o	e	o	e	o	e		
1	3	5	8	6	4	4	55	55	70	1.83
	1.14		.67		.02		.00			
2	7	13	19	14	8	9	129	128	163	4.48
	2.56		1.87		.04		.01			
3	3	8	3	9	1	5	95	80	102	13.26**
	3.13		3.73		3.59		2.81			
4	86	61	77	67	66	42	557	616	786	31.36***
	9.95†		1.56		14.16†		5.69†			
5	10	15	13	16	3	10	167	151	193	9.13*
	1.72		.70		5.08†		1.63			
6	20	18	20	20	12	12	177	179	229	.29
	.25		.01		.00		.03			
7	12	24	26	26	21	16	245	238	304	7.46
	5.78†		.00		1.49		.19			
8	81	63	79	68	41	43	601	629	802	8.40*
	5.41†		1.71		.05		1.23			
9	75	72	68	79	44	49	736	724	923	2.23
	.13		1.40		.49		.21			
0	12	25	21	27	5	17	282	251	320	20.49***
	6.76†		1.41		8.47†		3.85†			
NHP	2	7	6	7	5	5	74	68	87	4.17
	3.39		.26		.03		.49			
Total N	311		340		210		3118		3979	
χ²	40.22***		13.32		33.42***		16.14			103.10***

Table 72. Teacher Prediction Related to High-Point Scale for the Girls

High Scale	Predicted Delinquency		Predicted Emotional Problems		Both		No Prediction		Total N	χ²
	o	e	o	e	o	e	o	e		
1	0	0	2	1	0	0	12	12	14	1.23
	.30		.53		.40		.00			
2	1	1	6	5	1	2	51	51	59	.34
	.01		.16		.17		.00			
3	2	3	15	14	1	4	139	137	157	2.55
	.23		.12		2.16		.04			
4	26	16	84	79	46	23	748	786	904	32.24***
	5.77†		.37		24.22†		1.88			
5	8	10	45	49	6	14	500	486	559	5.67
	.44		.27		4.57†		.39			
6	4	7	32	34	8	10	342	336	386	1.71
	1.22		.08		.30		.11			
7	0	4	13	17	4	5	175	167	192	4.83
	3.50		.82		.13		.38			
8	9	8	47	36	10	10	351	363	417	3.85
	.30		3.15		.02		.38			
9	19	14	62	69	22	20	686	686	789	2.52
	1.62		.63		.27		.00			
0	4	10	46	47	6	14	490	475	546	8.28*
	3.43		.05		4.33†		.47			
NHP	2	1	4	7	0	2	79	74	85	4.17
	.17		1.56		2.10		.34			
Total N	75		356		104		3573		4108	
χ²	16.99		7.74		38.67***		3.99			67.39***

Table 73. Teacher Prediction Related to Low-Point Scale for the Boys

Low Scale	Predicted Delinquency		Predicted Emotional Problems		Both		No Prediction		Total N	χ²
	o	e	o	e	o	e	o	e		
1	29	32	39	35	28	22	323	330	419	
		.26		.37		1.52		.13		2.28
2	54	45	43	50	30	31	462	463	589	
		1.84		.90		.05		.00		2.79
3	13	18	14	20	20	13	191	187	238	
		1.44		1.85		4.35†		.08		7.72
4	1	7	4	8	2	5	84	72	91	
		5.09†		1.78		1.63		2.15		10.60*
5	70	52	60	58	46	36	510	539	686	
		5.99†		.08		2.53		1.60		10.20*
6	13	19	19	21	12	13	203	194	247	
		1.79		.17		.09		.40		2.45
7	4	4	6	5	2	3	46	46	58	
		.04		.25		.39		.00		.68
8	1	2	0	2	0	1	26	21	27	
		.58		2.30		1.40		1.09		5.37
9	13	27	26	30	5	19	307	276	351	
		7.11†		.44		9.94†		3.48		20.97***
0	20	25	24	27	15	17	265	255	324	
		.89		.42		.28		.41		2.00
NLP	107	94	125	104	66	65	936	970	1234	
		1.77		4.15		.01		1.22		7.15
Total N	325		360		226		3353		4264	
χ²	26.75**		12.71		22.19*		10.56			72.21***

Table 74. Teacher Prediction Related to Low-Point Scale for the Girls

Low Scale	Predicted Delinquency		Predicted Emotional Problems		Both		No Prediction		Total N	χ²
	o	e	o	e	o	e	o	e		
1	14	12	48	54	18	16	518	516	598	
		.33		.63		.34		.00		1.30
2	17	15	49	67	21	20	662	647	749	
		.27		5.02†		.09		.36		5.74
3	9	6	28	25	8	7	235	242	280	
		2.06		.31		.05		.19		2.61
4	0	2	9	7	0	2	71	69	80	
		1.60		.45		2.10		.05		4.20
5	7	12	54	55	13	16	535	526	609	
		2.22		.01		.56		.16		2.95
6	2	4	23	20	4	6	193	192	222	
		1.31		.45		.56		.01		2.33
7	1	1	1	4	0	1	47	42	49	
		.00		2.63		1.30		.52		4.45
8	0	0	1	1	1	0	10	10	12	
		.20		.00		1.63		.00		1.83
9	5	10	47	45	7	13	440	431	449	
		2.50		.10		2.84		.19		5.63
0	3	5	16	23	9	7	232	225	260	
		.93		2.34		.71		.25		4.23
NLP	29	20	115	89	33	26	807	850	984	
		4.29†		7.87†		2.01		2.16		16.33***
Total N	87		391		114		3750		4342	
χ²	15.71		19.81*		12.19		3.89			51.60**

Table 75. High 4 Profiles Related to Delinquency Rate for Boys Tested
Both in the Ninth and in the Twelfth Grade

Category	Number	Percentage of 9th-Grade High 4 Group	Percentage Delinquent
High 4 in 9th grade 311		100	38
Still high 4 in 12th grade 115		37	47
Changed to other high point in 12th grade 196		63	31
High 4 in 12th grade but other high point in 9th grade 297			35

Table 76. Ninth- and Twelfth-Grade Test-Retest Results
When Both Tests Were Valid[a]

Scale	Mean			Standard Deviation			Corre-lation
	9th Grade	12th Grade	Value of "t"	9th Grade	12th Grade	Value of "t"	
			BOYS				
L	3.9	3.4	7.35**	2.4	2.8	7.36**	.39**
F	6.2	4.6	17.20**	4.4	3.5	11.33**	.45**
K	13.8	15.2	12.96**	4.8	4.9	1.06	.52**
1	51	51		8.7	8.1	3.33**	.34**
2	52	51	3.94**	10.1	10.0	.47	.38**
3	52	54	9.90**	8.0	7.9	.59	.37**
4	58	59	3.85**	9.9	10.3	1.86	.36**
5	51	52	4.63**	8.8	9.4	3.24**	.45**
6	56	54	7.94**	10.2	8.8	6.85**	.32**
7	58	57	3.88**	10.4	9.8	2.80**	.37**
8	62	58	13.11**	12.7	11.0	6.80**	.37**
9	58	57	4.00**	10.6	10.8	.92	.47**
0	54	47	36.46**	8.4	9.0	3.60**	.54**
			GIRLS				
L	4.0	3.5	9.26**	2.3	2.2	2.33*	.50**
F	5.0	3.7	16.67**	3.7	3.0	10.97**	.49**
K	13.9	15.1	12.00**	4.7	4.8	1.15	.56**
1	48	49	5.85**	7.5	6.9	41.15**	.41**
2	49	49		8.9	8.7	1.17	.47**
3	51	54	15.79**	8.3	7.8	2.96**	.44**
4	57	57		10.0	10.0		.38**
5	53	51	9.52**	9.0	9.0		.43**
6	55	54	4.22**	10.0	9.0	5.13**	.36**
7	56	55	5.32**	8.5	8.5		.50**
8	58	56	9.09**	9.7	8.6	6.02**	.42**
9	56	54	7.87**	11.3	10.7	2.77**	.45**
0	54	52	10.93**	8.9	9.5	3.73**	.61**

[a] Level of significance is indicated by asterisks: ** significant at .01; * significant at .05. The sample sizes were 1922 for the boys, 2054 for the girls.

Table 77. Code Stability for the Boys

High Scale	Percentage of Boys in Test-Retest Group with Given High Point on 9th-Grade Test Code			Percentage of Boys with 9th-Grade High Point in 1st or 2nd Place on Retest Code			Percentage of Boys with 9th-Grade High Point among Three Lowest Points on Retest Code		
	<70	≧70	Total	<70	≧70	Total	<70	≧70	Total
1	0.9	0.9	1.8	8	22	15	0	7	3
2	2.1	2.0	4.1	16	39	27	14	6	10
3	2.5	0.2	2.7	37	44	38	2	0	2
4	10.5	7.7	18.2	51	75	60	0	0	0
5	3.3	1.3	4.6	44	73	52	8	0	6
6	3.2	2.6	5.8	26	16	22	5	1	3
7	3.7	4.0	7.7	24	38	31	4	1	3
8	5.9	12.7	18.6	31	39	37	6	3	4
9	9.6	11.4	21.0	41	59	50	3	4	4
0	6.2	1.3	7.5	31	55	34	10	0	9

Table 78. Code Stability for the Girls

High Scale	Percentage of Girls in Test-Retest Group with Given High Point on 9th-Grade Test Code			Percentage of Girls with 9th-Grade High Point in 1st or 2nd Place on Retest Code			Percentage of Girls with 9th-Grade High Point among Three Lowest Points on Retest Code		
	<70	≧70	Total	<70	≧70	Total	<70	≧70	Total
1	0.2	0.2	0.4	0	33	17	17	0	8
2	0.9	0.6	1.5	7	24	15	10	0	6
3	3.0	0.9	3.9	54	50	53	0	3	1
4	12.0	7.9	19.9	47	65	53	2	1	2
5	8.4	3.6	12.0	29	45	34	10	10	10
6	5.1	3.8	8.9	25	25	25	4	7	5
7	3.6	1.6	5.2	24	33	36	2	0	2
8	4.6	5.6	10.2	24	31	28	1	2	1
9	8.1	9.3	17.4	37	56	47	7	4	5
0	9.3	2.8	12.1	42	64	47	6	3	5

TABLE 79 157

Table 79. Items to Which Responses by a Statewide Random Sample of 100 Boys and 100 Girls Showed More Than a 17 Per Cent Change in Either Direction between the Ninth and Twelfth Grades[a]

Item	Percentage Responding "True"	
	9th Grade	12th Grade
BOYS		
* I am neither gaining nor losing weight.	22	56
I do not worry about catching diseases.	57	78
I seldom worry about my health.	53	72
I would like to wear expensive clothes.	37	68
I enjoy gambling for small stakes.	26	52
I enjoy social gatherings just to be with people.	57	81
* I believe that a person should never taste an alcoholic drink.	45	14
* It takes a lot of argument to convince most people of the truth.	67	47
I am apt to pass up something I want to do because others feel that I am not going about it in the right way.	38	18
I am quite often not in on the gossip and talk of the group I belong to.	53	33
These days I find it hard not to give up hope of amounting to something.	60	41
What others think of me does not bother me.	51	32
I tend to be interested in several different hobbies rather than to stick to one of them for a long time.	64	84
I would like to be a singer.	22	45
I have several times had a change of heart about my life work.	51	69
I like movie love scenes.	21	46
I like to flirt.	31	61
Sexual things disgust me.	29	10
I love to go to dances.	43	64
* I never attend a sexy show if I can avoid it.	51	17
I wish I were not bothered by thoughts about sex.	44	23
* I have been quite independent and free from family rule.	27	54
I would like to be an auto racer.	43	62
At times I have been so entertained by the cleverness of a crook that I have hoped he would get by with it.	31	49
Most people will use somewhat unfair means to gain profit or an advantage rather than to lose it.	57	38
I have never been in trouble with the law.	72	53
I deserve severe punishment for my sins.	64	46
* I am attracted by members of the opposite sex.	66	87
* I am very strongly attracted by members of my own sex.	49	25
GIRLS		
I used to keep a diary.	40	63
I am often afraid that I am going to blush.	59	38
I very much like horseback riding.	80	60
If I were a reporter I would very much like to report sporting news.	56	37
* I believe that a person should never taste an alcoholic drink.	43	24
* I have been quite independent and free from family rule.	21	42
At times I have very much wanted to leave home.	31	52
I feel that I have often been punished without cause.	38	20
* I am neither gaining nor losing weight.	46	66
I am not afraid of picking up a disease or germs from door knobs.	59	79
* I am very strongly attracted by members of my own sex.	44	19
* I am attracted by members of the opposite sex.	65	84
I like mannish women.	29	9
Usually I would prefer to work with women.	62	42
* I never attend a sexy show if I can avoid it.	62	42
I believe women ought to have as much sexual freedom as men.	58	40
I have often found people jealous of my good ideas, just because they had not thought of them first.	45	19

[a] Starred items appear on both lists, for boys and girls.

Table 79 — continued

Item	Percentage Responding "True"	
	9th Grade	12th Grade
Most people inwardly dislike putting themselves out to help other people.	48	27
My way of doing things is apt to be misunderstood by others.	44	25
People have often misunderstood my intentions when I was trying to put them right and be helpful.	62	41
I have often felt badly over being misunderstood when trying to keep someone from making a mistake.	65	47
When I take a new job, I like to be tipped off on who should be gotten next to.	46	24
I commonly wonder what hidden reason another person may have for doing something nice for me.	60	41
Most people make friends because friends are likely to be useful to them.	46	26
* It takes a lot of argument to convince most people of the truth.	57	39
I have often lost out on things because I couldn't make up my mind soon enough.	47	27
The future is too uncertain for a person to make serious plans.	40	17
If given the chance I could do some things that would be of great benefit to the world.	59	37
I like to read newspaper articles on crime.	50	69
I do not blame a person for taking advantage of someone who lays himself open to it.	52	31

Table 80. Items to Which Responses by a Statewide Random Sample of 100 Boys and 100 Girls Showed More Than 39 Per Cent Instability between the Ninth and Twelfth Grades

Item	Percentage Changing Response	
	"True" to "False"	"False" to "True"
BOYS		
Once in a while I think of things too bad to talk about.	22	20
My speech is the same as always (not faster or slower, or slurring; no hoarseness).	21	19
I like dramatics.	20	21
My conduct is largely controlled by the customs of those about me.	19	23
It makes me uncomfortable to put on a stunt at a party even when others are doing the same sort of things.	24	20
I should like to belong to several clubs or lodges.	19	24
I dream frequently about things that are best kept to myself.	22	20
People often disappoint me.	24	19
I feel unable to tell anyone all about myself.	24	21
When I was a child I didn't care to be a member of a crowd or gang.	19	21
When I am cornered I tell that portion of the truth which is not likely to hurt me.	26	21
It is unusual for me to express strong approval or disapproval of the actions of others.	22	22
GIRLS		
These days I find it hard not to give up hope of amounting to something.	28	24
Most people will use somewhat unfair means to gain profit or an advantage rather than to lose it.	21	19
I know who is responsible for most of my troubles.	24	22
It makes me impatient to have people ask my advice or otherwise interrupt me when I am working on something important.	22	18

Table 80 — continued

	Percentage Changing Response	
Item	"True" to "False"	"False" to "True"
I am always disgusted with the law when a criminal is freed through the arguments of a smart lawyer.	20	20
I like to keep people guessing what I'm going to do next.	19	21
I am apt to hide my feelings in some things, to the point that people may hurt me without their knowing about it.	23	18
If given the chance I would make a good leader of people.	23	18
I have never been made especially nervous over trouble that any members of my family have gotten into.	22	20
I prefer work which requires close attention, to work which allows me to be careless.	21	23
I do not try to cover up my poor opinion or pity of a person so that he won't know how I feel.	23	20
I think Lincoln was greater than Washington.	22	20

Table 81. Means and Standard Deviations for the 1947 and 1954 Ninth-Grade Boys[a]

High Scale	Mean			Standard Deviation		
	1947	1954	Diff.	1947	1954	**Diff.**
L	4.49	3.60	−.89**	2.17	2.24	+ .07
F	6.61	6.14	−.47	3.62	3.63	+ .01
K	13.82	12.97	−.85	4.33	4.55	+ .22
1	55	49	−6**	8.76	8.29	− .47
2	56	51	−5**	9.54	9.06	− .48
3	53	50	−3**	6.55	7.61	+1.06*
4	64	58	−6**	8.72	9.79	+1.07
5	50	50	0	7.18	8.98	+1.80
6	56	55	−1	8.61	10.18	+1.57*
7	58	56	−2	7.70	9.96	+2.26*
8	62	59	−3*	10.16	10.41	+ .25
9	61	59	−2	9.55	10.13	+ .58
0	54	55	+1	6.43	7.27	+ .84

[a] The number of subjects for 1947 was 101; for 1954, 112. The asterisks indicate level of significance: * significant at .05; ** significant at .01.

Table 82. Means and Standard Deviations for the 1947 and 1954 Ninth-Grade Girls[a]

High Scale	Mean			Standard Deviation		
	1947	1954	Diff.	1947	1954	Diff.
L	4.04	3.78	—.26	1.86	1.57	— .29
F	5.47	5.53	+.06	3.49	2.96	— .53
K	13.07	12.16	—.91	4.68	3.49	—1.19*
1	50	47	—3**	8.89	6.94	—1.95*
2	51	48	—3*	7.43	8.89	+1.46
3	52	50	—2	8.14	7.32	— .82
4	59	56	—3*	8.56	8.26	— .30
5	57	55	—2	8.68	9.50	+ .82
6	54	55	+1	10.78	9.52	—1.26
7	55	56	+1	8.67	7.81	— .86
8	58	59	+1	9.42	7.44	—1.98*
9	55	58	+3*	10.73	10.49	— .24
0	56	56	0	8.05	8.81	+ .76

[a] The number of subjects for 1947 was 81; for 1954, 124. The asterisks indicate level of significance: * significant at .05; ** significant at .01.

Table 83. Symmetrical Surface Correlations between Twins and Comparison with Test-Retest Correlations for a Three-Year Interval (from the Ninth to the Twelfth Grade)[a]

High Scale	Male Twins (N = 31)	Female Twins (N = 41)	Mixed Twins (N = 36)	Test-Retest[b]	
				Boys (N = 1922)	Girls (N = 2054)
L	—.06	.52**	.26	.39	.50
F	.07	.50**	.00	.45	.49
K	.38*	.55**	.13	.52	.56
1	.20	.21	.09	.34	.41
2	.12	.08	.14	.38	.47
3	.34	.15	.15	.37	.44
4	.31	.47**	—.06	.36	.38
5	.43*	.46**	—.47**	.45	.43
6	.27	.16	.09	.32	.36
7	—.02	.21	—.11	.37	.50
8	—.26	.23	.05	.37	.42
9	.24	.12	.49**	.47	.45
0	.47**	.53**	.07	.54	.61

[a] The asterisks indicate level of significance: * significant at .05; ** significant at .01.
[b] All test-retest correlations are significant at the ≥.01 level.

Table 84. Delinquency (at Levels 2, 3, and 4 for the Boys and 1, 2, 3, and 4
for the Girls) Related to the Variables

	Boys		Girls	
Variable	Distribution of Delinquents among Subgroupings of Each Variable[a]	Rate of Delinquency in Each Variable Category[a]	Distribution of Delinquents among Subgroupings of Each Variable	Rate of Delinquency in Each Variable Category
Socioeconomic status				
Day laborer	10.7%	30.5%	12.2%	18.0%
Semiskilled and				
slightly skilled	46.5	26.6	55.5	15.5
Farmer	11.4	12.2	10.7	5.7
Clerical	23.4	27.2	17.3	10.3
Professional and				
semiprofessional	8.0	24.8	4.3	6.9
Intelligence (percentile rank)				
1–15	14.5	22.7	10.6	10.2
16–39	22.2	25.7	30.6	13.7
40–68	30.3	24.3	26.3	9.2
69–90	23.8	24.7	24.9	10.3
91–100	9.1	19.5	7.5	6.2
High school rank (percentile)				
1–19	36.4	30.4	25.4	13.4
20–39	25.8	22.8	18.8	9.1
40–69	25.1	18.0	33.3	8.2
70–100	12.7	12.4	22.5	4.4
School status				
Dropout	30.9	39.1	45.7	31.2
Non-dropout	69.1	20.5	54.3	6.7
Parents' marital status				
Separated or divorced	9.7	37.1	13.1	21.3
Not separated or				
divorced	90.3	23.2	86.9	9.7
Total sample		24.0		10.4

[a] The distinction between the first and second column (and the third and fourth) should be emphasized. The Distribution column shows the percentages of all delinquents classified in each variable subgrouping; these percentages therefore add to 100 for the total variable category. The Rate column shows the percentage of subjects from the entire sample in each subgrouping that were rated as delinquent.

Table 85. Relationship between Delinquency and Neighborhood
for the Minneapolis Boys

	"High" Schools		"Low" Schools		Total Group	
Delinquency	Number	Cumulative Percentage	Number	Cumulative Percentage	Number	Cumulative Percentage
None	222	100	173	100	395	100
Contact only or minor ..	98	33	104	46	202	39
Severe	11	3	44	14	55	8
Total	331		321		652	

TABLES 86–106. RELATIONSHIPS BETWEEN ENVIRONMENTAL AND BEHAVIORAL
VARIABLES AND DELINQUENCY

Delinquency is here categorized into rating levels 0, 1, 2, 3, and 4. As for Tables 34–74, the reliability of the relationship in each cell is roughly suggested by a number that is derived from the difference between the observed number of subjects (o) and the statistically expected number of subjects (e). The derived number, a portion of χ^2, is obtained for each cell by the equation $(o - e)^2/e$. The sum of these numbers for each row and column makes up the χ^2 value. The χ^2 values are finally marked by asterisks if the values are large enough to support reliably the hypothesis that the observed data differ from margin expectations. The asterisks have the conventional meaning: * indicates significance at .05, ** at .01, *** at .001. A dagger (†) indicates that the observed number of cases in the cell probably differs significantly from the expected value. After computing the tables the numbers in the e columns were rounded to the nearest whole number to facilitate reading; the precision lost is negligible.

Table 86. Community Size Related to Delinquency for the Boys

Delinquency Rating	City		Suburbs		Towns over 5000 Population		Towns under 5000 Population		Farm		Total N	χ^2
	o	e	o	e	o	e	o	e	o	e		
0	365	415	616	671	943	1015	553	536	1187	1026	3664	
	6.11†		4.54†		5.15†		.55		25.13†			41.48***
1	65	67	75	108	193	164	102	86	156	166	591	
	.06		10.24†		5.21†		2.82		.56			18.89***
2, 3, 4	205	153	335	247	416	373	164	197	226	377	1346	
	17.99†		31.69†		4.96†		5.47†		60.48†			120.59***
Total N	635		1026		1552		819		1569		5601	
χ^2	24.16***		46.47***		15.32***		8.84*		86.17***			180.96***

Table 87. Community Size Related to Delinquency for the Girls

Delinquency Rating	City		Suburbs		Towns over 5000 Population		Towns under 5000 Population		Farm		Total N	χ^2
	o	e	o	e	o	e	o	e	o	e		
0	553	554	883	870	1295	1335	789	819	1425	1367	4945	
	.00		.19		1.20		1.09		2.44			4.92
1	15	26	23	41	82	62	68	38	43	64	231	
	4.59†		7.63†		6.23†		23.03†		6.84†			48.32***
2, 3, 4	50	38	65	60	113	93	57	57	58	95	343	
	3.50		.37		4.49†		.00		14.29†			22.65***
Total N	618		971		1490		914		1526		5519	
χ^2	8.09*		8.19*		11.92**		24.12***		23.57***			75.89***

Table 88. Socioeconomic Status Related to Delinquency for the Boys

Delinquency Rating	Professional and Semi-professional		Clerical		Farmer		Semiskilled and Slightly Skilled		Day Laborer		Total N	χ^2
	o	e	o	e	o	e	o	e	o	e		
0	275	273	702	731	941	790	1401	1479	250	297	3569	
		.02		1.12		28.99†		4.11†		7.44†		41.68***
1	37	44	108	117	114	127	251	238	64	48	574	
		1.08		.77		1.33		.72		5.49†		9.39
2, 3, 4	103	98	302	264	147	285	599	534	138	107	1289	
		.21		5.50†		66.97†		7.89†		8.78†		89.35***
Total N	415		1112		1202		2251		452		5432	
χ^2	1.31		7.39*		97.29***		12.72**		21.71***			140.42***

Table 89. Socioeconomic Status Related to Delinquency for the Girls

Delinquency Rating	Professional and Semi-professional		Clerical		Farmer		Semiskilled and Slightly Skilled		Day Laborer		Total N	χ^2
	o	e	o	e	o	e	o	e	o	e		
0	376	356	972	955	1140	1066	1958	2042	361	388	4807	
		1.11		.29		5.19†		3.46		1.85		11.90*
1	6	17	51	44	29	49	105	95	32	18	223	
		6.68†		1.01		8.42†		1.12		10.89†		28.12***
2, 3, 4	22	31	61	84	40	94	254	180	47	34	424	
		2.81		6.44†		31.02†		30.32†		4.79†		75.38***
Total N	404		1084		1209		2317		440		5454	
χ^2	10.60**		7.74*		44.63***		34.90***		17.53***			115.40***

Table 90. Parents' Marital Status Related to Delinquency for the Boys

Delinquency Rating	Separated or Divorced		Not Separated or Divorced		Total N	χ^2
	o	e	o	e		
0	177	229	3488	3436	3665	
		11.81†		.79		12.60***
1	43	37	547	553	590	
		1.01		.07		1.08
2	69	54	789	804	858	
		4.42†		.29		4.71*
3, 4	61	30	427	458	488	
		30.50†		2.03		32.53***
Total N	350		5251		5601	
χ^2	47.74***		3.18			50.92***

Table 91. Parents' Marital Status Related to Delinquency for the Girls

Delinquency Rating	Separated or Divorced		Not Separated or Divorced		Total N	χ^2
	o	e	o	e		
0	277	315	4668	4630	4945	5.00*
	4.68†		.32			
1	20	15	211	216	231	2.04
	1.91		.13			
2	35	15	197	217	232	29.45***
	27.57†		1.88			
3, 4	20	7	91	104	111	25.04***
	23.44†		1.60			
Total N	352		5167		5519	
χ^2	57.60***		3.93			61.53***

Table 92. Person with Whom the Subject Lives Related to Delinquency for the Boys

Delinquency Rating	Neither Parent		Stepparent		Father		Mother		Both Parents		Total N	χ^2
	o	e	o	e	o	e	o	e	o	e		
0	68	77	88	85	61	60	235	286	3306	3250	3758	11.37*
	1.12		.14		.01		9.13†		.97			
1	14	12	11	13	9	9	53	45	498	506	585	2.46
	.33		.37		.02		1.62		.12			
2	16	18	15	19	12	14	90	65	722	739	855	11.21*
	.15		.92		.21		9.52†		.41			
3, 4	19	10	14	11	9	8	55	37	393	424	490	19.48***
	7.84†		.82		.18		8.40†		2.24			
Total N	117		128		91		433		4919		5688	
χ^2	9.44*		2.25		.42		28.67***		3.74			44.52***

Table 93. Person with Whom the Subject Lives Related to Delinquency for the Girls

Delinquency Rating	Neither Parent		Stepparent		Father		Mother		Both Parents		Total N	χ^2
	o	e	o	e	o	e	o	e	o	e		
0	74	77	88	86	57	57	242	282	3176	3135	3637	6.34
	.13		.05		.00		5.62†		.54			
1	13	11	11	12	8	8	48	41	444	452	524	1.97
	.33		.16		.00		1.35		.13			
2, 3, 4	27	26	28	29	19	19	126	94	1008	1041	1208	12.37*
	.08		.01		.00		11.22†		1.06			
Total N	114		127		84		416		4628		5369	
χ^2	.54		.22		.00		18.19***		1.73			20.68**

Table 94. Number of Siblings Related to Delinquency for the Boys

Delinquency Rating	No Siblings		4 or Fewer Siblings		More Than 4 Siblings		Total N	χ^2
	o	e	o	e	o	e		
0	247	236	2215	2216	1198	1208	3660	
		.49		.00		.08		.57
1	31	38	343	357	215	194	589	
		1.29		.52		2.18		3.99
2, 3, 4........	83	87	828	814	433	444	1344	
		.16		.25		.25		.66
Total N	361		3386		1846		5593	
χ^2	1.94		.77		2.51			5.22

Table 95. Intelligence (Measured by ACE Score or IQ) Related to Delinquency for the Boys

Delinquency Rating	Intelligence Percentile Score										Total N	χ^2
	1–15		16–39		40–68		69–90		91–100			
	o	e	o	e	o	e	o	e	o	e		
0	560	552	724	744	1066	1075	824	832	431	403	3605	
		1.07		.52		.07		.07		1.95		3.68
1	92	89	119	120	175	173	132	134	64	65	582	
		.88		.01		.01		.04		.02		.96
2, 3, 4........	191	202	292	271	399	392	313	303	120	147	1315	
		.55		1.58		.13		.31		4.96		7.53
Total N	843		1135		1640		1269		615		5502	
χ^2	2.50		2.11		.21		.42		6.93			12.17

Table 96. Intelligence (Measured by ACE Score or IQ) Related to Delinquency for the Girls

Delinquency Rating	Intelligence Percentile Score										Total N	χ^2
	1–15		16–39		40–68		69–90		91–100			
	o	e	o	e	o	e	o	e	o	e		
0	521	521	1073	1117	1450	1433	1211	1212	640	612	4895	
		.00		1.71		.19		.00		1.26		3.16
1	26	24	67	52	54	67	62	56	18	28	227	
		.15		4.46†		2.35		.60		3.81		11.37*
2, 3, 4	33	35	104	75	93	97	77	82	24	41	331	
		.14		10.76†		.16		.29		7.31†		18.66***
Total N	580		1244		1597		1350		682		5453	
χ^2	.29		16.93***		2.70		.89		12.38**			33.19***

Table 97. High School Rank Related to Delinquency for the Boys

Delinquency Rating	High School Rank in Percentile										Total N	χ^2
	1–19		20–39		40–69		70–89		90–100			
	o	e	o	e	o	e	o	e	o	e		
0	643	762	685	720	940	890	503	444	257	212	3028	
	18.53†		1.75		2.84		7.78†		9.65†			40.55***
1	128	113	124	107	121	132	52	66	24	31	449	
	1.99		2.77		.90		2.93		1.74			10.33*
2, 3, 4	337	233	239	221	233	272	91	136	27	65	927	
	46.20†		1.53		5.70†		14.89†		22.05†			90.37***
Total N	1108		1048		1294		646		308		4404	
χ^2	66.72***		6.05*		9.44**		25.60***		33.44***			141.25***

Table 98. High School Rank Related to Delinquency for the Girls

Delinquency Rating	High School Rank in Percentile										Total N	χ^2
	1–19		20–39		40–69		70–89		90–100			
	o	e	o	e	o	e	o	e	o	e		
0	577	616	659	670	1318	1326	1135	1106	597	567	4286	
	2.42		.18		.05		.74		1.53			4.92
1	40	25	35	27	52	54	37	45	9	23	173	
	9.32†		2.37		.04		1.33		8.44†			21.50***
2, 3, 4	49	26	31	28	65	55	25	46	8	24	178	
	21.39†		.37		1.78		9.52†		10.31†			43.37***
Total N	666		725		1435		1197		614		4637	
χ^2	33.13***		2.92		1.87		11.59**		20.28***			69.79***

Table 99. School Dropout Related to Delinquency for the Boys

Delinquency Rating	Grade of Dropout										Total N	χ^2
	9th		10th		11th		12th		Non-Dropout			
	o	e	o	e	o	e	o	e	o	e		
0	74	86	169	196	152	227	74	132	2900	2728	3369	
	1.73		3.69		24.95†		25.42†		10.90†			66.69***
1	15	14	29	32	57	37	29	22	42	446	551	
	.06		.28		10.54†		2.54		1.41			14.83**
2, 3, 4	43	32	102	72	139	84	99	48	855	1002	1238	
	4.03†		12.50†		36.89†		52.58†		21.65†			127.65***
Total N	132		300		348		202		4176		5158	
χ^2	5.82		16.47***		72.38***		80.54***		33.96***			209.17***

Table 100. School Dropout Related to Delinquency for the Girls

Delinquency Rating	Grade of Dropout										Total N	χ²
	9th		10th		11th		12th		Non-Dropout			
	o	e	o	e	o	e	o	e	o	e		
0	41	57	156	192	210	286	128	162	4041	3879	4576	45.37***
	4.64†		6.65†		20.10†		7.21†		6.77†			
1	4	3	21	9	25	14	8	8	162	186	220	28.18***
	.51		15.13†		9.32†		.00		3.22			
2, 3, 4	19	4	37	13	84	19	45	11	126	264	311	494.80***
	58.46†		44.31†		215.11†		105.09†		71.83†			
Total N	64		214		319		181		4329		5107	
χ²	63.61***		66.09***		244.53***		112.30***		81.82***			568.35***

Table 101. Conduct Rating Related to Delinquency for the Boys

Delinquency Rating	Conduct Rating								Total N	χ²
	3 and 4		2		1		Good Conduct			
	o	e	o	e	o	e	o	e		
0	81	229	222	388	562	643	2714	2318	3579	244.90***
	95.83†		71.22†		10.27†		67.58†			
1	37	37	116	62	157	103	264	372	574	105.60***
	.00		46.29†		28.05†		31.26†			
2, 3, 4	229	81	250	137	255	228	532	820	1266	446.47***
	269.72†		92.28†		3.32		101.15†			
Total N	347		588		974		3510		5419	
χ²	365.55***		209.79***		41.64***		199.99***			816.97***

Table 102. Conduct Rating Related to Delinquency for the Girls

Delinquency Rating	Conduct Rating								Total N	χ²
	2, 3, 4		1		5 [a]		Good Conduct			
	o	e	o	e	o	e	o	e		
0	138	232	454	511	81	169	4158	3920	4831	104.69***
	38.34†		6.25†		45.59†		14.51†			
1	40	11	71	24	6	8	111	185	228	197.82***
	76.45†		91.27†		.50		29.60†			
2, 3, 4	81	16	44	34	101	11	100	265	326	1080.81***
	271.60†		2.68		704.22†		102.31†			
Total N	259		569		188		4369		5385	
χ²	386.39***		100.20***		750.31***		146.42***			1383.32***

[a] The rating for illegitimate pregnancy.

Table 103. Adjustment Rating Related to Delinquency for the Boys

Delinquency Rating	Adjustment Rating								Total N	χ^2
	3 and 4		2		1		Good Adjustment			
	o	e	o	e	o	e	o	e		
0	203	385	470	622	991	978	1918	1596	3582	
	86.25†		37.32†		.17		64.79			188.53***
1	77	62	149	101	185	158	168	258	579	
	3.47		23.29†		4.58†		31.40†			62.74***
2, 3, 4	305	138	326	222	309	349	338	570	1278	
	204.05†		48.72†		4.56†		94.17†			351.50***
Total N	585		945		1485		2424		5439	
χ^2	293.77***		109.33***		9.31*		190.36***			602.77***

Table 104. Adjustment Rating Related to Delinquency for the Girls

Delinquency Rating	Adjustment Rating								Total N	χ^2
	3 and 4		2		1		Good Adjustment			
	o	e	o	e	o	e	o	e		
0	156	249	443	549	1093	1085	3150	2958	4842	
	34.80†		20.57†		.06		12.44†			67.87***
1	26	12	63	26	58	52	83	141	230	
	17.09†		52.17†		.82		23.53†			93.61***
2, 3, 4	96	17	107	38	60	74	68	202	331	
	367.12†		128.09†		2.72		89.07†			587.00***
Total N	278		613		1211		3301		5403	
χ^2	419.01***		200.83***		3.60		125.04***			748.48***

Table 105. Teacher Prediction Related to Delinquency for the Boys

Delinquency Rating	Predicted Delinquency		Predicted Emotional Problems		Both		No Prediction		Total N	χ^2
	o	e	o	e	o	e	o	e		
	RATINGS OF BEFORE-TEST AND CONTINUOUS DELINQUENTS									
0	204	299	339	339	118	209	3002	2816	3663	
	30.18†		.00		39.89†		12.33†			82.40***
1	55	48	38	55	41	34	457	454	591	
	.96		5.10†		1.53		.02			7.61*
2, 3, 4	198	110	141	124	161	77	845	1034	1345	
	70.85†		2.24		91.97†		34.51†			199.57***
Total N	457		518		320		4304		5599	
χ^2	101.99***		7.34*		133.39***		46.86***			289.58***
	RATINGS OF AFTER-TEST DELINQUENTS ONLY									
0	204	275	339	342	118	182	3002	2864	3663	
	18.56†		.02		22.51†		6.68†			47.77***
1	29	31	25	38	23	20	330	318	407	
	.08		4.44†		.39		.44			5.35
2, 3, 4	153	80	115	99	114	53	681	831	1063	
	66.88†		2.52		70.94†		27.11†			167.45***
Total N	386		479		255		4013		5133	
χ^2	85.52***		6.98*		93.84***		34.23***			220.57***

Table 106. Teacher Prediction Related to Delinquency for the Girls

Delinquency Rating	Predicted Delinquency		Predicted Emotional Problems		Both		No Prediction		Total N	χ^2
	o	e	o	e	o	e	o	e		
	RATINGS OF BEFORE-TEST AND CONTINUOUS DELINQUENTS									
0	79	109	420	443	88	138	4358	4254	4945	
	8.40†		1.25		18.12†		2.53			30.30***
1	21	5	28	21	15	6	168	200	232	
	49.57†		2.49		11.12†		5.00†			68.18***
2, 3, 4	22	8	47	31	51	10	222	294	342	
	27.28†		8.65†		181.29†		17.72†			234.94***
Total N	122		495		154		4748		5519	
χ^2	85.25***		12.39**		210.53***		25.25***			333.42***
	RATINGS OF AFTER-TEST DELINQUENTS ONLY									
0	79	93	420	438	88	118	4358	4297	4945	
	1.97		.72		7.41†		.86			10.96**
1	8	2	16	12	2	3	106	115	132	
	12.10†		1.58		.39		.66			14.73***
2, 3, 4	13	5	37	24	37	6	180	232	267	
	12.80†		7.61†		1.07		11.66†			33.14***
Total N	100		473		127		4644		5344	
χ^2	26.87***		9.91**		8.87*		13.18**			58.83***

Table 107. Teacher Prediction of Delinquency Compared with the Occurrence of
Delinquency at Levels 2, 3, and 4 among the Statewide Boys

Variable	Percentage of Predicted Group in Each Category	Teacher-Predicted Percentage Divided by Actual Percentage in Category (Index = 1.00)	Teacher-Predicted Rate Divided by Actual Delinquency Rate (Index = 1.00)	Accuracy of Teacher Prediction (in Percentage) [a]
Socioeconomic status				
Day laborer	11.5	1.46	1.04	45
Semiskilled and slightly skilled	47.2	1.13	1.03	47
Farmer	19.5	.88	1.18	30
Clerical	17.0	.83	.75	51
Professional and semi-professional	4.9	.64	.45	54
Intelligence (percentile rank)				
1–15	19.7	1.54	1.13	44
16–39	29.3	1.17	1.13	38
40–68	31.2	1.09	1.04	50
69–90	15.0	.68	.63	47
91–100	4.9	.43	.54	54
High school rank (percentile)				
1–19	53.3	2.12	1.48	46
20–39	29.5	1.23	1.13	39
40–69	13.8	.47	.55	28
70–100	3.4	.16	.26	29
Dropout	40.8	2.33	1.32	52
Broken family	10.7	1.67	1.07	54
Total sample	13.9			45

[a] The number of boys who were delinquent at levels 2, 3, and 4 in the teacher prediction group divided by the total number in the teacher prediction group.

Table 108. Teacher Prediction of Delinquency Compared with the Occurrence of
Delinquency at Levels 1, 2, 3, and 4 among the Statewide Girls

Variable	Percentage of Predicted Group in Each Category	Teacher-Predicted Percentage Divided by Actual Percentage in Category (Index = 1.00)	Teacher-Predicted Rate Divided by Actual Delinquency Rate (Index = 1.00)	Accuracy of Teacher Prediction (in Percentage) [a]
Socioeconomic status				
Day laborer	13.6	1.79	1.13	53
Semiskilled and slightly skilled	51.5	1.23	.92	38
Farmer	20.1	.89	1.32	26
Clerical	12.9	.63	.76	38
Professional and semi-professional	1.9	.25	.27	20
Intelligence (percentile rank)				
1–15	20.4	1.89	1.85	35
16–39	31.5	1.39	1.05	40
40–68	34.1	1.16	1.31	40
69–90	11.5	.47	.46	39
91–100	2.6	.21	.34	29
High school rank (percentile)				
1–19	39.9	2.75	1.60	44
20–39	27.5	1.76	1.45	21
40–69	23.2	.75	.70	16
70–100	9.4	.24	.41	15
Dropout	43.8	3.02	.95	51
Broken family	17.3	2.70	1.33	39
Total sample	5.0			38

[a] The number of girls who were delinquent at levels 1, 2, 3, and 4 in the teacher prediction group divided by the total number in the teacher prediction group.

Table 109. MMPI Prediction of Delinquency Compared with the Occurrence of
Delinquency at Levels 2, 3, and 4 among the Statewide Boys

Variable	Percentage of Predicted Group in Each Category	MMPI-Predicted Percentage Divided by Actual Percentage in Category (Index = 1.00)	MMPI-Predicted Rate Divided by Actual Delinquency Rate (Index = 1.00)	Accuracy of MMPI Prediction (in Percentage)[a]
Socioeconomic status				
Day laborer	8.2	1.04	.75	32
Semiskilled and slightly skilled	47.3	1.13	1.04	41
Farmer	12.6	.57	1.14	26
Clerical	24.4	1.19	1.06	37
Professional and semi-professional	7.4	.96	.93	35
Intelligence (percentile rank)				
1–15	9.0	.70	.60	46
16–39	19.4	.77	.88	32
40–68	35.9	1.26	1.20	39
69–90	24.6	1.11	1.03	37
91–100	11.0	.96	1.22	31
High school rank (percentile)				
1–19	24.7	.98	.69	45
20–39	25.8	1.08	1.00	36
40–69	31.9	1.09	1.27	25
70–100	17.6	.81	1.35	23
Dropout	20.0	1.14	.65	60
Broken family	9.8	1.53	.98	47
Total sample	13.9			37

[a] The number of boys who were delinquent at levels 2, 3, and 4 in the MMPI prediction group divided by the total number in the MMPI prediction group.

Table 110. MMPI Prediction of Delinquency Compared with the Occurrence of
Delinquency at Levels 1, 2, 3, and 4 among the Statewide Girls

Variable	Percentage of Predicted Group in Each Category	MMPI-Predicted Percentage Divided by Actual Percentage in Category (Index = 1.00)	MMPI-Predicted Rate Divided by Actual Delinquency Rate (Index = 1.00)	Accuracy of MMPI Prediction (in Percentage)[a]
Socioeconomic status				
Day laborer	9.1	1.20	.76	
Semiskilled and slightly skilled	46.4	1.11	.83	
Farmer	13.6	.60	1.23	
Clerical	26.0	1.27	1.53	
Professional and semi-professional	5.0	.65	1.25	
Intelligence (percentile rank)				
1–15	12.5	1.16	1.14	
16–39	26.1	1.15	.87	
40–68	30.5	1.03	1.17	
69–90	25.3	1.02	1.01	
91–100	10.1	.82	1.26	
High school rank (percentile)				
1–19	17.3	1.19	.79	
20–39	16.7	1.07	.88	
40–69	32.0	1.04	.97	
70–100	33.9	.87	1.47	
Dropout	30.2	2.08	.66	
Broken family	10.6	1.66	.82	
Total sample	4.5			26

[a] The number of girls who were delinquent at levels 1, 2, 3, and 4 in the MMPI prediction group divided by the total number in the MMPI prediction group.

Table 111. Means and Standard Deviations on Each MMPI Scale for the
Nondelinquent and Delinquent Minneapolis Boys (Valid Tests Only)[a]

High Scale	Nondelinquents (N = 1096)		Delinquents (N = 714)	
	Mean	S.D.	Mean	S.D.
L	3.7	2.00	3.6	1.98
F	5.6	3.47	6.4	13.50
K	13.6	4.72	13.6	4.73
1	51.4	8.46	51.7	8.50
2	52.0	9.20	51.4	9.06
3	51.6	8.03	51.7	7.82
4	57.7	10.29	61.9	10.56***
5	52.7	8.96	50.7	8.24***
6	52.1	8.83	53.4	9.15
7	56.0	9.72	56.4	9.94
8	58.4	10.65	60.6	10.90***
9	56.5	10.63	59.2	11.22***
0	52.8	8.26	51.9	7.86

[a] The asterisks indicate significance at .001.

TABLES 112–115. RELATIONSHIPS BETWEEN ADOLESCENT PERSONALITY AND DELINQUENCY

The values in this series of chi-square tables were derived as for Tables 34–74 and 86–106. Asterisks, marking the χ^2 values large enough to support reliably the hypothesis that the observed data differ from margin expectations, have the conventional meaning: * indicates significance at .05, ** at .01, *** at .001. A dagger (†) indicates that the observed number of cases in the cell (o) probably differs significantly from the expected value (e). After computing the tables the numbers in the e columns were rounded to the nearest whole number to facilitate reading; the precision lost is negligible.

Table 112. High-Point Scale Related to Delinquency for the Boys

High Scale	Delinquency Rating								Total N	χ^2
	3 and 4		2		1		0			
	o	e	o	e	o	e	o	e		
1	6	6	9	10	12	7	41	45	68	
		.01		.16		3.20		.31		3.68
2	11	13	19	24	14	17	114	104	158	
		.43		1.04		.41		.98		2.86
3	3	9	13	15	9	10	75	66	100	
		3.56		.32		.21		1.29		5.38
4	110	66	144	118	89	82	431	509	774	
		29.87†		5.83†		.69		11.98†		48.37***
5	8	16	17	29	22	20	144	126	191	
		4.15†		5.03†		.18		2.70		12.06**
6	12	19	37	34	24	24	151	147	224	
		2.58		.25		.01		.09		2.93
7	17	26	50	46	24	32	211	199	302	
		2.89		.37		1.91		.77		5.94
8	61	67	128	121	89	84	517	523	795	
		.63		.40		.34		.07		1.44
9	86	77	136	138	103	96	585	599	910	
		1.01		.04		.54		.30		1.89
0	11	27	36	48	19	33	251	208	317	
		9.40†		3.09		6.21†		8.66†		27.36***
NHP	8	7	8	13	8	9	61	56	85	
		.09		1.86		.09		.47		2.51
Total N	333		597		413		2581		3924	
χ^2	54.62***		18.39*		13.79		27.62**			114.42***

Table 113. High-Point Scale Related to Delinquency for the Girls

High Scale	2, 3, 4		1		0		Total N	χ²
	o	e	o	e	o	e		
1	0	1	0	1	12	11	12	1.33
	.70		.50		.13			
2	1	4	0	2	57	52	58	4.65
	1.79		2.40		.46			
3	4	9	7	6	144	139	155	3.22
	3.02		.04		.16			
4	90	52	48	37	742	791	880	33.35***
	26.79†		3.55		3.01			
5	22	33	19	23	511	496	552	4.82
	3.67		.70		.45			
6	22	23	11	16	349	343	382	1.63
	.03		1.51		.09			
7	9	12	10	8	173	173	192	1.04
	.54		.50		.00			
8	23	24	18	17	369	369	410	.14
	.09		.05		.00			
9	55	46	37	32	681	695	773	2.67
	1.68		.72		.27			
0	14	32	17	22	507	483	538	12.65**
	10.21†		1.30		1.14			
NHP	1	5	1	4	82	75	84	5.55
	3.20		1.79		.56			
Total N	241		168		3627		4036	
χ²	51.72***		13.06		6.27			71.05***

Table 114. Low-Point Scale Related to Delinquency for the Boys

Low Scale	3 and 4		2		1		0		Total N	χ²
	o	e	o	e	o	e	o	e		
1	35	35	73	64	25	37	280	277	413	5.45
	.00		1.24		4.17		.04			
2	51	48	97	88	57	52	362	380	567	2.55
	.21		.92		.59		.83			
3	20	19	32	35	23	21	154	153	229	.61
	.03		.35		.23		.00			
4	1	8	9	14	10	8	71	61	91	9.70*
	5.83†		1.84		.35		1.68			
5	68	55	122	102	48	60	421	441	659	9.88*
	2.82		3.79		2.33		.94			
6	16	20	35	37	19	22	170	161	240	1.90
	.87		.13		.36		.54			
7	7	5	6	9	10	5	34	38	57	6.79
	1.01		.89		4.43		.46			
8	0	2	5	4	3	2	18	17	26	2.62
	2.20		.25		.15		.02			
9	17	29	32	53	25	31	269	230	343	21.27***
	4.90†		8.45†		1.20		6.72†			
0	28	27	47	50	36	29	209	214	320	1.96
	.04		.15		1.64		.13			
NLP	105	100	183	184	119	108	778	794	1185	1.80
	.27		.01		1.21		.31			
Total N	348		641		375		2766		4130	
χ²	18.18		18.02		16.66		11.67			64.53***

Table 115. Low-Point Scale Related to Delinquency for the Girls

Low Scale	Delinquency Rating 2, 3, 4 o	e	1 o	e	0 o	e	Total N	χ²
1	35	30	26	19	521	533	582	
	1.03		2.41		.28			3.72
2	39	37	28	24	664	670	731	
	.10		.63		.05			.78
3	9	13	6	9	251	244	266	
	1.50		.89		.22			2.61
4	2	4	2	3	75	72	79	
	1.00		.14		.09			1.23
5	29	30	13	19	541	534	583	
	.01		2.06		.09			2.16
6	12	11	10	7	194	198	216	
	.09		1.18		.08			1.35
7	0	2	3	2	45	44	48	
	2.40		1.23		.02			3.65
8	1	1	0	0	10	10	11	
	.27		.40		.00			.67
9	10	24	9	16	465	444	484	
	8.58†		3.06		1.04			12.68**
0	14	13	9	8	228	230	251	
	.13		.06		.02			.21
NLP	61	47	32	31	835	850	928	
	4.10†		.06		.28			4.44
Total N	212		138		3829		4179	
χ²	19.21*		12.12		2.17			33.50*

Table 116. Frequency of Delinquency (Levels 1, 2, 3, and 4) and Dropouts
in Each Two-High-Point Code Class[a]

Code Class	Boys Percentage of Delinquents T < 70	T ≥ 70[b]	Total	Percentage of Dropouts	Girls Percentage of Delinquents	Percentage of Dropouts
		INVALID PROFILES				
L ≥ 10		23		20	5	18
F = 16–21		41		32	28	32
F ≥ 22		45		48	21	29
? ≥ 40		37		16	13	13
		VALID PROFILES				
Indet.[c]	30	41	34	10	8	13
No high point	28	0	28	14	2	7
1–	67	0	67†	33†	0†	0†
12	43	33	40†	10†	0†	50†
13	30	69	44	11	9†	9†
14	36	41	39	21	20†	20†
15	0	0	0†	0†	25†	50†
16	0	33	20†	20†	0†	0†
17	25	18	21†	5†	0†	0†
18	36	40	39	11	20†	30†
19	10	60	27†	20†	0†	100†
10	38	33	35†	29†	0†	0†
Total 1	32	42	37	16	12	26

[a] An asterisk (*) indicates that the two-point code is among the fifteen most common for each sex; italics set off the corresponding percentages. A dagger (†) is used to indicate that there are fewer than eleven in the total two-point code class.

[b] The height of the first point only in each code class was considered.

[c] Included in the "indeterminate" class are all codes with underscoring on the first three or more high points. If underscoring occurred on the first two high points only, one-half a tally was assigned to the first high point and one-half a tally to the second high point.

TABLE 116 175

Table 116 — continued

Code Class	Boys			Percentage of Dropouts	Girls	
	Percentage of Delinquents				Percentage of Delinquents	Percentage of Dropouts
	T < 70	T ≧ 70	Total			
2–	21	0	21	36	0†	20†
21	20	33	25†	6†	0†	0†
23	25	14	21†	16†	0†	21†
24	44	32	39	25	0	12
25	8	33	21	8	0†	33†
26	36	20	31†	0†	0†	9†
27	40	33	35	18	0†	8†
28	47	15	25	14	11†	33†
29	37	0	23	7	0†	25†
20	29	18	24	24	2	21
Total 2	33	23	28	19	2	19
3–	40	0	40	13	7	0
31	30	33	31	4	9	12
32	24	0	20†	10†	5	5
34	23	0	22	9	8	18
35	33	0	33†	11†	0	13
36	23	100	26	4	7	12
37	13	33	17	0	13	13
38	20	100	24†	10†	7	11
39	28	0	26	5	13	20
30	25	0	25†	0†	0†	0†
Total 3	26	26	26	7	7	13
4–	35	67	37	16	7	9
41	28	22	25	36	25	33
42	32	46	39	17	7	17
43*	28	40	31	14	10	15
45*	46	52	48	11	13	15
46*	43	60	51	20	22	26
47*	29	43	36	17	10	13
48*	43	55	50	21	17	21
49*	50	60	54	25	20	18
40	52	14	44	17	14	19
Total 4	40	51	45	20	15	18
5–	10	0	10	10	9	9
51	0	0	0†	0†	9†	0†
52	15	33	23	9	4	18
53	5	44	17	10	4	12
54*	24	39	28	11	6	16
56	24	21	23	10	9	13
57	43	31	40	7	4	11
58	22	27	24	5	9	17
59*	44	28	39	9	9	11
50	26	9	22	9	9	11
Total 5	24	28	26	9	8	12
6–	53	0	50	10	4	4
61	0	0	0†	0†	0†	0†
62	10	50	21†	14†	5†	10†
63	13	29	16	0	2	12
64	31	44	38	22	11	17
65	39	53	44	6	4	19
67	13	33	23	23	11	6
68	26	24	24	15	10	17
69	42	47	44	20	5	10
60	18	11	16	20	5	5
Total 6	29	34	31	16	8	12

Table 116 — continued

Code Class	Boys				Girls	
	Percentage of Delinquents			Percentage of Dropouts	Percentage of Delinquents	Percentage of Dropouts
	T < 70	T ≧ 70	Total			
7–	20	0	20†	0†	13	13
71	50	50	50†	20†	0†	0†
72	14	17	15	8	0	0
73	35	0	23	7	8	8
74	34	48	41	21	12	7
75	24	50	30	0	11	11
76	36	24	31	10	9	5
78*	45	21	28	18	9	14
79	22	31	26	13	11	5
70	26	33	29	10	6	5
Total 7	31	27	29	14	9	9
8–	8	0	8	17	9	0
81	42	52	49	19	25†	30†
82	58	29	34	34	6†	17†
83	23	50	31	14	14	11
84*	33	38	36	26	11	13
85	11	24	17	15	7	13
86*	28	42	38	26	8	20
87*	35	34	35	19	12	14
89*	36	38	37	20	10	25
80	18	30	23	20	6	19
Total 8	30	37	35	22	10	17
9–*	41	33	40	11	6	10
91	33	22	30	9	9†	9†
92	46	11	36	15	8†	15†
93	33	44	35	7	2	4
94*	41	48	45	17	17	17
95*	21	34	28	10	13	16
96*	29	42	37	12	16	18
97*	27	35	32	8	7	11
98*	31	34	33	12	12	15
90	22	44	28	18	6	17
Total 9	34	39	36	13	12	15
0–	33	33	33	18	3	5
01	9	0	8†	8†	15†	15†
02	8	17	10	1	7	11
03	16	0	15†	8†	0	11
04	22	50	25	12	5	10
05*	12	0	11	5	9	9
06	20	55	26	14	7	15
07*	25	30	27	13	7	6
08	22	18	21	13	4	11
09	17	25	18	13	4	43
Total 0	21	27	22	11	6	9
Total valid sample ...	31	38	34	15	10	14

Table 117. Sample Distribution of Scores on the De Scale and the Distribution
of Scores of the Delinquents[a]

De Score	Number of Sample	Accumulative Number of Sample		Number at Delinquency Levels 2, 3, 4	Accumulative Number of Delinquents	
		Low to High Score	High to Low Score		Low to High Score	High to Low Score
28 0		224	0	0	52	0
26 1		224	1	1	52	1
24 1		223	2	1	51	2
22 5		222	7	1	50	3
20 6		217	13	2	49	5
18 21		211	34	5	47	10
16 16		190	50	4	42	14
14 35		174	85	14	38	28
12 34		139	119	6	24	34
10 39		105	158	10	18	44
8 41		66	199	5	8	49
6 11		25	210	1	3	50
4 14		14	224	2	2	52
2 0		0	224	0	0	52

[a] Mean = 12.4; S.D. = 4.47; T score 70 = raw score 21.

Table 118. Time of Dropout Related to the Variables for the Boys

Variable	Grade of Dropout						
	9 and 10		11 and 12		All Dropouts		
	No.	Percentage of Category	No.	Percentage of Category	No.	Percentage of Category	Percentage of Total Dropouts
Community size							
Duluth and suburbs 81		5	177	12	258	17	26
Towns 172		8	226	10	398	18	40
Farm 196		13	150	10	346	24	34
Total dropout 449			553		1002		100
Socioeconomic status							
Day laborer 77		19	79	19	156	38	17
Semiskilled and slightly skilled 149		7	237	11	386	19	41
Farmer 132		12	110	10	242	21	26
Clerical 49		5	88	8	137	13	14
Professional and semi-professional 7		2	8	3	15	5	2
Total dropout 414			522		936		100
Parents' marital status							
Separated or divorced 53		17	51	16	104	34	10
Not separated or divorced .396		8	502	10	898	18	90
Total dropout 449			553		1002		100
Intelligence (percentile rank)							
1–39 251		14	280	15	531	29	57
40–68 125		8	180	11	305	19	33
69–100 21		2	74	4	95	6	10
Total dropout 397			534		931		100

Table 119. Time of Dropout Related to the Variables for the Girls

| | | Grade of Dropout | | | | |
| | | 9 and 10 | | 11 and 12 | | All Dropouts | |
Variable	No.	Percent-age of Category	No.	Percent-age of Category	No.	Percent-age of Category	Percentage of Total Dropouts
Community size							
Duluth and suburbs	75	5	164	11	239	16	29
Towns	146	6	220	10	366	16	45
Farm	81	6	129	9	210	15	26
Total dropout	302		513		815		100
Socioeconomic status							
Day laborer	54	14	66	18	120	32	16
Semiskilled and slightly							
skilled	128	6	240	12	368	18	49
Farmer	45	4	83	7	128	11	17
Clerical	37	4	78	8	115	12	15
Professional and semi-							
professional	8	2	12	3	20	5	3
Total dropout	272		479		751		100
Parents' marital status							
Separated or divorced	38	12	69	23	107	35	13
Not separated or divorced	264	5	444	9	708	15	87
Total dropout	302		513		815		100
Intelligence (percentile rank)							
1–39	148	9	217	12	365	21	47
40–68	100	7	181	12	281	19	36
69–100	32	2	97	5	129	7	17
Total dropout	280		495		775		100

TABLES 120–133. RELATIONSHIPS BETWEEN ENVIRONMENTAL, BEHAVIORAL, AND PERSONALITY VARIABLES AND SCHOOL DROPOUT

The values in this series of chi-square tables (except for Table 129, which provides data in a different form) were derived as for Tables 34–74, 86–106, and 112–115. Asterisks, marking the χ^2 values large enough to support reliably the hypothesis that the observed data differ from margin expectations, have the conventional meaning: * indicates significance at .05, ** at .01, *** at .001. A dagger (†) indicates that the observed number of cases in the cell (o) probably differs significantly from the expected value (e). After computing the tables the numbers in the e column were rounded to the nearest whole number to facilitate reading; the precision lost is negligible.

Table 120. High-Point Scale and Reason for School Dropout for the Boys

High Scale	Failing or Lack of Interest		Work or Military Service		Total N	χ^2
	o	e	o	e		
1	7	5	3	5	10	
		.47		.56		1.03
2	15	13	9	11	24	
		.28		.33		.61
3	2	2	1	1	3	
		.10		.11		.21
4	53	57	51	47	104	
		.25		.31		.56
5	3	6	8	5	11	
		1.50		1.80		3.30
6	11	11	10	10	21	
		.00		.00		.00
7	10	16	19	13	29	
		2.13		2.55		4.68
8	68	64	49	53	117	
		.26		.32		.58
9	41	39	31	33	72	
		.07		.09		.16
0	19	17	12	14	31	
		.26		.31		.57
NHP	5	4	3	4	8	
		.08		.10		.18
Total N	234		196		430	
χ^2	5.40		6.48			11.88

Table 121. Community Size Related to School Dropout for the Boys

Grade of Dropout	Duluth and Suburbs		Towns		Farm		Total N	χ^2
	o	e	o	e	o	e		
9th	17	41	58	60	66	40	141	
		14.15†		.06		16.99†		31.20***
10th	64	90	114	131	130	87	308	
		7.42†		2.19		20.93†		30.54***
11th	100	102	148	149	103	99	351	
		.05		.01		.13		.19
12th	77	59	78	86	47	57	202	
		5.56†		.72		1.83		8.11*
Non-dropout	1256	1222	1809	1781	1125	1187	4190	
		.96		.44		3.25		4.65
Total N	1514		2207		1471		5192	
χ^2	28.14***		3.42		43.13***			74.69***

Table 122. Community Size Related to School Dropout for the Girls

Grade of Dropout	Duluth and Suburbs o	e	Towns o	e	Farm o	e	Total N	χ²
9th	16	22	39	33	21	21	76	
		1.59		1.13		.00		2.72
10th	59	65	107	98	60	63	226	
		.59		.85		.13		1.57
11th	106	95	138	143	85	92	329	
		1.32		.15		.48		1.95
12th	58	53	82	80	44	51	184	
		.47		.07		1.01		1.55
Non-dropout	1248	1252	1869	1882	1226	1209	4343	
		.01		.09		.24		.34
Total N	1487		2235		1436		5158	
χ²	3.98		2.29		1.86			8.13

Table 123. Socioeconomic Status Related to School Dropout for the Boys

Grade of Dropout	Professional and Semi-professional o	e	Clerical o	e	Farmer o	e	Semiskilled and Slightly Skilled o	e	Day Laborer o	e	Total N	χ²
9th	1	7	7	26	42	29	50	54	27	10	127	
		5.34†		14.26†		5.40†		.23		26.50†		51.73***
10th	6	16	42	60	90	66	99	121	50	24	287	
		6.51†		5.25†		8.30†		4.00†		29.53†		53.59***
11th	5	19	49	68	70	76	159	138	45	27	328	
		10.04†		5.41†		.47		3.13		12.00†		31.05***
12th	3	11	39	40	40	45	78	82	34	16	194	
		5.82†		.04		.53		.18		20.60†		27.17***
Non-dropout	266	228	890	832	902	927	1696	1688	250	329	4004	
		6.41†		3.99†		.68		.04		19.01†		30.13***
Total N	281		1027		1144		2082		406		4940	
χ²	34.12***		28.95***		15.38**		7.58		107.64***			193.67***

Table 124. Socioeconomic Status Related to School Dropout for the Girls

Grade of Dropout	Professional and Semi-professional o	e	Clerical o	e	Farmer o	e	Semiskilled and Slightly Skilled o	e	Day Laborer o	e	Total N	χ²
9th and 10th	8	20	37	55	45	63	128	114	54	20	272	
		7.20†		5.67†		4.90†		1.62		55.34†		74.73***
11th and 12th	12	35	78	96	83	110	240	201	66	36	479	
		15.29†		3.44		6.71†		7.40†		25.00†		57.84***
Non-dropout	346	311	885	849	1017	972	1726	1778	254	318	4228	
		3.99†		1.51		2.06		1.53		12.74†		21.83***
Total N	366		1000		1145		2094		374		4979	
χ²	26.48***		10.62**		13.67**		10.55**		93.08***			154.40***

Table 125. Parents' Marital Status Related to School Dropout for the Boys

Grade of Dropout	Separated or Divorced		Not Separated or Divorced		Total N	χ^2
	o	e	o	e		
9th	17	8	124	133	141	
	8.80†		.56			9.36**
10th	36	18	272	290	308	
	16.83†		1.07			17.90***
11th	34	21	317	330	351	
	8.05†		.51			8.56**
12th	17	12	185	190	202	
	2.00		.13			2.13
Non-dropout	206	250	3982	3938	4188	
	7.78†		.49			8.27**
Total N	310		4880		5190	
χ^2	43.46***		2.76			46.22***

Table 126. Parents' Marital Status Related to School Dropout for the Girls

Grade of Dropout	Separated or Divorced		Not Separated or Divorced		Total N	χ^2
	o	e	o	e		
9th	10	5	66	71	76	
	6.72†		.42			7.14**
10th	28	13	198	213	226	
	16.25†		1.02			17.27***
11th	43	19	286	310	329	
	28.71†		1.80			30.51***
12th	26	11	158	173	184	
	21.39†		1.33			22.72***
Non-dropout	197	256	4146	4087	4343	
	13.60†		.85			14.45***
Total N	304		4854		5158	
χ^2	86.67***		5.42			92.09***

Table 127. Intelligence (Measured by ACE Score or IQ) Related to School Dropout for the Boys

Grade of Dropout	Intelligence Percentile Score						Total N	χ^2
	1–39		40–68		69–100			
	o	e	o	e	o	e		
9th	87	45	32	39	5	41	124	
	40.03†		1.13		31.22†			72.38***
10th	164	98	93	85	16	89	273	
	43.56†		.73		60.26†			104.55***
11th	180	121	110	104	45	110	335	
	28.89†		.30		38.16†			67.35***
12th	100	72	70	62	29	65	199	
	11.08†		1.03		20.10†			32.21***
Non-dropout	1313	1508	1287	1302	1579	1369	4179	
	25.22†		.17		32.21†			57.60***
Total N	1844		1592		1674		5110	
χ^2	148.78***		3.36		181.95***			334.09***

Table 128. Intelligence (Measured by ACE Score or IQ) Related to School Dropout for the Girls

Grade of Dropout	Intelligence Percentile Score						Total N	χ^2
	1–39		40–68		69–100			
	o	e	o	e	o	e		
9th	41	23	18	20	10	26	69	
	13.45†		.18		9.76†			23.39***
10th	107	71	82	61	22	79	211	
	18.13†		7.39†		41.22†			66.74***
11th	132	105	119	90	62	118	313	
	6.66†		9.20†		26.29†			42.15***
12th	85	61	62	52	35	68	182	
	9.16†		1.76		16.16†			27.08***
Non-dropout	1357	1461	1191	1249	1787	1625	4335	
	7.38†		2.67		16.07†			26.12***
Total N	1722		1472		1916		5110	
χ^2	54.78***		21.20***		109.50***			185.48***

Table 129. Dropout Related to Teacher Prediction

| Teacher Prediction | Boys | | | Girls | | |
	Number Predicted	Number of Dropouts	Per-centage	Number Predicted	Number of Dropouts	Per-centage
Delinquency	409	179	44	101	45	45
Emotional troubles	468	128	27	444	108	24
Delinquency and emotional troubles	289	145	50	136	78	57
Total delinquency	698	324	46	237	123	52

Table 130. High-Point Scale Related to Time of School Dropout for the Boys

High Scale	Accumulative Dropouts										Total N	χ^2
	Before 10th Grade		Before 11th Grade		Before 12th Grade		Before Graduation		Non-Dropout			
	o	e	o	e	o	e	o	e	o	e		
1	1	2	7	5	11	9	12	11	53	54	65	
	.23		1.13		.44		.03		.00			.03
2	7	4	16	10	28	20	32	26	113	119	145	
	3.50		2.88		3.20		1.66		.35			2.01
3	0	2	2	7	4	12	7	16	82	73	89	
	2.20		3.12		5.60†		4.82†		1.03			5.85*
4	22	17	69	51	122	97	157	124	547	580	704	
	1.40		6.19†		6.39†		8.90†		1.90			10.80***
5	3	4	8	13	15	24	16	30	157	143	173	
	.34		1.68		3.31		6.82†		1.45			8.27**
6	11	5	18	15	29	29	35	37	175	173	210	
	6.83†		.48		.00		.10		.02			.12
7	7	7	17	21	35	39	42	50	242	234	284	
	.00		.63		.45		1.28		.27			1.55
8	20	18	70	54	138	103	177	131	567	613	744	
	.22		4.67†		12.21†		16.24†		3.47			19.71***
9	12	20	40	61	80	116	112	148	731	695	843	
	3.46		7.40†		11.33†		8.89†		1.90			10.79***
0	4	7	13	21	30	41	37	52	259	244	296	
	1.42		3.36		2.86		4.38†		.93			5.31*
NHP	1	2	4	6	9	11	12	14	68	66	80	
	.43		.56		.36		.31		.07			.38
Total N	88		264		501		639		2994		3633	
χ^2	20.03		32.10		46.15		53.43***		11.39			64.82***

Table 131. High-Point Scale Related to Time of School Dropout for the Girls

High Scale	Before 10th Grade o	e	Before 11th Grade o	e	Before 12th Grade o	e	Before Graduation o	e	Non-Dropout o	e	Total N	χ²
Accumulative Dropouts												
1	0	0	2	1	5	2	6	2	8	12	14	
		.20		1.80		6.41		6.56		1.22		7.78
2	0	1	7	3	11	6	13	8	40	45	53	
		.80		5.80		3.31		2.81		.51		3.32
3	4	2	10	8	14	18	21	23	127	125	148	
		1.72		.40		.81		.16		.00		.16
4	12	12	60	46	139	100	168	128	659	699	827	
		.00		4.26†		15.59†		12.57†		2.30		14.87***
5	9	7	30	30	52	64	70	82	460	448	530	
		.30		.01		2.18		1.76		.32		2.08
6	5	5	12	20	36	42	43	54	309	298	352	
		.00		2.95		.97		2.39		.44		2.83
7	2	3	7	10	16	22	18	28	165	155	183	
		.14		1.00		1.64		3.75		.69		4.44*
8	8	5	26	21	53	45	77	59	301	319	378	
		1.25		1.19		1.24		5.85†		1.07		6.92**
9	8	10	35	40	91	87	117	112	607	612	724	
		.51		.67		.17		.22		.04		.26
0	6	7	19	28	36	61	48	78	457	427	505	
		.20		2.89		10.12†		11.60†		2.12		13.72***
NHP	0	1	3	5	4	10	6	13	76	69	82	
		1.20		.56		3.52		3.53		.65		4.18*
Total N	54		211		457		587		3209		3796	
χ²	6.32		21.53		45.96		51.20**		9.36			60.56***

Table 132. Low-Point Scale Related to Time of School Dropout for the Boys

Low Scale	Before 10th Grade o	e	Before 11th Grade o	e	Before 12th Grade o	e	Before Graduation o	e	Non-Dropout o	e	Total N	χ²
Accumulative Dropouts												
1	11	8	32	28	49	51	66	66	314	314	380	
		.80		.60		.09		.00		.00		.00
2	8	12	21	39	46	72	65	92	470	443	535	
		1.28		8.52†		9.45†		8.07†		1.68		9.75**
3	7	5	18	16	28	30	39	38	181	182	220	
		.90		.20		.09		.03		.01		.04
4	1	2	4	6	4	12	6	15	80	71	86	
		.43		.84		4.98†		5.23†		1.09		6.32*
5	16	14	66	46	121	84	145	108	480	517	625	
		.35		8.80†		16.08†		12.76†		2.66		15.42***
6	1	5	8	16	27	30	38	39	186	185	224	
		3.20		4.30†		.34		.01		.00		.01
7	0	1	4	4	4	8	5	10	51	46	56	
		1.20		.00		1.63		2.28		.48		2.76
8	1	1	1	2	2	3	2	5	24	22	26	
		.27		.43		.64		1.39		.29		1.68
9	3	7	18	24	35	43	40	56	283	267	323	
		2.45		1.37		1.66		4.25†		.92		5.17*
0	4	6	7	21	15	39	25	50	264	239	289	
		.90		9.51†		14.68†		12.43†		2.59		15.02***
NLP	34	25	106	82	192	151	239	193	879	925	1118	
		3.41		6.96†		11.38†		10.96†		2.29		13.25***
Total N	86		285		523		670		3212		3882	
χ²	15.19		41.53		61.02		57.41***		12.01			69.42***

Table 133. Low-Point Scale Related to Time of School Dropout for the Girls

Low Scale	Before 10th Grade o	e	Before 11th Grade o	e	Before 12th Grade o	e	Before Graduation o	e	Non-Dropout o	e	Total N	χ^2
1	5	8	30	32	67	69	86	88	478	476	564	
	1.19		.08		.05		.06		.01			.07
2	6	10	23	38	69	84	94	108	593	579	687	
	1.54		6.24†		2.65		1.72		.32			2.04
3	5	4	19	14	42	30	49	39	199	209	248	
	.54		1.87		4.52		2.68		.50			3.18
4	0	1	1	4	2	9	3	11	67	59	70	
	1.10		2.16		4.97†		5.82†		1.08			6.90**
5	5	8	27	31	60	68	77	87	480	470	557	
	1.13		.57		.94		1.19		.22			1.41
6	4	3	13	12	26	25	31	33	178	176	209	
	.33		.14		.01		.22		.04			.26
7	1	1	3	3	5	6	6	7	40	39	46	
	.13		.06		.06		.20		.04			.24
8	1	0	2	1	3	1	3	2	9	10	12	
	3.20		2.41		1.50		.64		.12			.76
9	4	7	19	26	38	56	50	72	407	385	457	
	1.02		1.70		5.68†		6.52†		1.21			7.73**
0	1	3	7	13	23	28	33	36	199	196	232	
	1.60		2.77		.99		.30		.06			.36
NLP	24	13	78	49	149	108	189	138	694	745	883	
	10.05†		16.56†		15.75†		18.59†		3.45			22.04***
Total N	57		222		484		621		3344		3965	
χ^2	21.83		34.56		37.12		37.94***		7.05			44.99**

References and Index

REFERENCES

1. Ball, J. C. *Social Deviancy and Adolescent Personality*. Lexington: University of Kentucky Press, 1962.
2. Berkowitz, B. "The Juvenile Aid Bureau of the New York City Police," *Nervous Child*, 11:42–47 (1955).
3. Bruce, A. A., A. J. Harno, E. W. Burgess, and J. Landesco. *Parole and the Indeterminate Sentence*. Springfield, Ill.: Illinois State Board of Parole, 1928.
4. Capwell, Dora F. "Personality Patterns of Adolescent Girls. II. Delinquents and Non-Delinquents," *Journal of Applied Psychology*, 29:289–97 (1945).
5. Community Health and Welfare Council of Hennepin County, Research Department. *Juvenile Delinquency in the Greater Minneapolis Area: A Statistical Report of Juvenile Delinquency during 1960 in Minneapolis and Its Suburbs*.
6. Dahlstrom, W. G., and G. S. Welsh. *An MMPI Handbook: A Guide to Use in Clinical Practice and Research*. Minneapolis: University of Minnesota Press, 1960.
7. Drake, L. E., and E. R. Oetting. *An MMPI Codebook for Counselors*. Minneapolis: University of Minnesota Press, 1959.
8. Edwards, A. L. *The Social Desirability Variable in Personality Assessment and Research*. New York: Dryden, 1957.
9. Glueck, S., and Eleanor T. Glueck. *One Thousand Juvenile Delinquents*. Cambridge, Mass.: Harvard University Press, 1934.
10. Glueck, S., and Eleanor T. Glueck. *Juvenile Delinquents Grown Up*. New York: Commonwealth Fund, 1940.
11. Glueck, S., and Eleanor T. Glueck. *Unraveling Juvenile Delinquency*. New York: Commonwealth Fund, 1950.
12. Gottesman, I. I. "The Psychogenetics of Personality." Unpublished Ph.D. thesis, University of Minnesota, 1960. Summarized in part in "Differential Inheritance of the Psychoneuroses," *Eugenics Quarterly*, 9:223–27 (1962).
13. Gough, H. G., and D. Peterson. "The Identification and Measurement of Predispositional Factors in Crime and Delinquency," *Journal of Consulting Psychology*, 16:207–12 (1952).
14. Hathaway, S. R., and P. E. Meehl. *An Atlas for the Clinical Use of the MMPI*. Minneapolis: University of Minnesota Press, 1951.
15. Hathaway, S. R., and E. D. Monachesi. *Analyzing and Predicting Juvenile Delinquency with the MMPI*. Minneapolis: University of Minnesota Press, 1953.
16. Hathaway, S. R., and E. D. Monachesi. "The Personalities of Predelinquent Boys," *Journal of Criminal Law, Criminology, and Political Science*, 48:149–63 (1957).
17. Hathaway, S. R., and E. D. Monachesi. *An Atlas of Juvenile MMPI Profiles*. Minneapolis: University of Minnesota Press, 1961.
18. Held, Virginia P. "What Can We Do about 'J.D.'?" *Reporter*, 21:12–18 (August 20, 1959).
19. Kvaraceus, W. C. *K D Proneness Scale and Check List*. Yonkers-on-Hudson, N.Y.: World Book Company, 1953.
20. Kvaraceus, W. C. *The Community and the Delinquent*. Yonkers-on-Hudson, N.Y.: World Book Company, 1954.
21. Lane, Ellen A., and G. W. Albee. "Childhood and Intercurrent Intellectual Performance of Adult Schizophrenics." Paper read at the annual meeting of the American Psychological Association,

St. Louis, August 30, 1962. Published under same title by G. W. Albee, Ellen A. Lane, Clare Corcoran, and Ann Werneke in *Journal of Consulting Psychology*, 27:364–66 (1963).

22. Laune, F. F. *Predicting Criminality*. Studies in Social Science, No. 1. Chicago: Northwestern University, 1936.
23. Meehl, P. E., and S. R. Hathaway. "The K Factor as a Suppressor Variable in the MMPI," *Journal of Applied Psychology*, 30:525–64 (1946).
24. *Minnesota Scale for Parental Occupations*. Minneapolis: Institute of Child Welfare.
25. Monachesi, E. D. *Prediction Factors in Probation*. Hanover, N.H.: Sociological Press, 1932.
26. Powers, E., and Helen Witmer. *An Experiment in the Prevention of Delinquency*. New York: Columbia University Press, 1951.
27. Sanders, B. S. "Testing Parole Prediction," *Proceedings of the Sixty-Fifth Annual Congress of the American Prison Association*. 1935. Pp. 222–33.
28. Sarbin, T. R., and D. S. Jones. "Intra-Personal Factors in Delinquency: A Preliminary Report," *Nervous Child*, 11:23–27 (1955).
29. United Community Fund of San Francisco, Social Planning Department. *Juvenile Delinquency: An Analysis of Theory and Research towards a Program of Action*. January 1961. P. 29.
30. Vincent, C. E. *Unmarried Mothers*. New York: Free Press of Glencoe, 1961.
31. Vold, G. B. *Prediction Methods and Parole*. Hanover, N.H.: Sociological Press, 1931.
32. Weeks, A. H. "Predicting Juvenile Delinquency," *American Sociological Review*, 8:40–46 (1943).
33. Welsh, G. S., and W. G. Dahlstrom. *Basic Readings on the MMPI in Psychology and Medicine*. Minneapolis: University of Minnesota Press, 1956.
34. Wirt, R. D., and P. F. Briggs. "Personality and Environmental Factors in the Development of Delinquency," *Psychological Monographs*, 73, No. 485 (1959).